Flagging the Problem

A new approach to mental health

DR HARRY BARRY

This book is dedicated to Niall, his parents John and Anne, and all his family and friends. It is also dedicated to Jason Smurfit, his uncle Michael Smurfit and all those who have lost loved ones to the white flag of suicide. Niall and Jason, you are not forgotten by those who love you in this world, and we pray you are happy in the next.

First published in 2007 by Liberties Press, Ireland
This revised and updated edition published in 2017 by Orion Spring,
an imprint of The Orion Publishing Group Ltd
Carmelite House, 50 Victoria Embankment
London EC4Y 0DZ

An Hachette UK Company

1 3 5 7 9 10 8 6 4 2

A CIP catalogue record for this book is
available from the British Library.

ISBN: 978 1 4091 7445 5

Typeset by Input Data Services Ltd, Somerset

Printed in Great Britain by CPI Group (UK) Ltd, Croydon, CR0 4YY

MIX
Paper from
responsible sources
FSC® C104740

www.orionbooks.co.uk

Praise for *Flagging the Problem*

It's that rare thing – a medical book that can be read by lay people and health professionals alike. Dr Barry demystifies subjects that touch so many of our lives and he does so with compassion, wisdom and vast professional knowledge.

Cathy Kelly, author and UNICEF ambassador

This is a superb book; it looks at mental-health problems in a fresh and accessible way. The use of an innovative 'flag' method to explain mood disorders offers a unique insight into depression. *Flagging the Problem* could help save lives that might otherwise be lost to suicide.

Dr Muiris Houston, Medical Correspondent, The Irish Times

This is an important book. It provides a new approach to mental health and the intricacy of the variables that influence it. Written with compassion and creativity and informed by decades of General Practice insights, Dr Harry Barry helps the reader to understand the complexity of the normal mood system and the distress of depression, anxiety, addiction and suicide.

Marie Murray, Director of Student Counselling Services at University College Dublin

Depression is the scourge of the twenty-first century. Dr Barry, in *Flagging the Problem*, offers a unique insight into this illness from a biological/sociological/cognitive perspective, and in this wonderful book has married together all three insights. In particular he defines the hidden dynamic underlying the reluctance of the sufferer to come for help. This is a 'must read' for public and professionals alike.

Enda Murphy, Cognitive Behaviour Therapist and Project Director, ICGP

Dr Barry has produced an innovative, highly readable, challenging text which focuses on the core mental-health disorders associated with suicide. The book will be of major benefit to doctors working in primary care, clinical psychologists and other professionals in the mental-health arena.

Professor Ted Dinan, MD, PhD, DSc,
Department of Psychiatry, University College Cork

A Note to Readers

This book was originally published in 2007 as the first part of the *Flag* Series. In preparation for the launch of the series in the UK and abroad, I have taken the opportunity to refresh and update the whole series. I have updated therefore some parts of *Flagging the Problem* to include some new insights into what is an ever-changing field.

All names, occupations and other details used in this book are allegorical in nature.

CONTENTS

FOREWORD

It is a sad fact that many families have experienced the suicide of a relative. We all ask ourselves why it happened and what more could have been done to prevent it.

When that death involves a young person with their whole life ahead of them, the grief that we feel for them is so much greater. We can remember them as happy children and we can see the opportunities that were ahead of them. We wonder how they reached a point when the thought of life became so bleak for them, and whether, no matter how much we tried, we failed them in providing the hope, the help and the encouragement that they needed.

In Ireland we are living through a period when we have more money, and more opportunities for work and leisure, than ever before, yet many of our young people, particularly our young men, find themselves living in a world of despair and drug addiction that ends with their suicide and a legacy of pain for those they leave behind.

Dr Harold Barry's experiences, his research and his findings provide a valuable source of information for the medical profession and for anyone who is trying to help a young person to change their life around, or who, sadly, is trying to come to terms with the suicide of someone they have been close to.

This book could save lives: I believe that it should be dedicated to all those young people whose lives came to such an unhappy and unnecessary end. They have not been forgotten, they are still loved, we still grieve for them and we still treasure memories of the time when they were happy and looking forward to each day with excitement and enthusiasm. They have been the inspiration for Dr Barry's book, which will help us to understand why these lives were lost and what can be done to help prevent other young people from giving up on the glorious journey that is life.

Dr Michael W. J. Smurfit
In memory of my nephew, Jason Smurfit

INTRODUCTION

It is a chilling statistic that as you read this introduction today, at least one person in Ireland will be preparing to end their life by suicide. Even more alarming is the fact that there is a significant chance that this individual will be under the age of thirty-five. Suicide claims the lives of approximately 450 people each year in Ireland.

Niall, whose story is told in the 'White Flag' section of this book, was one of these people. The main aim of his father John, an inspiration to many because of the way he spoke out publicly about his son's suicide, was that other families could be spared the pain of losing a loved one. Families which have fallen victim to suicide are forever haunted by the question: 'Why?' This book was born out of a search for an answer to this question.

As a family doctor, dealing with the problems of depression, addiction, anxiety and suicide are part of my job. In the past ten years, general practitioners have witnessed a major upheaval in Irish society, brought about by the Celtic Tiger and the increased prosperity that has accompanied this economic boom followed by one of the greatest economic depressions in the last hundred years. 'Stress' and 'fatigue' are words heard in all surgeries on a daily basis. 'Alcohol misuse' and 'substance abuse' are not far behind. Thankfully, more and more patients are beginning to speak freely about their symptoms of depression and anxiety, particularly men in their late twenties and early thirties. Nonetheless, it is my belief that the numbers presenting are only the tip of the iceberg. Most suffer in silence, hiding behind a mask of normality. This book is aimed at these people in particular, and their friends and families, whose role is often vital in encouraging people to discuss their mental-health problems.

Four things which I have noticed in the course of my professional life over thirty-five years are:

1. A lack of awareness or understanding of the ways in which illness can disrupt normal mental health. This includes an inability to accept that the mind is a function of the brain.
2. A misunderstanding of mental illness – that it is a 'weakness' without a biological basis. Just as diabetes is an illness caused by biological abnormalities in our pancreas, depression, anxiety and addiction are illnesses caused, at least in part, by biological abnormalities of the brain.
3. The huge stigma which has been attached to sufferers of these illnesses, and also, by association, to the families of these sufferers.
4. The enduring myth that psychiatrists and psychologists are the only experts who can deal with these illnesses. The family doctor will deal with a large number of such cases on a daily basis, yet this treatment option is often overlooked by both the general public and the media. This is in no way to denigrate the invaluable contribution made by psychiatrists or psychologists. Recent data released by the Irish College of General Practitioners suggests, however, that from the large pool of biological illnesses, which include depression, diabetes and heart disease, very few cases will be treated by a specialist. Meanwhile, although many cases of mental illness are treated by the family doctor, the majority remain undiagnosed.

In the last five years, there has been an explosion of information, based on scientific research, in areas such as neuro-imaging, genetics, neurophysiology and molecular biology. This has led to a transformation in our understanding of how the brain functions, as well as of illnesses such as depression, anxiety and addiction. It marks the beginning of a long and promising journey which may lead to a complete understanding of the brain and the illnesses which affect it. I have attempted to combine these recent findings with my thirty-five years of clinical experience to produce a book which not only deals with how to stay mentally healthy but also reveals the symptoms of mental illness together with their underlying biological causes.

The book uses a unique system to explain the biology behind these illnesses. During my research, I realised that the first letters of the main components of the biological mood system (the Frontal and Limbic mood departments, the Adrenal gland and the stress hormone Glucocortisol) make up the word 'FLAG'. Based on this, I have used a colour-coded flag system throughout the book.

The colour coding for the various sections is as follows:
- The Green Flag Normal mood: green indicating normality and balance
- The Red Flag Depression: red as the symbol of warning or danger
- The Yellow Flag Anxiety: yellow as the symbol of fear
- The Purple Flag Addiction: purple as the symbol of pleasure and excess
- The White Flag Suicide: white as the symbol of surrender

This system will, I feel, make it easier for the reader to visualise the illnesses, their symptoms and biology.

The most important part of the book, for me, is the explanation of the symptoms of the Red Flag of depression, and how they are caused. If enough people become aware of the warning signs and symptoms of depression, we will have taken a giant step towards preventing many potential cases of suicide.

The driving force behind this book is hope. For those in Ireland and in many parts of the developed world who are suffering from depression, addiction, anxiety and suicidal thoughts, the candle of hope has gone out. This candle needs to be relit, bringing with it the possibility of a new life where the pain and suffering caused by these illnesses can be alleviated. If this book does nothing more than provide a flame of hope to one person whose life seems to them to be so grey, hopeless and empty that ending it appears to be the only solution, and encourages them to come forward for help, then it has been well worth writing.

Let this be Niall's legacy.

PART ONE

The Green Flag:
The Normal Mood System

1: THE MOOD SYSTEM

Mood is an 'emotional state which lasts for a reasonably long period of time, often hours or days'. It differs from simple emotions like fear, anger, sadness or happiness in that it is of longer duration, is usually less intense, and is less likely to have been triggered by outside events. It is usually positive or negative, i.e. manifests itself in the person feeling 'up' or 'down'. Behaviour, on the other hand, relates to how we act or react to different circumstances in our internal or external environment. It can be conscious or unconscious, and is often strongly influenced by our emotions. These two important functions in our lives, along with our ability to cope with stress, are controlled by a highly organized mood system.

Most of us take normal mood and behaviour (otherwise known as good mental health) for granted. For others who are not so fortunate, disruption of this delicate system through biological illnesses such as depression, anxiety and addiction causes great upset, and sometimes havoc, in their lives.

Many people do not like to discuss issues like depression, anxiety or suicide. Somehow, these words convey an implied weakness or a basic flaw in the personality of those who are suffering from mental illness. Fear lies at the basis of our reluctance to talk about or admit to these conditions. This fear is deeply rooted in a long-standing ignorance and lack of knowledge as to how the brain in particular works.

The majority of mental illnesses arise from a common biological source: problems arising within our 'mood system'. In order to understand these illnesses, it is necessary to understand how the mood system works.

What Is The Mood System?

'Mood system' is a term I have coined to try to simplify for the reader what is, in fact, a highly complex internal biological network within the body. The function of this network is to keep in balance our emotions, behaviour and responses to stress of any kind. So let's take a look at the main components of this system.

Most emotional experiences and behavioural responses are mediated by two departments in the brain – which we'll call our 'mood departments' – one situated at the front of the brain, the other in the centre. These two mood departments are connected by a number of telephone-like cables which are vital for the smooth running of these areas of the brain. Outside of the brain, the mood system is completed by glands situated in our abdomen (perched on top of each of our kidneys), and the hormones this gland produces. This gland and its hormones are key players in our stress response, as we will see later.

So to sum up, these two mood departments, the mood cables connecting them, the adrenal gland in our abdomen and the stress hormones it produces, make up our 'mood system'. The slightest disruption to this delicately balanced system can cause mayhem throughout the body.

The brain is a great integrator of information, so most parts of this organ have an input into every decision we make. It is also extremely adaptable and, like all good computers, is adept at moving information around from one area to another, depending on circumstances. The brain lies at the heart of the mood system because it processes our emotions, creates our thoughts and moods, is the 'biological' source of the mind, and is responsible for instigating our emotional and behavioural responses.

The next section is a discussion of the brain and how it works, and this is followed by an examination of our mood system and how it is organised. I must preface all of this with a caveat. We are only at an early stage in our understanding of the brain: although a large amount of research has been carried out in this area, it remains cloaked in mystery. It is likely to take many years for us to have a complete understanding of the way the brain works – and indeed we may never develop such an understanding. Although functions such as the creation of mood or the control of behaviour will be assigned to different parts of the brain, much of what follows is merely educated guesswork by the world's leading experts in the field.

What Is The Brain?

Aptly described as the 'boss organ' of the body, the brain is analogous to the central processor of a computer. It receives, compiles and evaluates information both from within the body and from the external environment, makes the necessary decisions, and issues instructions to every other organ structure in the body.

The brain is composed of around 10 billion cells. These cells are of two basic types:

1. *Neurons:* Neurons are the decision-makers. They are individual cells which receive, process and pass on information. Like all other cells in the body, neurons are fluid-filled units surrounded by a fine cell membrane, which helps them to remain distinct from one another. In the centre of each neuron lie the chromosomes which in turn contain our genes. Neurons constitute only 10 percent of adult brain cells.
2. *Glial cells:* Glial cells are the support cells. These cells support, protect and nourish the neurons. The glial cells make up the remaining 90 percent of adult brain cells. Many researchers now feel that glial cells may play a much greater role in brain function than was previously thought.

As with any large company, the brain assigns various functions and responsibilities to each department. This organisation mainly involves the neurons; the glial cells are the support staff, servicing all the neurons, regardless of where they are in the organisation.

Within such a large organisational structure, good communication is a prerequisite of efficient operation for the brain. Adjacent neurons must be able to communicate unimpeded, and departments must also be able to exchange important information easily. In order to address this concern, the brain – again like a company – has an excellent 'telephone system' installed, with cables connecting units within a particular department and also linking one department to another. These cables are of great importance in dealing with our mood system.

The Brain: It's Good To Talk

The brain has an ingenious means of passing on information from one neuron to another. Each cell has the ability to activate itself electrically and to pass this charge on to the next cell, causing it to activate also. As each neuron is an isolated cell, the brain has developed a practical way of sending information from one neuron to another.

Between neurons in the brain are hundreds of small gaps or meeting points, known as synapses. The neuron which is passing on information produces chemical messengers which it releases in a small bubble into each of these gaps. These chemical messengers are called neurotransmitters, as they are transmitting messages between two neurons. The neurotransmitters cross the gap, attaching to receptors on the surface of the neighbouring neuron, re-leasing their information and returning to their cell of origin to await further instructions. As soon as this information has been communicated to the next cell, that cell may also decide to fire, based on the information it has received, repeating the process and activating the next neuron. A pathway is formed.

The receptor is like a lock on a door that can only be opened using a key with two notches – the chemical messenger. Receptors are hugely important in our understanding of all illnesses. They are usually generated in the middle of the cell and transported to its outer membranes, where they are positioned to respond to the relevant chemical messengers. Some receptors are designed simply to encourage the cell to fire, others to communicate more detailed messages to the genes at the core of the cell. All this activity shares one key objective: the flow of information. When individual neurons are banded together into long cables, the information can travel long distances to other sections of the brain.

All of these communications between neighbouring cells and departments in the brain take place at lightning speed and occur constantly. Each individual neuron has up to a thousand synapses. A conservative estimate of the number of synapses in our brain is 100 trillion. This fact alone highlights the challenge faced by brain researchers!

The Brain: The Messengers

About two hundred chemical messengers, or neurotransmitters, mediate brain functioning. Of these, the six most influential present in our mood system are:

(i) *Serotonin:* Probably the best-known neurotransmitter. It is responsible for mood, memory, sleep, and the control of impulsive behaviour.

(ii) *Noradrenalin:* Has an important role to play in the stress response. It is also important in sleep and mood, and is responsible for a person's drive/motivation.

(iii) *Dopamine:* Creates a sense of joy and pleasure. It can have an effect on mood and also, when tampered with, addiction.

(iv) *Glutamate:* This is present in almost every neuron in the brain. It differs from the first three neurotransmitters in this regard, which, as we will see, are mainly confined to their individual mood cables. Its function is a general 'housekeeping' one and is related to stimulating neurons into action. It is little surprise, therefore, that this transmitter, along with dopamine, is involved in schizophrenia, and, along with serotonin and noradrenaline, in depression.

(v) *GABA:* This messenger, which is present in about 40 percent of the cells in our brain, is essential in preventing the brain from over-stimulating itself, leading to seizure and death. Its job is to balance out the effect of glutamate by relaxing neurons.

(vi) *Peptides:* These are a group of roaming messengers that are released by neurons. They disperse throughout the brain and attach themselves to cell receptors elsewhere, communicating information to the genes of those cells. They are central to the way in which a person handles stress and anxiety.

Two common examples of peptides are:

1. *Endorphins:* Chemicals which induce a state of euphoria, released particularly during exercise.
2. *Stress peptides:* Primarily released to help a person cope with stress. Prolonged or excessive release of these messengers (CRH in particular), however, can result in illnesses of the mood system.

The Mood System: Mood Departments

There are two main mood departments:

Frontal Mood Department

This department, as its name implies, is situated anatomically at the front of the brain, within the frontal lobe. Most of this part of the brain is taken up by the most important structure we will deal with in this book: the prefrontal cortex. (Both the right and left side of the brain contain individual frontal mood departments.) The frontal mood department prefrontal cortex is the thinking (thought-producing), decision-making part of the mood system (the so called 'logical brain'). Its functions, partly related to mood but mostly related to behaviour, are as follows:

(i) Analysing situations (particularly if they are new to the individual) and making judgements and decisions based on information received. This includes future planning
(ii) Managing short-term memory
(iii) Preventing impulsive and destructive behaviour, including self-injurious behaviour and aggressive acts towards others
(iv) Helping to produce and maintain normal mood and producing positive thinking. This department may also be the source of self-consciousness

The *prefrontal cortexes* (which themselves are composed of different small functioning units) on either side of the brain have different functions. They take up most of the frontal lobes and constitute 29 percent of the total grey matter of the brain; they are therefore of great importance in our lives.

Of primary interest in relation to mental illness is the left-frontal prefrontal cortex. This mediates positive thoughts and impulsive behaviour, and is often called the 'executive decision-maker'. For the most part, when the prefrontal cortex is discussed, the left prefrontal cortex will be the area that is being referred to. This part of the brain is very influential in both depression and suicide.

Limbic Mood Department

This department lies in the centre of the brain. It is usually described as the limbic system. It is the part of the mood system that deals with emotion (the so called 'emotional brain'). Composed of different sections with corresponding functions, the limbic system is responsible for:

- The way in which a person responds to stress
- The preservation of normal mood
- Feelings of joy and pleasure
- Processing of memory
- Appetite for both food and sex

Within the limbic mood department, there are several sections, which we will call 'boxes', each of which is involved in its own functions:

(i) *'Memory box' (hippocampus):* This is where memory is generated, filtered and organised before being sent to other parts of the brain for storage. It is also involved in the retrieval of such memories. It plays a key role in putting these recalled memories into context, and in spatial memory. This box becomes very active when we are sleeping, particularly when we are dreaming. It is likely that memories are consolidated at these times.

(ii) *'Stress box' (amygdala):* This unit controls the response to perceived threats both from within the body and from the external environment. Most experts feel that it is also the main processor of the primary emotions of fear, hate, love and anger. It is integral to stress and anxiety and plays a large part in how the brain stores emotions related to unpleasant memories, memories which may or may not be consciously accessible. The negative thinking prevalent in depression probably originates here (or, more accurately, the emotions associated with the negative thinking). This box is larger in males than in females.

(iii) *'Pleasure box' (nucleus accumbens):* This section is activated when we are participating in rewarding activities such as eating food, drinking alcohol, having sex, and so on. In the biological illness of addiction, this box becomes affected by abuse.

The two mood departments, which control emotion and behaviour/logic, are in constant communication. When this communication breaks down – and indeed when communication is disrupted within sections of each mood department – the brain descends into chaos, and illness is a likely consequence.

It has been shown that there is a greater flow of information from the *amygdala* to the *prefrontal cortex* than vice versa, probably for evolutionary survival reasons. This may explain why our emotions (such as fear) frequently overpower our thoughts and behaviour, but unfortunately we often have difficulty in persuading our thoughts and behaviour to overrule our emotions! As we will see in the section on the Yellow Flag, it is hard for a person in the middle of a panic attack to 'think' their way out of the way they feel.

As a general rule, in the course of normal life, our emotional brain will win out in a battle between the two! If you don't believe me, ask somebody in love to behave in a sensible and rational manner. Thankfully, in this case the 'heart' usually wins out. Another example would be passing a Chinese takeaway and battling between the logical brain informing us that getting a takeaway will not help our attempts to keep our weight down, and the emotional mind imagining a good tuck-in! Guess which one often wins?

Ideally, in relation to extreme negativity, the prefrontal cortex or prefrontal cortex should exert a large degree of control over the stress box. Not only can the prefrontal cortex produce positive thoughts, it can also switch off, rationalise and overrule overtly negative emotional thoughts that originate in the stress box. For this reason, many experts believe that depression and suicide result in part from a malfunctioning, mainly left-sided prefrontal cortex.

Before leaving the two mood departments, it is worth mentioning the role that both play in memory. We know that the memory box is essential to the formation of all memories and to the ability of the brain to store, retrieve and put in context such memories. It is the destruction of this box that leads to the profound memory loss seen in dementia, and to the memory loss so commonly seen in depression.

The stress box, in comparison, assigns an emotional content (often negative) not only to our thoughts but also to our memories, particularly distressing ones. The stress box, therefore, does not so much store the negative memories we all have (these memories are stored throughout the brain) as assign a negative emotion (such as fear, sadness, anger or anxiety) to the memory.

The stress and memory boxes work very closely together. Both are usually involved in the formation of memories. The latter is felt to be involved in creating, storing and recalling the memory; the former with the emotions associated with it. The inappropriate assignation of excess negativity from this box to both memories and thoughts is the secret to the negative thinking that is so prominent in depression, and to the symptoms of anxiety, both of which we will be dealing with later. Both of these boxes also link in with the pleasure box, so that enjoyable feelings are also stored away in our memories. This, as we will see later, is important in addiction.

The Mood System: Mood Cables

The two mood departments (and their individual sections) are in constant communication with all other parts of the brain, but in particular are constantly receiving, assimilating and passing on information (through a variety of neural pathways) to each other.

An important channel of communication between the two mood departments (and their individual sections) is a series of three long collections of neurons, which will be referred to as mood cables. Each cable will be named after the predominant chemical messenger used by neurons in that particular cable. Because they are so important to the normal health of the mood system, we will be dealing with these cables throughout this book.

Because the information carried by each neuron has to travel a distance from its source, the brain uses its glial support cells to manufacture, and surround the cells with a white insulation-type material (similar to that used in electrical wires in our homes) called myelin. This speeds up the passage of information along the neurons. The three main mood cables and their corresponding control boxes are:

(i) *The dopamine mood cable:* The dopamine control box is situated below the limbic mood department at the base of the brain. The dopamine cable travels from this box and continues through the limbic mood department before moving on to the frontal mood department and other structures. It uses the neurotransmitter dopamine, which is produced and mediated by the dopamine control box.

Of the brain's one billion neurons, a modest forty thousand make up this cable. The wellbeing of the entire mood system depends on this small structure, however. This cable produces feelings of joy and pleasure, and its malfunctioning is linked to depression, addiction and schizophrenia.

(ii) *The serotonin mood cable:* The serotonin control box is also situated at the base of the brain. The serotonin cable runs from this box through all sections of the limbic mood department, connects with the frontal mood department, and then moves on to pass information to almost every part of the brain. This cable's connections with the memory and prefrontal cortexes are of particular importance. This cable uses the neurotransmitter serotonin to communicate, which is produced and mediated by the serotonin control box.

Similar to the dopamine cable, the serotonin cable is composed of a relatively small number of neurons. What it lacks in size, it makes up for in significance by virtue of the massive number of connections it makes with all the sections of the mood system, and indeed with the rest of the brain. This is the primary mood cable, which regulates mood, sleep, concentration, memory, appetite, sexual drive, stress and destructive behaviour.

Naturally, then, if it malfunctions, this can lead to depression, suicide, anti-social behaviour, addiction and anxiety. Women seem to produce serotonin at a much lower rate than men, which may partially explain the higher rates of anxiety and depression that are present in females.

(iii) *The noradrenalin mood cable:* The source of this cable also lies in the brain stem, i.e. the noradrenalin control box. From here it travels up through the limbic and frontal mood departments before dispersing throughout the brain. It has a strong connection with the stress box. The main chemical messenger used by this cable is noradrenalin, the production of which mediated by the noradrenalin control box. It is also composed of a relatively small number of neurons (around twenty-five thousand). It keeps us alert, vigilant, driven, sleeping normally, and it also helps us to manage stress. It does not operate properly in patients suffering from depression and anxiety.

The peptide system: Alongside the three cables above there is another messenger system. This will be called the 'Peptide System.' Peptides are messengers released by neurons in the brain which travel to both local and distant areas of the brain. As mentioned previously, stress peptides and endorphins are two of the most prominent. Peptides (CRH in particular) have a major role to play in depression, anxiety, and suicide.

All three control boxes have a rich supply of glucocortisol receptors and as a result are very vulnerable to excessively high levels of this hormone, as seen in chronic stress and depression.

The Mood System: The Adrenal Stress Gland

The mood system is completed by the adrenal glands, which are found – in a somewhat unlikely location – a good distance from the brain, on top of the kidneys. The stress box sends messages to these glands, via the bloodstream and the nervous system. Following these instructions, the adrenal glands produce three important hormones: adrenalin, noradrenalin (both of which prepare the body to respond when faced with a sudden threat) and glucocortisol.

The Mood System: The Glucocortisol Stress Hormone

The adrenal glands, when instructed by the limbic mood department, produce glucocortisol. This hormone is used to fight stress, illness and infection. It tackles stress by activating pathways which release the energy necessary for the body to cope. The immune system, which fights illness, is very susceptible to fluctuating levels of this hormone. Glucocortisol also affects body fat, sugar levels and bones, is influential in heart disease, and plays a role in the brain's capacity to form memories. This hormone is normally elevated during daytime, and declines at night: this helps keep a person alert during the day and enables them to sleep at night.

When the mood cables and departments are severely disrupted through stress and depression, these normal daily patterns will be destroyed. The system will be bombarded with this hormone day and night. It will travel back to the brain via the bloodstream, where, in a vicious cycle, it will damage the mood cables and departments even more. Glucocortisol can be described as the body's heavy artillery for dealing with stress. In the case of an over-supply of the hormone, however – where it runs out of its usual targets – this heavy artillery begins to fight the brain itself, resulting in damage to the memory box in particular.

The Mood System: The Flag

By now, one can see how interwoven all the parts of the mood system are. Interference with any one section can result in widespread malfunction.

As mentioned in the introduction, a useful way of conceptualising the mood system is to take the first letter of the mood departments, (Frontal and Limbic), the first letter of the stress gland (Adrenal), the first letter of our stress hormone (Glucocortisol), and combine them to form the word 'FLAG'. In the model seen below, the mood departments are displayed, as is the stress gland and hormone.

Flags have universal appeal. Beaches during the summertime warrant careful examination of the lifeguard's flags: red warns of danger, yellow encourages vigilance, and green indicates safety. This book deals with normal mood and the various biological illnesses which affect the mood system. These illnesses will be colour-coded using flags. The Green Flag indicates normal mood and behaviour. This is the desirable state, yet for many people is only reached with great difficulty. The Red Flag warns of the inner turmoil and dangerous symptoms that depression can bring. The Yellow Flag of increased vigilance aptly describes the paralysing, cautious, fearful state in which those with anxiety disorders find themselves. The Purple Flag of addiction refers to an infatuation with the pleasures of alcohol, drugs and other addictive substances and activities. Finally, the White Flag of suicide signals acceptance of defeat, and the surrender of the mood system to the illness that has been plaguing it.

An interesting modern approach to the mood system within the brain itself is to consider the brain as a neural 'mood circuit' which links the bottom of the brain (which contains the control boxes associated with the main mood cables), the emotional limbic department in the middle of the brain, and the logical frontal mood departments at the top, together. Most mental illnesses are caused by difficulties when this circuit breaks down. If we could shift our understanding of illnesses like depression to encompass this concept of a neural mood circuit, it would revolutionise both our understanding of and our approach to managing this condition. For those who would like to understand this in more detail I refer them to *Flagging the Therapy*.

In attempting to understand the biology of the brain and mood system, it is possible to overlook the unique nature of humanity and individuality. It is important not to see the brain and the individual person as mutually exclusive. It is also important not to see the body or the mind as being somehow distinct from the brain. What affects one will inevitably also impinge on the other. This is why we must look at all illnesses holistically. The mind (both emotional and logical) is a function of the brain, just as blood flow is a function of the heart. So by definition, mental illness – and any approach to dealing with it – must involve the brain itself.

There are those who may worry that, by studying the brain in this way, we are dehumanising or devaluing the human person. Others are concerned that it denigrates the role of religion or spirituality. All these are valid and genuine concerns. But the greatest gift that we have (whatever the origin of this gift) is the ability to observe ourselves and learn about both the universe and our own beings. We can and should be using this gift to ease the sufferings of others.

The family doctor is in a unique position to observe all the highs and lows of human existence – from the joy of the birth of a baby to the mourning of death, with all its unanswered questions. This provides a strong motivation for us to learn as much as possible from current scientific research, in order to alleviate the suffering related to biological illnesses which affect the mood system, particularly in relation to depression and suicide.

Just as the study of coronary heart disease has greatly assisted in the understanding and treatment of this condition, so too have discoveries into the workings of the brain assisted in the understanding and treatment of mental illness. Such study can never diminish the uniqueness of humans beings! The only way to break the taboo of mental illness is to delve into the mystery of how the brain works. Fear of discussing psychiatric conditions is often built on ignorance and a lack of understanding. Human beings are extraordinary organisms! The ability of the brain to examine itself is an extraordinary one, and should be utilised for the benefit of others.

Summary

1   The brain is composed of ten billion individual cells. There are two main types of such cells – neurons, which make all the important decisions, and glial cells, which nourish and protect the neurons. Only 10 percent of all cells in the brain are neurons, with glial cells making up the remainder. Neurons and glial cells in the brain are organised into various departments with particular functions.

2   Each neuron stands alone, with lots of small meeting points or gaps (called synapses) present between separate cells. Through these synapses, each neuron talks to hundreds of its closest neighbours. It does so by sending messengers from one cell to another across these gaps in order to communicate information. These messengers are called neurotransmitters, and play a pivotal role in how the brain operates. There are three important

neurotransmitters that are crucial to the mood system: serotonin, no-radrenalin and dopamine. Another group of neurotransmitters released by neurons into these synapses are called peptides. These roaming messengers 'wander off' to pass important messages to other parts of the brain rather than activating the cells closest to them. Of these messages, the two most important are endorphins (released during exercise) and stress peptides (released during stress).

3   Within the brain, there are two main mood departments: the frontal, situated at the front of the brain, and the limbic system, in the centre of the brain.

4   The frontal mood department is mainly composed of a section we will refer to as the prefrontal cortex. This department or box (sometimes called the logical brain) plays a major role in our thinking and behaviour. Its main functions relate to short-term memory, the processing of positive and negative thoughts, analysing and decision-making, future planning, and the control of impulsive thoughts and actions.

5   The limbic mood department plays a major role in regulating our emotions (and is sometimes called the emotional brain). It has three main sections: the stress box (amygdala), memory box (hippocampus) and pleasure box (nucleus accumbens). The primary responsibilities of this department are the regulation of mood, the processing of memory, response to stress, and our experience of joy and pleasure.

6   Our two mood departments are connected by three long telephone-like mood cables. These cables will be named after the main neurotransmitter involved in their operation and are responsible for the smooth running of the mood system. The three cables concerned are the serotonin cable (which deals with mood, sleep, appetite, sex and control of impulsive behaviour), the noradrenalin cable (which deals with energy, drive, concentration, mood, sleep and the stress response) and the dopamine cable (which deals with mood and the sense of joy and pleasure that is extrapolated from positive experiences).

7   The mood system is completed by the adrenal stress gland (situated in the abdomen on top of our kidneys – and the core stress hormone glucocortisol.

When under stress for any length of time, the adrenal stress gland helps the system to cope. As we will see later, however, sustained activity in this gland over a prolonged period can give rise to numerous problems in our mood system.

8   A useful way of combining all this information to form a unified concept is to take the first letter of the two mood departments, the frontal and limbic system (*F* and *L*), the first letter of the adrenal stress gland (*A*) and the first letter of the stress hormone glucocortisol (*G*) to form the word *FLAG*. Flags have universal significance in our lives. A green flag suggests that all is well, red flags warn of danger, and yellow, purple and white flags can be taken to stand for, respectively, fear, debauchery and surrender. Based on these concepts, the Green Flag represents normal mood, and the Red Flag represents depression. Anxiety is represented by the Yellow Flag, the Purple Flag signals addiction, and suicide will be indicated by the White Flag. All of these illnesses and conditions originate from a widespread dysfunction within the mood system and will be dealt with in subsequent chapters.

9   Although particular functions will be assigned to each of the mood departments and their individual sections, it is important to realise that there is a substantial flow of information between them. These departments also communicate with all other parts of the brain. A modern approach to the mood system is to consider all the above as being part of a neural 'mood circuit'. Interference with this circuit is the basis for many mental illnesses. When a decision has to be made, there is normally a balanced discussion between the logical, thinking section of our mood system (the frontal department) and the emotional section (the limbic system). Sometimes, emotions prevail, and on other occasions the rational psyche dominates. This balance is a vital and healthy one. When the mood system is functioning properly, decisions that have been reached are balanced and informed. When an illness like depression spreads throughout the brain, this balance is disturbed. A serious consequence of this disruption is suicidal thoughts.

10 Finally, in discussing the workings of the brain and mood system, it must be noted that a person is more than simply a conglomeration of neurons

and neurotransmitters! The mystery of consciousness undoubtedly originates from the brain. The whole is indeed greater than the sum of its parts, and it will be difficult for any study of the brain to capture fully the elusive yet undeniable essence of humanity. We are indeed special and unique!

2: THE DEVELOPMENT OF THE BRAIN AND THE MOOD SYSTEM

Exciting new research has made a great deal of information on the brain, its mood system, and the illnesses that affect it available to us. The advent of neuro-imaging – the use of scanning to document the development and functioning of the brain – has opened up a new chapter in the understanding and treatment of mental illness.

The Development of the Brain

The brain begins its lengthy journey in the womb, around eighteen days after conception. Within three months, hundreds of billions of neurons have been formed, and they are organised rapidly into the different sections which will make up the future adult brain. These cells only survive if they manage to communicate with other neurons within a certain time period via the synapses.

By six months after birth, the brain has developed too many neurons, so it carries out a selective pruning of the neurons. It is a case of survival of the fittest: developing cells must start communicating or die, as those that are unable to form synapses are destroyed. This pruning process is a very important stage in the development of the brain. Illnesses such as autism, bipolar depression and schizophrenia may in part result from abnormal pruning.

At birth, most of the neurons we need for life are already present. It was accepted in the past by the scientific and medical community that, by age twelve, the brain was fully formed and that no new neurons could be formed. It is now known that this is not true and that, in fact, the development of the brain is a dynamic and ongoing process. The memory box is extremely underdeveloped under the age of three: this explains why we have few memories of our existence prior to this age!

Between ages six and twelve, the brain experiences a massive growth in the number of connections between individual neurons. This process reaches its peak just before puberty. Once again, another large pruning process has to occur, or efficiency suffers. Between twelve and twenty-five years of age, a massive reorganisation of the neurons and their synapses occurs. This is probably activated by a combination of our genes working together and the massive release of sex hormones which occurs between ages twelve and eighteen. The neurons themselves do not die during this stage; rather, the connections between them are selectively destroyed. The result is a reduction in the number of synapses but an increase in overall efficiency. Along with this pruning, there is a further increase in the speed of conduction between cells and departments of the brain, due to other cellular changes.

The pruning process begins at the back of the brain, and continues through the limbic system, situated in the centre of the brain, before finally reaching the frontal lobe. Thus, it starts with parts of the brain that are responsible for vision, hearing and coordination, before moving to areas which control emotions, and eventually finishing up in a section of the brain which controls behaviour and decision-making. By the person's early to mid-twenties, most of this work has been completed, and all the brain can do is attempt to improve its speed of conduction and renew dead cells in areas such as the memory box.

From this age onwards, the number of neurons will decline. Over the age of fifty, illnesses such as Alzheimer's and vascular damage to the brain may accelerate this process, resulting in dementia. The three main mood cables also begin to shrink as we age. This, as we will see later, may explain in part the arrival of depression in this group. Alcohol, lack of exercise, and failure to utilise mental faculties also accelerates the loss of neurons. Nonetheless, most of us will retain sufficient neurons to keep us functioning adequately for the duration of our lives.

The Development of the Mood System

New research into brain development has improved our understanding of how the mood system evolves from the womb to full maturity by the mid-twenties. In the last few months in the womb, during the massive pruning process, the frontal mood department seems to become particularly vulnerable to damage. If certain genetic vulnerability or intra-uterine environmental influences are present, a susceptibility to illnesses such as schizophrenia, autism and bipolar depression may become established at this stage; these illnesses will not reveal their presence until later, however. Recently, the frontal mood department has been demonstrated to be of greater importance in unipolar (or simple) depression than was previously believed. Therefore genetic or intra-uterine environmental influences may turn out to be a causal factor in this illness as well.

In childhood, major stress factors such as abuse and loss interact with genetic vulnerability to create a lifelong predisposition for people to react inappropriately to stress. The behaviour and stress boxes seem to be the most vulnerable targets for the creation of such a lifelong susceptibility. This predisposition may, as will be shown later, explain the emergence of depression, anxiety and addiction in the lives of such people.

The pruning process from the age of twelve to the early to mid-twenties is a vital period in the development of the mood system. The limbic system is dealt with first, before the brain moves on to its final objective, the maturing of the prefrontal cortex in the frontal lobes.

As the limbic system is responsible for how we feel, it is inevitable that feelings will run riot under the massive influence of our sex hormones from the age of twelve to eighteen. If we feel down, the pain will be more intense; and the same applies to positive emotions. As the immature prefrontal cortex can exercise only a weak control over the limbic system at this stage, emotions will influence thoughts and actions more than common sense. This explains the excessive behaviour of many teenagers: their exuberance and great enthusiasm on the one hand, and their apparently complete disregard for the consequences of their actions on the other. Lacking effective control over the prefrontal cortex, teenagers engage in impulsive and often reckless behaviour, including binge drinking, unprotected sex and joyriding. This is why the teenage years are so turbulent for those going through them – and for the parents of teenagers.

By the early to mid-twenties, the brain's 'commander-in-chief', the prefrontal cortex, has begun to exert its control over the great surge of emotions originating from the limbic mood department. Parents have observed their good-humoured, sociable eight- to ten-year-old undergoing extraordinary behavioural changes and becoming an impossible thirteen- to seventeen-year-old who demonstrates huge swings in mood and behaviour – only for the process to be reversed again as their offspring enter their twenties. This explains why teenagers are reached more easily by appealing to their emotions rather than to reason. Then, finally, out of the caterpillar stage of mood development emerges the butterfly of maturity.

This phased development of the teenage or young-adult mood system has huge implications for how messages relating to smoking, alcohol and drug misuse are communicated to young people. These are an issue because our pleasure box, dopamine cable and limbic system are much more active during this phase of development, due to an inability to exert control on the part of the prefrontal cortex, which is still immature. The pleasure that such activities brings outweighs the inevitable negative consequences of these activities in the mind of the teenager.

There is increasing focus on why most illnesses of the mood system, particularly depression and anxiety, often appear for the first time when a person is between fifteen and twenty-five years of age. It is speculated that the answers lie at earlier stages of development, both in the womb and in early childhood. Abnormalities originating from genetic or early environmental influences, or both, seem to weaken the mood structures, making them prone to breaking down during the emotional stress barrage of the teenage years. The behaviour and stress boxes in particular are very vulnerable during this early stage. A vicious circle can then ensue, with the affected individual becoming prone to further bouts of depression and anxiety in the future.

Schizophrenia also often develops during this phase of development. Scientists are of the opinion that this illness originates from poor development of the frontal lobe prefrontal cortex in the womb. When pruning takes place, from ages twelve to twenty-five, this deficiency is exacerbated, and the illness appears. Of concern recently is the increasing number of cases where abuse of drugs, particularly cocaine and marijuana, is triggering schizophrenia, because the use of these drugs affects the pruning process. This, unfortunately, may delay a diagnosis of schizophrenia, as many of the symptoms of schizophrenia may be attributed to the drug use itself.

If those in the twelve-to-twenty-five age group (particularly the under-fifteens) begin to misuse alcohol, drugs and nicotine from an early stage, the risk of a later, full-blown addiction increases, especially if the person comes from an 'addictive background' (a home where the parents may have been addicted to nicotine, alcohol, gambling or illegal drugs). This explains why so many young people in Ireland are hardened drinkers in many cases by the age of twenty-one. Many have started drinking from an early age, and as a result their dopamine and limbic system becomes hooked on the pleasurable feelings that alcohol can bring, and binge drinking becomes the norm rather than an aberration.

A similar situation exists with regard to smoking: we now know that if we expose the immature brain and mood system to nicotine before the age of eighteen, the chances of members of this group becoming long-term smokers dramatically increases. We live in a culture where alcohol and nicotine are freely available and where many young people (unlike in previous decades) are in a position, both financially and in terms of the freedom they enjoy, to avail themselves of both: the interaction of an immature mood system with modern Irish life is leading to problems. Lastly, suicide is unfortunately very common in the fifteen-to-twenty-five age group. One could query whether the individual's stage of development is a contributing factor to this situation: common sense dictates that it is. Firstly, at this age emotions are running wild due to the person's over-active limbic system. Secondly, illnesses such as depression and schizophrenia may appear. Thirdly, the dopamine/pleasure box is highly susceptible to the effects of alcohol and other drugs. Lastly, and possibly most importantly, the prefrontal cortex – which controls impulsive and violent behaviour – is slowly maturing from the mid-teens to the early and mid-twenties.

When the immaturity of the prefrontal cortex is combined with an illness like depression, impulsive suicidal thoughts and behaviours become more likely.

Before leaving this section, it is worthwhile to reflect briefly on the development of personality (defined as the consistent emotional thought and behaviour patterns of an individual) as opposed to that of the mood system. All of us, from a very early age, begin to show distinct personality traits; as a result, we differ in how we look at life, which consequently determines how we behave. There is a large genetic component to the development of our individual personalities, but positive and negative early childhood experiences also play a role. Some of us will be extroverted, and others more introverted and cautious. Lots of us have developed set behavioural patterns by adulthood. Our reactions to most life situations will of course be influenced by the type of person we have become. It is likely that key departments of the brain, like our prefrontal cortex, play an important role in determining our personality.

This is supported by neuro-imaging research which shows that extroverts have a very active left side of the prefrontal cortex and that those who are more introverted and cautious show more activity in the right side of this box. Since the former have a lower incidence of depression and the latter a higher incidence of anxiety, it is clear that in some areas our mood system and personality intermingle.

One of the difficulties that professionals encounter when dealing with mental-health issues is that many people assume that an illness like depression is simply a weakness of personality. This implies that, firstly, it is personality development that is at fault and, secondly, that those with this illness are in some way inferior to others. This thinking also extends to suicide: many people erroneously believe that those who commit suicide are generally suffering from a major personality problem and should be considered to be weak individuals.

Such perspectives are of course completely misguided. Personality is important in how we cope with many of life's difficulties and stresses, and it is also important in how an illness like depression might express itself. An anxious person by personality might show a lot more anxiety features if they develop depression; an impulsive or aggressive person might display their depression through heavy drinking or by lashing out in bursts of anger, or they may be more likely to self-harm. Men sometimes exhibit all three. Those with perfectionist personalities may become severely self-critical or negative in their thinking if they develop this illness.

It is not a defect in the development of our personality, however, or a weakness in character that leads to depression and suicide, but rather illness infecting the mood system. Rather, personality is more relevant when it comes to how the illness will manifest itself in a particular person.

The need to make this distinction is one of the driving forces behind this book. All of us need to try to understand that, despite the relationship between personality and mood, the two things are essentially different.

Environment Versus Genes in the Development of the Mood System

Whether it is our genes or our environment that controls the healthy development of our mood system is an age-old debate. It is now accepted, however, that there is a dynamic relationship between our genes and the way in which we interact with our environment, and that this relationship continues right through our lives. Everything begins with the genes we inherit. So what are our genes?

Each cell in the brain – like every cell in the body – contains a 'book' of instructions and information called DNA. This book is broken up into chapters and paragraphs which instruct the individual cell to make special proteins to perform particular functions. Each paragraph can be considered to be a gene. It is estimated that each human being has around a hundred thousand genes, which together control all the functions of the body and mind.

In the case of the mood system, a number of these paragraphs, or genes, determine the workings and functions of each cell in the mood cables and departments. If we combine these paragraphs together, a chapter on how each of our individual mood systems function is formed. The problem is that multiple flaws in these instructions – analogous to spelling or grammatical mistakes in a sentence – can lead to a malfunction in the development of our mood system.

Environment also plays a key role in the development of the mood system. From conception to the point when brain maturity is reached, at age twenty-five, a variety of environmental factors can influence our genes, predisposing them to malfunction at a later stage. In the womb, such influences include alcohol, nicotine, drugs and viral illnesses which affect the mother. In childhood, the influences include severe physical or sexual abuse, loss or separation of a parent, or any major trauma.

In adolescence, it is recognised that abuse, severe loss, and alcohol and substance misuse can also affect the genes. One other factor that is often overlooked in this crucial period of development is nutrition. From the womb to age twenty-five, the presence or absence of vital building blocks from our diet may also play a role in the development of the mood system. We will be dealing with this subject in more detail later.

The way in which environmental factors influence the development of the mood system has to be mediated through our genes. This is because everything that happens in the neurons of our mood system is controlled by the genes. In some people, environmental factors may interact with genes which are programmed to malfunction (to a greater or lesser extent) from the beginning.

Some illnesses of the mood system appear in the teenage years, when the limbic system is only maturing. During this phase of development, environmental triggers seem to activate underlying genetic or early-development malfunctions, causing these illnesses to appear. Researchers also speculate that the stress factors noted above in childhood and early adolescence combine with malfunctioning genes to produce a lifelong vulnerability to stress in adult life. This may lead to depression and anxiety later.

A useful way of looking at how genes and environmental factors interact in relation to the development of many common illnesses (including those affecting the mood system) is to use the analogy of a profit-and-loss sheet. All of us have genes which predispose us towards illnesses, and other genes which protect us from the same illnesses. In some of us, the genetic balance is tipped in favour of us developing or expressing this illness if environmental factors are favourable.

On the other side of the equation, all of us will experience both positive and negative environmental influences in our lives (both in our past and in our present) which may make it more likely that such illnesses develop. Once again, the overall balance can reduce or increase our chance of developing these illnesses. When we put these two sets of genetic and environmental balances together, we can assess our risks of developing such illnesses. (If the overall balance is tipped in the wrong direction, then it is likely that these illnesses will appear at some stage in our lives.)

Common examples of such conditions are coronary heart disease, diabetes and depression. In coronary heart disease, for example, the genetic predisposition may be towards overproducing cholesterol in the liver, combined with a tendency for the body's immune system to attack this fat within the wall of the coronary arteries; these factors may predispose some towards developing angina and dying from a heart attack. The environmental factors in this case might be poor diet, lack of exercise, smoking and stress. When we put all these factors together, the person's overall risk of developing CHD will be high. In general the stronger the genetic predisposition, the more likely the illness will be expressed, often at a younger age. As we will see later depression is another classical example of this delicate balance.

To conclude, it is the complex interaction between our genes and the environment that lies at the core of the development of the mood system. A proper understanding of the causes of mental illness therefore depends heavily on a comprehensive knowledge of this interaction – a knowledge which researchers have so far been unable to develop.

3: THE 'STRESS SYSTEM'

One of the main functions of the mood system is to control the stress system. Stress is a universal phenomenon: everyone experiences periods of acute stress (such as exam pressure) and chronic stress (including financial pressures and job difficulties). The body also has to deal with the internal stress of infection and illness. Stress is now felt to be pivotal to the creation and maintenance of certain mental illnesses such as depression and anxiety.

Stress is not always a bad thing, however: it is the way in which the body deals with stress which is crucial. We will also examine how chronic activation of the stress system can lead to many difficulties relating to our general health, even in the absence of mood-system illnesses.

The Biology of the Stress System

The body's stress response is coordinated by the stress box, situated in the limbic mood department. When under attack from any internal or external stress, the frontal mood department prefrontal cortex activates the stress box. The stress box then releases CRH, one of the peptide messengers. This in turn activates two areas in the brain: the hormone control box and the brain stem, both of which send information to the adrenal stress glands, through the bloodstream and the spinal cord respectively.

The brain stem instructs the adrenal glands to release adrenalin and nor-adrenalin into the blood stream. This instant response to stress occurs in a period lasting anything from a few seconds to several minutes. The hormones adrenalin and noradrenalin prepare the body for combating the immediate threat. Heart rate increases, blood pressure rises, the mind is vigilant and alert, the mouth becomes dry, and the stomach starts to churn. The body is diverting resources away from non-essential organs towards those which will be used in combat to maximise the person's chances of survival. This is known informally as a 'fight or flight' reaction. The hormone control box also receives instructions from the stress box, and sends a message via the bloodstream to the adrenal stress glands, instructing them to release glucocortisol. This is a longer process and can last anything from a few minutes to several hours. Glucocortisol is a vital hormone, and is involved in making glucose available to all the cells in the body. Every cell in the body, including the neurons in the brain, has receptors for this hormone. Glucocortisol also helps to break down fats in order for the body to release more energy.

Both adrenalin and glucocortisol feed back to the brain. When the stress or threat has lifted, they encourage the stress box to switch off. Everything then goes back to normal. When stress becomes prolonged or chronic, however, problems begin to arise. Whereas the immediate effects of stimulation of the adrenal gland to produce adrenalin and noradrenalin usually settle, the production of glucocortisol continues, and has the following negative effects on the mood system:

Effects On Mood Cables

The three main mood cables originate from their control boxes, situated below the limbic system. Each box is responsible for controlling its own cable, so interference with them will automatically damage the cable in question. Chronic stress forces the stress system to produce too much glucocortisol, and this interferes with the mood control boxes in the following ways:

- *Serotonin mood control box and cable:* Persistently high glucocortisol levels deplete serotonin levels in this box and cable, and have a negative effect on serotonin receptors. This combination of damage to the brain results in mood, memory and sleep difficulties.
- *Noradrenalin mood control box and cable:* Initially, stress encourages this box and cable to be highly active, but continually high glucocortisol levels

eventually deplete the noradrenalin reserves. Initial tension and vigilance becomes severe exhaustion. Chronic stress also results in reduced concentration and drive, and sleep disturbance. Overstimulation of the noradrenalin cable results in a 'tired but wired' state.

- *Dopamine control box and cable:* Stress initially activates this system, producing a temporary high. Again, however, it does not take long for the supplies of this neurotransmitter to become depleted, and activities which are normally rewarding then become tiring and laborious. Our normal enjoyment of life becomes impaired.

Those who have been exposed to long periods of sustained stress will be familiar with this lack of energy, drive, concentration, appetite and libido.

Effects On Mood Departments

The relentless bombardment of stress peptides and glucocortisol due to stress also affects the two mood departments.

- *Frontal mood department:* The prefrontal cortex is very sensitive to both stress peptides and glucocortisol, making it vulnerable to an attack. As this box produces positive thoughts and reduces impulsive actions, it is no surprise that, under sustained stress, negativity and impulsiveness begin to manifest themselves.

    Some experts believe that the susceptibility of the left-side of the prefrontal cortex to stress triggers depression. In certain people, this vulnerability may be pre-programmed by genetics and early environmental factors, possibly due to a shortage of glial support cells. For these people, depression is a ticking time bomb, awaiting detonation from a bout of stress.

- *Limbic mood department:* Due to the heightened activity of the stress box, anxiety and negativity will be a likely adjunct to stress. The major casualty in this department during stress, however, is the memory box, which is rich in glucocortisol receptors. The memory box requires the presence of this hormone for routine memory formation, but the presence of excessive amounts has a counter-productive effect. The latter interferes with the routine production of memories and also prevents new nerve cells from developing, resulting in memory and concentration impairment. A similar process occurs, as we will see later, in depression.

Effects On General Health

While it may sound from what we have seen above as though stress is the body's most dangerous adversary, it is in fact a key ally. A healthy stress system is very important to our general physical wellbeing. Constant bouts of acute and chronic stress can, however, give rise to various problems. For instance, high blood pressure, stroke and cardiac problems result from heightened levels of adrenalin and noradrenalin. Immune-system damage and the clumping together of platelets (an important component of our blood's clotting system) due to an excess of glucocortisol give rise to infection and heart attacks, respectively. The body's ability to defend against a potentially fatal illness like cancer may also be compromised.

Summary

1   The stress box in the limbic mood department is in charge of the whole stress system. During times of stress, this box activates two major pathways. One works via the brain stem (especially in response to acute stress) by sending instructions to the adrenal stress glands to release adrenalin and noradrenalin into the bloodstream. The presence of these hormones gives rise to symptoms such as dry mouth, palpitations, stomach churning, sweating and alertness. These feelings are common before an important exam or job interview.

2   The second pathway works via the hormone control box (especially in response to chronic stress) by sending instructions to the adrenal glands to release the stress hormone glucocortisol. This prepares the body for a longer fight by reorganising its energy reserves to tackle the threat exclusively.

3   When the threat has passed, the body restores levels of these hormones to within normal parameters again.

4   When the person feels under constant threat, however, and stress is

prolonged, levels of glucocortisol may remain high. This damages the mood cables and mood departments. It also increases the risk of heart attack and damages the immune system, making the body vulnerable to infection.

5   The effects of chronic stress on our mood system are fatigue, poor concentration, reduced drive, sleep problems and an inability to derive any pleasure from life.

The Interaction between the Mood and Stress Systems

The stress system and mood system are intertwined. This intertwining underlies all the illnesses discussed in this book. For most people, periods of chronic stress are inevitable, but normally the mood system is robust enough to survive the onslaught of stress hormones. The body is designed to help the person cope with stress, not force the person to succumb to it. That is not to say that a period of normal stress will be without fatigue, poor concentration, sleep disturbance and a general dissatisfaction in life. These complaints will be temporary ones, however, and will subside when the perceived threat has passed.

Some people do not recover from chronic stress so easily, however, because their mood system becomes dysfunctional when they are faced with stressful situations. Their system does not bounce back from stress in a normal fashion, and is more likely to deteriorate rapidly until the more serious conditions of depression, anxiety and substance abuse (if they are vulnerable to this) seize control of their brains.

Further research may reveal more about the relationship between the stress and mood systems. This will not only foster a better understanding of these illnesses but may also provide radically different and more effective treatments than the ones that are presently available.

4: THE SYSTEMS AND BIOLOGY OF NORMAL MOOD

Having explored the nature and function of the mood system, the Green Flag of normal mood and behaviour will now be discussed. For many people who are unaware that they are suffering from depression, anxiety and addiction, what they consider normal may be a horrendous experience for someone who is free of these illnesses. To understand what it means to be depressed, anxious and dependent on addictive substances, one first has to be aware of the features, biology and course of normal mood.

The Green Flag Checklist

When asked about their mood, people are likely to respond that they feel 'up', 'down', or simply 'fine'. When a doctor is asked to make the same assessment about a person, he or she will apply much more stringent criteria before reaching a conclusion. A doctor is likely to check for the prevalence of a number of key symptoms which will give a better indication of the state of the person's mood. The checklist of symptoms on the next page is designed to identify problems in the mood system.

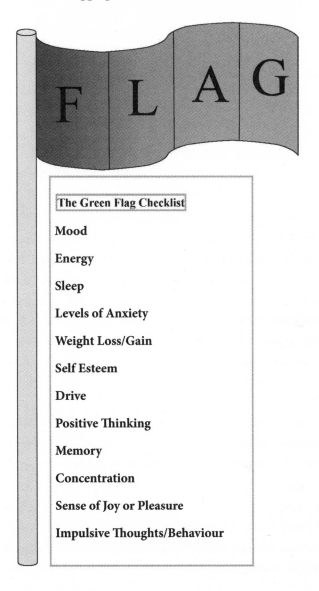

Figure 1: The Green Flag Checklist

How Can I Tell If My Mood System Is Well?
Mood

This is arguably the easiest to assess. All of us will regularly experience feelings of happiness and sadness in our lives. These emotions originate from our limbic mood department (probably mediated through our serotonin and dopamine systems). It is possible to feel both these emotions within minutes of each other, due to the situation in which one finds oneself; it is also possible to experience more prolonged phases of positivity, and negativity. These variations are normal, and are heavily influenced by normal life events such as relationships.

If mood drops down to a level where it becomes debilitating, however, there is cause for concern, particularly if low mood lasts for a sustained period (of between two to four weeks). If it continues past this point, the Red Flag of depression may have arrived. The longer this low mood persists, the higher the risk of such a bout deepening. It is important, therefore, for people in this situation to seek help as early as possible; indeed, these early weeks should be seen as a critical warning period.

Sometimes the opposite may occur, and mood may rise to an unnaturally high level. While this may not appear to be cause for complaint, it constitutes an equally vital warning of impending illness. In both cases, help should be sought to assess the cause of the mood changes.

Energy

Exhaustion is not just a symptom of mental illness; it is a feature of life. It can result from intense physical or mental activity, or from stress, and is usually corrected by an adequate amount of rest and sleep. When stress or illnesses are absent, a person usually has sufficient energy to cope with day-to-day activities. If the mood system is not functioning properly, however, a paralysing fatigue can emerge. This leaves a person physically and emotionally drained. In the absence of any physical ailment, this is an important sign that the mood system is experiencing difficulties.

Sleep

Normal sleeping patterns are a function of the mood system. Sleep allows the brain to rest and provides an opportunity for minor damage inflicted during the brain's day-to-day operation to be repaired. It is also an opportunity for the brain to reorganize the memories of the day. The most notable warning sign of a malfunctioning mood system is a disturbance of these patterns. This can range from difficulty in falling asleep, awakening too early, awakening periodically throughout the night, or feeling exhausted upon waking in the morning.

Depression, anxiety and addiction all create sleep-pattern disturbance. As sleeping patterns are highly individual, a warning sign is a drastic change in the usual pattern. Some people prefer eight to ten hours' sleep, whereas others function well on only four to six hours. The need for sleep tends to decrease as a person gets older. There is no set 'abnormal' sleeping pattern, but if a person's sleep deviates from its usual pattern, it can be considered abnormal for them – and a possible indicator of mood problems.

Levels of Anxiety

Anxiety, which can be defined as a state of apprehension, fear or worry, is a normal reaction when faced with final exams, a driving test or a first date, for instance. When these feelings are unremitting and evoked by even the most benign of situations, however, to a point where they begin to interfere with a person's day-to-day functioning, it is indicative of illness.

For those suffering from a long-term anxiety disorder, this paralysing anxiety is all they know. Others suffering from depression or addiction may be familiar with this feeling too. The persistent fear that such people experience originates in the mood system.

Appetite

This refers to the satisfaction that is sought from eating and sexual activity. Metabolic rates differ from person to person: some people will struggle to keep their weight at a healthy level, for instance, whereas others will remain slim apparently regardless of what they eat. As with sleep, it is not the appetite itself that is an indicator of illness, but a sudden change in that appetite.

Depression can suppress appetite, resulting in a loss of interest in food, with consequent rapid weight loss. It can also increase appetite, as the mood system attempts to compensate for the declining pleasure derived from eating. A loss of interest in sex is also common. As with eating, however, a small number of those affected will experience increased libido. If the appetite for food and sex remains constant, it is a good sign that the mood system is functioning normally.

Self-esteem

This symptom is often well-concealed, and hidden even from the person affected by it. It concerns our perception of ourselves. In illnesses such as depression, feelings of self-worth are greatly diminished. Questions to ask yourself include: Do you feel uncomfortable in the presence of others? Do you think your ideas and feelings are unimportant? Do you feel useless? Do you constantly evaluate yourself negatively? Do you accept yourself 'unconditionally'?

If you are well, you will feel comfortable with others and confident in yourself. You may doubt yourself in certain situations, but in general you will feel good about yourself. If you answer 'yes' to these questions, and in particular 'no' to the last one, you may be suffering from low self-esteem.

Drive

Motivation and drive are highly individual. Some people have a strong drive to excel at work, while others focus on their relationships or aim for sporting achievement, and so on. Others may be of a more relaxed disposition, and may be content with their current situation. If your drive has been extremely low for a long time, however, and you do not have much interest in anything, or if you suddenly find yourself not doing activities which you would normally be involved in, because you simply 'can't be bothered', this may be an indication that you are suffering from an illness such as depression.

Positive Thinking

Positive thinking involves an interpretation of the world, and our relationship with others, that is optimistic, hopeful and upbeat. Some personalities are prone to pessimism, and see the 'glass' as being half- empty. This common attitude could also be interpreted as cautious, realistic and sensible. When this pessimism becomes almost apocalyptic, however, and the person starts to wonder what the point of the glass existing in the first place is, it is likely that a mood disorder affecting thought processes is present.

Memory

At first glance, this seems an unlikely symptom, and is often overlooked by those not familiar with mental illness. Memory loss is normally associated in the mind of the layperson with Alzheimer's disease or dementia. Memory disturbance is also a feature of mood disorders, however, as the processing of memory is embedded deep in the mood system. This becomes evident when those suffering from depression and anxiety struggle to remember even the simplest of things, making their life chaotic and confusing. For instance, not being able to remember things at work will impair performance, and can be perceived as incompetence, whereas the cause is in fact a widespread malfunction of the mood system. Students both at school and university will suffer from this condition even more, as their success in examinations depends in large part on their ability to commit information to memory.

Concentration

Concentration – the ability to focus one's attention on a particular task for a length of time, and to process information received efficiently – has a direct effect on memory. Obviously, if concentration cannot be achieved, there is nothing to commit to memory! People suffering from depression or anxiety will find it difficult to read a book or newspaper, watch a film, or finish any task they start. This has serious negative ramifications for those who are at work or in full-time education.

Sense of Joy or Pleasure

Normal sources of pleasure in life include relationships, sex, food and alcohol. Hence the joy and pleasure that are extrapolated from such activities are major incentives to a person's participation in a full and active life. Without such rewards, the world appears an empty and meaningless place.

For those suffering from mental illness, the world is exactly that. As the reward system is a component of the mood system, general malfunction in the latter results in a generalised lack of enjoyment. The negative thinking outlined above can only be confirmed and exacerbated by this absence of positive biological feedback from the environment. Known officially as 'anhedonia', this vacuum of pleasure is a trademark symptom of depression.

Impulsive Thoughts and Behaviour

Some individuals are naturally impulsive, novelty-seeking risk-takers, whereas others are of a more cautious disposition. It is the job of the mood system to regulate impulses that will result in potentially harmful consequences if the person indulges them.

If the mood system is not working, a person's rational inhibitions are often diminished. In such cases, suicide, self-mutilation and violence directed towards others may become acceptable, reasonable and often unavoidable. When a person is going through a difficult period, fleeting and impulsive thoughts of self-harm can emerge. These thoughts are quickly and forcefully eliminated by the mood system when it is working normally. In illnesses such as depression and addiction, however, the ability to control these thoughts is substantially impaired, and the person in some cases may begin to elaborate on such thoughts and plan in detail how they will carry out the violent acts. Recurrent thoughts of self-harm, and how it can be achieved, are an indicator of serious mood-system disturbance.

Having read this checklist, you should have a clearer indication of your mood state, and whether it is really 'fine'. As we have seen, mood is not just a feeling of well-being but a cluster of different functions, all of which originate from the same system in the brain. The majority of people reading this list will find their mood system to be in good working order. Others will realise that they may be ill, and require support, empathy and assistance from those around them.

Whether or not you are suffering from, or at risk of, a mood problem is determined by the amount of the aforementioned symptoms you can relate to. Whether you feel you have been having some of these difficulties for a long time, or if you have noticed them appearing only recently, you should contact a health professional for further assessment. Difficulties which have lasted longer than four weeks warrant careful investigation by your doctor.

As a general rule, illness in the mood system results in a 'domino effect': the longer it remains untreated, the more the symptoms appear. For this reason, it is recommended that the Green Flag checklist be consulted on a regular basis. Early detection facilitates early treatment, and the damage to the brain caused by such illness can then be minimised.

One advantage of a healthy mood system is that the immune system will be strong and capable of fighting infection, illness and cancer cells. Other advantages are a decreased risk of osteoporosis and heart attacks. Those who are sceptical about the direct link between mental illness and general illness should note that those who are suffering from a serious bout of depression, for example, are five times more likely to suffer a heart attack than an average person.

The body and the mood system are interdependent. If mood is normal, general health is improved. This is not to say that someone who is free from mental illness will remain immune from other diseases, but they are better protected against them.

Biology of the Green Flag

If the flag is green, then the mood departments, mood cables, glands and hormones are all working smoothly and within normal parameters.In this case, the various boxes which control memory, stress and behaviour are doing what they were designed to do: promoting homeostasis, or balance within the body. The adrenal stress glands are producing adequate, but not excessive, amounts of its two main hormones, adrenalin and glucocortisol. Responses to stress, illness and disease are not impaired. The immune system is working efficiently, and the heart and bones are not in any immediate danger.

Course of the Green Flag

The flag will be green for the majority of a person's life. It is almost inevitable that it will change colour at some stage. Many people go through periods of depression, anxiety or addiction, and some will spend their whole lives dealing with these illnesses. Statistically speaking, between 10 and 15 percent of the population will experience a bout of the Red Flag of depression at some stage. Others will be paralysed by the Yellow Flag of anxiety, or will fall victim to the Purple Flag of addiction.

The Green Flag's most formidable adversary (genes and early environment aside) is stress, for which the fast pace of modern life is a breeding ground. Other challenges to the Green Glag include alcohol abuse, relationship break-down, and isolation.

Over the last five years, there has been a huge focus on healthy living in Ireland. Diet assessment, cholesterol measurement, prostate checking, breast screening, and cervical smears are seen as critical to the health of the nation. Yet the health of our mood system is not discussed. Such neglect is not only allowing mental illness to remain undetected and run rampant but is also, as has been discussed, increasing the chances of various illnesses, such as heart disease and cancer.

5: HOW TO KEEP YOUR MOOD SYSTEM HEALTHY

The Top Ten Ways of Keeping Your Mood System Healthy

Follow the Green Flag Checklist

As one should regularly check for the presence of a tumour to protect against testicular and breast cancer, reviewing the Green Flag checklist regularly ensures that you have a good chance of detecting mental illness at an early stage. If significant symptoms are persistent, medical advice should be sought.

Reduce Personal Stress

The key to fighting stress is identifying its cause. This will be different for each person. For most people, work, commuting, family problems, and relationship and financial difficulties are common sources of stress.

Solutions to work-related stress may include working part-time, reducing commuting times by working closer to home and, as a last resort, removing oneself from stressful working situations. Relationship or family problems should be dealt with as quickly as possible. Financial situations should be constantly reviewed, especially bills and credit cards, to prevent debt-related pressure and stress emerging.

Another important cause of stress in our lives is unrealistic self-expectations. Many of us do not accept ourselves as being genuinely human – that is, 'warts and all'. If we fail – as all of us will regularly do – to reach the often impossibly high goals we set ourselves, we become our own worst critics. We often extend these ideal standards to others and are disappointed when they too fail to reach them. Learning to accept ourselves unconditionally and to look at others in the same way is a vital component of mental health. Examining various areas of our lives with this core concept in mind will help ensure that the Green Flag flies!

Exercise

Exercise is a powerful stimulant of the mood system. The euphoria-inducing chemicals known as endorphins which are released during exercise provide both energy and relaxation. Exercise also stimulates the dopamine system, alleviating symptoms of mental fatigue. The memory box in particular benefits greatly from exercises like walking and swimming, which encourage the creation of new neurons.

Thirty to forty minutes of exercise per day is ideal for maintaining a healthy mood system. All forms of exercise deliver similar benefits, so it is simply a case of personal preference. Apart from controlling weight and helping the heart, exercise will also help to keep the flag green.

Get Back to Nature

Shopping centres and busy department stores drain a person's energy – along with their bank account! Walking in the countryside – or by our lakes, sea shores, or rivers – fishing and swimming are all excellent ways of clearing the mind and providing much-needed relaxation for body, mind and spirit. The emotional part of the brain is particularly affected in a positive manner by interaction with Mother Nature.

Relax and Contemplate

For those who live in or near cities, the world is a noisy place. Traffic, television, computer games and mobile phones break the silence which is necessary for relaxation. People often return from work, where they have been staring at a computer screen all day, to stare at a television screen all night.

Our mood system needs periods of calm and silence. Activities such as yoga, meditation or massage, or just going for a walk, fulfil this requirement. Time for quiet contemplation also helps to keep the flag green.

Improve Your Diet

You are what you eat, and the mood system does not escape this concept. Instant dinners, sugary food, and takeaway treats, although convenient, are damaging to the body. Although it takes time and energy to cook properly, the rewards for mood are great.

Fresh fruit and vegetables, fish, grains, meat and water help the system cope with day-to-day life. Cooking in olive oil, and reducing the intake of meat, dairy products (apart from eggs) and vegetable oils, and increasing the consumption of fish and soya is a good place to start.

Changes like this will reduce the likelihood of obesity and diabetes, and it should also be pointed out that up to a third of the energy derived from food is used by the brain, and that the mood system itself depends on certain vitamins and minerals. These include vitamin C, the B vitamins, zinc and magnesium. Supplements which help to keep the mood system healthy include the whole family of B vitamins, vitamin C, Omega 6 oils like evening primrose, and Omega 3 fish oils (so called because oily fish like mackerel, herring, tuna, salmon and sardines are the best natural source of such oils).

There has been a great deal of interest in these oils in recent years. They contain essential fatty acids which are usually absent from the Western diet. The body cannot manufacture these acids on its own, so it relies on either diet (in the form of oily fish, flax seeds or flax oil, walnuts and some green vegetables) or supplements to ensure the efficient operation of the mood system.

The most important oils are EPA (Eicosapentaenoic Acid) and DHA (Docosahexaenoic Acid). These are essential for the smooth running of our mood cables, helping to build the receptor sites for neurotransmitters and in the day-to-day maintenance of the cell membranes of our neurons. DHA is significant in the formation of the foetal brain in the womb, the neurological development of children under five, and general heart function.

Most brands of Omega 3 oils contain a mixture of EPA and DHA. Some experts believe that capsules containing higher doses of pure EPA (without vitamin E and with smaller amounts of DHA) are of more value when dealing with illnesses of the mood system, like depression. The recommended dose for the average healthy person who does not have such illnesses is probably 250 to

500 milligrammes, or two portions of oily fish a week. (The only exception is for people who are also on anticoagulants (blood thinners).)

Omega 3 oils have also been shown to reduce deaths from heart attacks by 30 percent and sudden death by 45 percent in heart watch prevention trials. (This programme, run by family doctors and practice nurses, monitors the continuing health of those who have either had a heart attack, or who have required a coronary artery bypass or stent to maintain the patency of the blood vessels serving the heart.) Whilst there seems to be a benefit from taking higher doses in such cases, the general view is that two helpings of oily fish (equivalent to 500 milligrammes) per week, or low doses of these essential fatty acids, is generally sufficient.

It is interesting to note that, in parts of the world, such as Japan, where there is a higher consumption of oily fish, there seems to be a lower risk of breast cancer, depression and coronary heart disease. This suggests the importance of diet in general, and possibly fish oils in particular, in preventing these illnesses. Whether this will prove to be of significance, only time and further research will tell.

A diet rich in these essential fats should begin from infancy onwards. Our typical diet in the West often lacks the building blocks necessary for the development of a healthy body and mind. Just observe the contents of the lunchbox or 'deli diet' of the typical school-going child. Some schools are challenging this trend and are at the forefront of encouraging healthy eating habits. This is a very welcome development.

A close examination of the contents of the average supermarket trolley will often reveal a huge dependency on tins and packets, large bottles of high-sugar-content or caffeinated drinks, and a notable absence of fruit and vegetables. Fast-sugar-release foods like white bread and rolls, white rice, confectionery, processed meals and so on have become the norm in a cash-rich, time-poor economy. Are we at risk of becoming an overfed, undernourished generation? Obesity may prove to be one of the major health problems over the next few decades. The obvious medical consequences of this are diabetes and coronary heart disease.

The consequences for the young person's developing mood system are equally alarming. The brain requires proper nutrition for normal growth, development and function. The widespread ignorance of this information could turn out to be one of the casual factors in the increasing prevalence of child behavioural problems and depression in the under-twenty-five age group. Most parents worry about the increasing rates of depression in young men and women, but they rarely consider the role of proper diet, exercise and supplements in the prevention of depression.

It is advisable that young people eat plenty of freshly prepared and cooked healthy food, together with regular portions of fruit and vegetables. Soft drinks should be replaced with milk, water or fruit juices. Growing children, teenagers and young adults should, unless they are eating a proper healthy diet high in fruit, vegetables and oily fish, take B vitamins and fish-oil supplements. Age twelve to twenty-five, in particular, is a period of dramatic brain and mood-system development, and a supply of these essential fatty acids is essential. If we wait until late in the teen years to implement these dietary changes, the benefits are greatly reduced.

Watch Your Alcohol Intake

Alcohol, when taken in moderation, helps a person to relax, especially in social situations. There is no major health risk associated with alcohol if it is used in a sensible manner. Nonetheless, alcohol is classified as a depressive substance, and in genetically vulnerable people its misuse can lead to addiction. Alcohol misuse leaves a person depressed and irritable and can also result in a greater risk of impulsive, violent behaviour.

The international guidelines set arbitrary weekly limits of 21 units for males and 14 units for females (1 unit = 1 glass of beer, or 1 small glass of wine (125 mls) of 8 to 9 percent strength; 2 units = 1 pint of beer, 1 average size (175 mls) glass of wine of 12 percent strength, or 1 large measure of spirits).

Some experts regard 21 to 50 units of alcohol per week as hazardous, and more than 50 units as harmful. In practice, this weekly allowance is sometimes consumed on a single night. When 12 units of more (6 pints of beer, or 6 measures of spirits) are consumed in one sitting, it is classified as a binge. Alcohol is best consumed in small amounts, or with food.

Some useful guidelines to healthy drinking should include the following:

- Try if at all possible to avoid binge drinking
- Learn to drink slowly rather than gulping down alcoholic drinks
- Be aware of what constitutes 'safe' drinking by memorising the limits given above
- If you feel guilty when approached about your drinking habits, then it is quite likely that you have a problem
- Avoid drinking as a means of overcoming shyness or boredom, or as a solution to any other problem
- Have a number of alcohol-free days every week
- Taking food with alcohol is always preferable to drinking on an empty stomach
- Avoid buying rounds where possible
- Avoid using alcohol to self-medicate during times of stress, anxiety and low mood
- If you are finding Mondays difficult due to excessive alcohol intake over the weekend, you need to review your drinking habits
- Do not allow friends or workmates to dictate your personal drinking patterns
- Do not be afraid to say 'no'

Heavy drinking over the age of fifty-five to sixty can be extremely harmful, and results in an increased risk of falls, interaction with medication, impotence, sleep and memory problems, depression and dementia. The older you get, the less alcohol you should consume. Unfortunately, in practice the reverse is often the case.

It is frequently in the aftermath of a binge-drinking session that the underlying symptoms of illnesses such as depression begin to rise to the surface, in the form of decreased mood, anxiety, and suicidal thoughts and actions. Heavy alcohol intake is not compatible with the Green Flag.

Spirituality

Religion and spirituality are commonly misunderstood terms. Religion is a specific system of beliefs; spirituality relates to a more general search for the meaning of existence. This search can bring peace and harmony. Many rush through life without reflecting on its meaning or relevance. Time spent on such reflection may be beneficial to mental health. Many experts feel that the increased incidence of depression and suicide particularly in the young may lie partially in the absence of such a focus. The religious structures that existed before and are now in dramatic decline may not have been perfect, but their removal has left a vacuum. Whether or not the filling of this vacuum is of any benefit to those at risk of mental illness is for the individual to decide.

Lifestyle

We seem to be living in a world where our lifestyle has become increasingly unhealthy. We are often overweight or obese. We are obsessed with world of technology, becoming very individualistic in our behaviour and less community based.

Advertising gives the impression that if one generates and consumes a great deal of money, life will be perfect. Those who feel as though they cannot reach such lofty materialistic heights may start to feel that they are failures. In short, the pressures on young people to achieve and consume are immense.

As long as this ideology is predominant, the Green Flag is under threat. Consumerism is an empty promise, and its rewards are without substance. While impulse buying is thought to be mediated by dopamine, and people often feel better after a shopping spree, this positive effect on the mood system is short-lived.

Communication

Just as neurons in the brain only survive the harsh and unforgiving pruning process by communicating with others around them, people can only survive the harsh and unforgiving events in life by doing the same. Loneliness is one of the hidden enemies of normal mood and happiness.

Equally, as a breakdown in communication between neurons results in illness, a breakdown in communication between partners or families results in separation and divorce. This can lead to a major assault on the Green Flag.

In particular, men in such situations find it difficult to admit to feelings of sadness, confusion and loss, as it is often not socially acceptable for them to do so. So instead of reaching out for help, they conceal their emotions. This repression creates problems in the mood system, and increases the risk of depression and suicide. It is important for both men and women to express freely how they feel, without experiencing humiliation or rejection for being honest and open.

An absence of emotional expression makes the Green Flag difficult to maintain. It is advisable to keep lines of communication with significant others open, to set aside time to converse with them without any distractions, and to allow them to express any feelings of unhappiness.

Conclusion

For the mood system to remain healthy, proper diet, taking dietary supplements, exercise, meditation, communication, monitoring of stress, and moderating alcohol intake are all important. If these changes are made, improvements to our physical and mental health may not be the only benefits: a feeling of peace and tranquillity is also likely to result. Try it and see. You will be amazed at the results!

PART TWO

The Red Flag: Depression

1: SIMPLE DEPRESSION

Depression has been clouded by myth for a long time: it is often believed that it is a weakness, a personal flaw in the sufferer. This myth leads to a fear of discussing the problem. The fear results in silence, which maintains ignorance. Such ignorance compounds the sufferer's misery and effectively seals their fate. It is time to break this myth. Depression is not a weakness: it is a biological illness which damages the body's mood system. It presents with distinct symptoms, operates via well-known biological mechanisms and, most importantly, is in many cases easily treatable.

In order to break this myth, depression must be regarded in the same light as diabetes and heart disease – illnesses resulting from genetic and environmental interaction. The brain is classified as an organ just like the heart, liver and lungs, and is just as vulnerable to malfunction and illness as these organs.

Generally, a diabetic does not ignore their symptoms and view them as a weakness; rather, they seek medical help and treatment that will keep them alive. The chronic suffering, health risks, damage to quality of life, and mortality rates associated with diabetes are also associated with depression, so why should the sufferer not react in the same way as a diabetic?

The symptoms evident in depression (negative thinking, low mood, fatigue, lack of pleasure, suicidal thoughts, and so on) leave the victim ill-equipped to deal with society's ignorance about the condition. Statements like: 'Pull yourself together!' and 'Snap out of it!' are not only naive but counterproductive. Such ultimatums make the sufferer feel responsible for their own condition, and weak for not being able to defend against it. If they could 'snap out of it', they would do so instantly, but they can't, and as this is seen as the only solution by society, they conclude that they are not going to get better. Thus such statements end up making the depression worse.

The time has come to promote an understanding of this illness, and to support those who have suffered in silence for so long. This chapter deals with the symptoms, causes, course and treatment of the biological illness of depression. There is also a question-and-answer section for those who are trying to understand their own illness, or the illness of a person close to them.

Symptoms of the Red Flag of Depression

Some people reading this chapter will suspect that either they themselves, or someone close to them, are suffering from depression, but need more information on the subject. Others will know that either they, or a person close to them, are definitely suffering from depression, and are seeking to understand the condition. To help such people identify and understand this illness, the following is a list of symptoms that the depressed person may be experiencing, and a description of how these symptoms will manifest themselves to those around them.

Low Mood

'I feel weighed down by hopelessness and sadness. It is a physical pain in my heart, and no one understands how terrible it feels.'

John, a nineteen-year-old undergraduate student who has developed depression on moving away from his family for the first time, to live in a flat in Dublin. He is successfully hiding his depression from his family and friends. Alcohol relieves the pain for short periods, but its embrace is fleeting and illusory.

Low mood is an overwhelming feeling of inner sadness, gloom and despair. It is the main warning sign that the mood system is in trouble. Even when the mood system is operating normally, mood swings are inevitable, and are easily influenced by life circumstances.

Low mood, however, is different to 'feeling blue'; those who have not experienced it will not understand the distinction. In depression, these feelings are overpowering and devastating. To people with depression, particularly if the condition is severe, it feels like having fallen down a deep dark well: the individual is alone, hurt, and unable to communicate with others. As they feel that there is no chance of receiving help, or of climbing out on their own, they lie inactive and succumb to their inevitable fate. The feelings of pain they experience may be beyond the comprehension of an outsider.

What John feels:

- A deep emotional pain so intense he would gladly replace it with any physical pain
- Enduring despair, sadness and inner turmoil
- Frustration that no one understands his pain, or cares about it
- An increasing reliance on alcohol to numb the pain

What those close to John may observe:

- He may smile less, and his emotional reactions may often be subdued
- At times he may suddenly lash out in anger at those closest to them
- He may be drinking excessively
- He may withdraw into his room, listen to dark angry music, play video games, or use Internet chat rooms

Fatigue

'The simplest of tasks drains me of all my energy. I just want to sleep all the time.'

Mary, a twenty-seven-year-old mother with two small children, who has started to develop symptoms of depression following a series of stressful events, in particular the death of a close friend from cancer.

Exhaustion is an inevitable consequence of intense and stressful physical or mental activity. In depression, however, a more serious form of exhaustion emerges. This form of exhaustion is best described as fatigue: it is a complete lack of energy, resulting in an inability to perform the easiest of tasks.

What Mary feels:

- Completely sapped of energy
- Normal functioning becomes a battle: work, shopping and other day-to-day activities all require a level of effort she cannot muster
- Unrefreshed by sleep
- Unrelenting exhaustion all the time
- A further drop in self-esteem and a feeling of uselessness, as she is not able to complete even the most mundane activities

What those close to Mary may observe:

- She may return to bed frequently in the middle of the day
- She complains that she is tired all the time, and is prone to yawning and falling asleep
- She is having difficulties completing normal activities
- At times she appears listless and apathetic
- She appears to be acting in a lazy fashion

Sleep Difficulties

'Why can't I sleep when I'm tired all the time? I lie awake all night, or if I do manage to fall asleep, I wake early. It's so frustrating.'

Thomas, a thirty-two-year-old successful businessman, who has been suffering from undiagnosed bouts of depression for more than a decade.

Sleep disturbance can refer to a sudden change in a person's normal sleeping pattern, or a long-standing pattern of sleeping which is broken, fitful and un-satisfactory. It presents most commonly in depression as pure insomnia.

What Thomas experiences:

- Difficulties falling asleep despite the fact that he is exhausted
- Early-morning waking
- Waking intermittently throughout the night
- Unpleasant nightmares
- Somnolence during the day
- An increased reliance on alcohol to induce sleep

What those close to Thomas will observe:

- He walks around the house at night looking for things to do
- He lies awake for a long time before falling asleep
- He is exhausted in the morning
- He may return to bed during the day when the opportunity presents itself
- He regularly drinks alcohol before going to bed

Anxiety

'I am constantly on a high state of alertness, and I always feel under pressure. I cannot cope when something goes wrong. I sometimes feel panicky for no obvious reason.'

Peter, aged twenty-two, who for the previous three years has successfully hidden how he feels.

Anxiety often occurs alongside depression, and can be described as constant panic, tension and worry about things going wrong. It is a vicious circle because anxiety uses up so much energy that the person is too tired to deal with the situations of which they are afraid. This results in further anxiety when other situations arise, as the first ones have not been tackled.

What Peter feels:

- Agitated and irritable
- Worried about not being able to perform simple tasks properly
- Excessively fatigued

- Episodes of panic
- A reluctance to start new tasks or take on new responsibilities

What those close to Peter will observe:

- He appears tense and often 'snaps' when asked a simple question
- Restlessness
- Sensitivity to criticism
- Regular alcohol intake, often drinking alone or at odd times
- Persistent inability to make decisions
- He may complain of physical irregularities such as headaches, palpitations and stomach pains

Weight Loss or Weight Gain

'I'm just not hungry any more. Food does not look appetising and it's too much energy to eat. Hopefully I will waste away into nothing.'

Catherine, a single parent aged twenty-four. The stress of coping with a small child on social welfare, living in a small, poorly equipped flat, and with a partner who abuses alcohol (and her), has triggered a bout of depression. She has lost more than a stone in weight. Her diet (already poor due to lack of money and knowledge about nutrition) has been reduced to coffee and cigarettes.

Or:

'Eating has become a habit for me. It distracts me from how I feel for a while. Then I feel worse as I get fatter and uglier, but who is going to look twice at me anyway?'

Michael, who, although presenting an outer image of seeming normality, has suffered for years with poor self-esteem. Now, at the age of thirty, he is grossly obese from years of using food as a coping mechanism for his bouts of low mood.

Usually in depression, a sudden and complete loss of interest in food ensues. The weight loss prevalent in depression does not usually result from a person's negative self-image and dissatisfaction with their appearance, however: it occurs because eating becomes a laborious chore that yields no enjoyment. Sometimes, although not as often, the depressed person will eat excessively because it makes them feel better, and weight gain becomes the symptom to look out for.

What Catherine experiences:

- A sudden and absolute lack of interest in food
- Difficulty in finishing a meal
- A tendency to regard food as one area of life that she can control
- Decreased energy
- Weight loss

What those close to Catherine will observe:

- A rejection of food when it is offered
- A seeming loss of any interest in food
- Visible weight loss
- Irritation when friends try to encourage her to eat
- That she seems to be withdrawing 'into herself'

What Michael experiences:

- A desire to hide his true feelings behind his large girth and a mask of seeming good humour
- An increasing craving for food to numb his emotional pain
- A complete lack of interest in his personal appearance
- A feeling that food is the one area of his life that he can control
- A deep seated lack of self worth: 'I'm just a fat, useless nobody'
- A denial of the consequences of his obesity: 'After all, who will notice if I was gone anyway'

What those close to Michael may observe:

- He takes no interest in his appearance
- He rejects any offers of help or advice
- He has complete disregard for the consequences of his obesity
- He seems to binge-eat at every opportunity
- Although he is always smiling, it seems to be 'skin deep'

Loss of Self-Esteem

'I am ashamed of the weak, useless, boring, incompetent failure that I am. People hate spending time with me.'

Carl, a twenty-four-year-old mechanic whose quiet disposition and painful shyness has disguised his inner torment from those close to him. Depression visited him first at the age of seventeen and has been an unwelcome but frequent visitor ever since.

Self-esteem refers to whether we love and value ourselves unconditionally. Depressed people feel unloved, unworthy, and of no value. It is a common and distressing set of symptoms.

How Carl feels:

- Of no value or use to society
- An unnecessary burden on others
- That his opinions are irrelevant
- Completely non-accepting of himself

What those close to Carl will observe:

- He has become self-absorbed
- He avoids and withdraws from social interaction
- He makes negative comments about himself
- He is reluctant to express his opinions

Loss of Drive

'I don't enjoy any of the activities that I used to. It all seems like so much effort now, and I don't see the point.'

Maura, a twenty-four-year-old working mother who developed depression three months after the birth of her first child.

Drive refers to a person's willingness to participate in an activity. This is usually absent in depression, and results in idleness. Loss of drive is compounded by fatigue, as the person lacks either the will or the means to do anything.

What Maura feels:

- Apathy, an inability to see the point of any activity
- A lack of purpose
- A pervasive boredom with regard to life

What those close to Maura will observe:

- Avoidance of tasks and situations
- Unwillingness to become involved in normal activities
- A dissolving of ambition and goals

Negative Thinking

'I cannot wait till I am dead. Then I will be at peace, the loneliness and hurt will be gone. I cannot go on, not like this. I have often thought of trying to explain how I feel to those closest to me: to share the pain. But what would be the point. After all, there's nothing they or anyone else can do to help, and I would only be burdening them with my troubles.'

Andrew, a twenty-six-year-old postgraduate student, suffering from his second major bout of depression. Andrew, like many others with this illness, is having relationship difficulties with his girlfriend, blaming her for not seeing his pain, and using alcohol in large amounts. This does little, however, to silence his negative thoughts that he does not deserve to live: he reasons that no one, including her, would notice if he was gone.

Negative thinking is a distorted and often false interpretation of the world (sometimes called 'rumination') which focuses exclusively on unpleasant events and results in pessimistic predictions. Although to others this thinking seems odd and irrational, to the depressed person it is an important explanation as to why they feel the way they do. Because they view the world and their own existence as being empty and futile, there is no point in seeking help: they feel that it is unlikely that anything can be done. This fosters a sense of predestined and unavoidable suffering, and explains why they isolate themselves, and in certain cases rationalise suicide.

What Andrew feels:

- An inability to see the positive aspects of anything or anyone (including his girlfriend, who cares deeply for him), particularly himself
- A sense of futility about existence in general
- Pessimism about the prospects of treatment
- A conviction that his life is not salvageable
- That he deserves the pain he is feeling
- That the hidden cigarette burns he occasionally inflicts on himself to ease the emotional pain are 'all he deserves'

What those close to Andrew will observe:

- A predominantly negative verbal assessment of health, family, friends and himself that seems to bear no relation to reality
- A decline in goal-oriented behaviour, as he is not working towards anything
- A refusal of help from anyone
- Occasional bursts of anger (particularly after drinking alcohol) that nobody can understand the world (of negativity) he lives in

Poor Memory

'I have become increasingly forgetful, and have difficulty remembering the simplest of things, like what I did yesterday.'

Noreen, a single, very busy twenty-seven-year-old manager who is struggling to cope with her day-to-day duties due to depression triggered by a prolonged period of sustained stress.

Depression reduces short-term memory – the ability to retain information concerning recent events. Naturally, if this continues, the capacity to form, store and retrieve long-term information is also adversely affected. This, combined with damage to the part of the brain which filters and organises the storage and retrieval of long-term memories, leads to chaos in the life of the person.

What Noreen experiences:

- Difficulties remembering exceptionally simple things, e.g. repeating what she has just read in a newspaper
- A reduction in the effectiveness of studying and memorising data, regardless of the amount of time she spends on it
- Difficulty performing in a job in which memory is an important component

What those close to Noreen will observe:

- Noticeable and often bizarre forgetfulness, bordering on eccentricity
- Exasperation when trying to remember data
- Slowed performance in the workplace

Reduced Concentration

'I don't read any more, it is too much effort to make sense out of the words, and it is becoming difficult to pay attention to anything.'

George, a seventeen-year-old student, struggling to study as he battles internally with a bout of unrecognised depression

Concentration is the ability to focus exclusively on a task for its duration, from start to completion. Concentration is a prerequisite for learning to occur. One cannot commit to memory what one is not paying attention to. Furthermore, the initial performance of a task in work, for example, demands concentration. Subsequent improved performance depends on memory. Without the initial concentration, this cannot be achieved, and new skills cannot be learnt.

What George experiences:

- Easily distracted when performing any task, particularly in relation to the upcoming exam
- An inability to focus on individual words when reading a newspaper or a book
- Study that is unproductive and constantly broken up by his mind wandering
- A pile-up of projects and tasks, all of which are unfinished
- An increasing sense of panic as the exam looms and his ability to prepare seems to diminish

What those close to George will observe:

- Unfinished projects and tasks, or projects that have been completed taking an extremely long time
- What seems like laziness in relation to his studies
- Impaired performance at school, university or work
- He will read much less, if at all

Lack of Pleasure (Anhedonia)

'I can barely manage a smile any more. I'm sick of people telling me to "cheer up" or "it can't be that bad". It is, and it's much worse than they can imagine.'

Paula, aged twenty-eight, who was sexually abused at the age of nine and has had bouts of depression for the previous five years.

An inability to enjoy anything that life has to offer is one of the trademark symptoms of depression.

How Paula feels:

- Complete indifference to activities which would normally be considered enjoyable
- Dejected, wondering what the point is of going anywhere or doing anything
- Curious and confused as to why people enjoy and participate in activities like sport, socialising and eating out

What those close to Paula will observe:

- Her face may seem blank and emotionless
- She rarely smiles or laughs
- She seems to avoid social situations
- It takes a lot to persuade her to take part in any optional activity

Suicidal Thoughts

'The world will be a much better place without me. I am a burden on everyone and they won't miss me at all.'

Jack, who is twenty-nine, has already quietly planned in great detail how he will end the pain he is experiencing. If his depression is not recognised and remains untreated, he may soon put these thoughts into action. This is made more likely by a dramatic increase in alcohol consumption to numb the pain of the recent breakup with his girlfriend.

Suicidal thoughts are the most perilous symptom of depression. Sometimes a healthy mind will experience impulsive thoughts of self-harm, but such thoughts will be fleeting due to the brain's ability to control them. In depression, however, this control is lacking, and urges to self-harm may become habitual. The suicidal thoughts are bolstered and rationalised by low self-esteem, low mood, and a generally negative outlook on life. If these impulses become too strong, the person may feel compelled to cut themselves or attempt suicide. Death becomes something to look forward to, and is seen as a favour to those around them. The combination of alcohol and suicidal thoughts should be avoided: alcohol makes it easier for the depressed person to act on their suicidal thoughts.

How Jack feels:

- The only way to end this intense emotional pain is to kill himself
- A feeling of helplessness and hopelessness
- A burden on everyone around him
- A craving for the peace and quiet that death will bring
- A compulsion to do anything that will result in self-injury
- An inability to see any future for himself
- That his girlfriend was right to leave him, as he is worthless and deserves to be left on his own
- A sense of isolation
- A sense of relief in working out in detail how he will end it all

What those close to the Jack may observe:

- Gradual physical and emotional withdrawal from loved ones
- Spending increased time on his own
- An increased amount of time spent in front of computer games or in Internet chat rooms
- Increased dependence on alcohol
- Throwaway statements such as 'Wouldn't it be a lot easier if I just killed myself'

The Red Flag Checklist

The above symptoms are summarised in the Red Flag checklist.

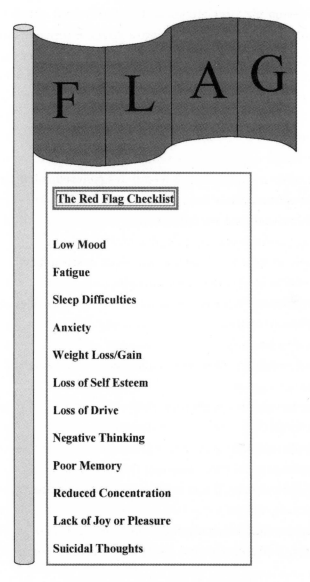

Figure 2: *The Reg Flag checklist*

This is a useful tool for assessing the health of our mood system. These symptoms can be summarised as a combination of 'physical' symptoms such as fatigue and sleep difficulties and 'psychological' ones such as low mood and negative thinking. This physical and emotional cocktail makes the condition difficult both to recognise and to treat. The mystery and secrecy that cloud and maintain depression can only be lifted by a frank and open discussion of these symptoms.

How many of the above symptoms does a person need to have in order to conclude that he or she is depressed? Technically, the doctor will diagnose 'major depression' (the commonest form) as depressed mood for more than two weeks, combined with at least four of the above additional symptoms, particularly difficulties with sleep, appetite, fatigue, feelings of worthlessness, and anhedonia.

Most people with the Red Flag will usually experience the majority of these symptoms, of which low mood, negative thinking, reduced self-esteem and sleep or appetite disturbance are the most common. Reduced energy and concentration are not as obvious, but are usually just as prevalent. The crux of the issue is that, if these symptoms are consistently present for a period of two to four weeks or longer, it is likely that the person is suffering from a mood disorder and needs to get help.

The longer an episode of depression continues, the more of these symptoms appear. As a result, early detection and treatment is vital before the person's life is completely disrupted, or even in some cases destroyed. References to suicide should be regarded as the most alarming symptom of depression because they are often a quiet cry for help, and warrant immediate referral to a specialist.

Lastly, as many of these symptoms reflect internal states, and not overt behaviour, it can be difficult for those around the depressed person to notice that anything is wrong. Fatigue, low mood, anxiety, anhedonia, reduced self-esteem, and thoughts of suicide are not readily observable, especially to a person who is not looking for them. This is why it is crucial to encourage people to talk about how they feel.

The illnesses of depression, anxiety and addiction all revolve around and are sustained by emotional disturbance. The mood system is responsible for these emotions; illness affecting this system leads to such disturbances.

If you have read through the above section and are experiencing many of the symptoms of depression, your mood system is in trouble, and you need to seek help. Depression is an illness, and is eminently treatable. The symptoms that are causing such misery in your life can be successfully eliminated.

If you suspect that you are living with somebody who may be depressed, sit them down in a quiet room, and ask them to talk to you about how they are feeling. Let them know that you care, and that they are worth a lot to you. Remember, they will probably think that you hate even spending time with them, and that they cannot be helped, so it is important to reassure them that this is not the case.

If major suicidal thoughts are present, the mood system is in real trouble. It is an indication that the depression is taking over complete control of the brain. If you or anyone close to you is feeling suicidal, help must be sought and alcohol avoided till the situation is brought under control.

The Biology of the Red Flag

Of all the illnesses that can affect the mood system, depression causes the greatest disruption. The symptoms outlined above cover every aspect of the mood system. The causes of this illness and its exact neurological mechanisms will take some time for researchers to understand fully. Science is only beginning to explain the workings of the brain, and how an illness like depression operates. New research continues to lift the veil from that mystery. Taking this into consideration, we will look at what is known to date about the biological causes of depression.

There may be many people reading this chapter who are not particularly interested in the biological underpinnings of depression. To cater for them, following this section is a summary of the main biological findings relating to depression. Others may be curious about the specifics of how the condition operates.

The whole 'flag system' is in chaos, but why? This is the question that modern researchers are struggling to answer. At the moment, it seems likely that some of us are programmed (by virtue of genes and our early environment) to be particularly vulnerable to stress. In such people, once the stress response has been activated, particularly in a chronic fashion, the mood departments and cables come under sustained attack, and the whole neural mood circuit starts to malfunction.

This, in turn, impairs the ability of the mood system to shut down the stress response. So a vicious circle ensues, and the mood system deteriorates, until the symptoms of depression increase and take over the person's life.

In chronic depression, there may not be any trigger: the mood system can just break down. This may be due to previous structural damage to various departments, such as the prefrontal cortex in particular, and also the memory box, from earlier episodes. Therefore, the more episodes of depression the brain has to deal with, the more likely it is that depression will occur again in the future. This is why detection and treatment of initial episodes is crucial.

The genetic vulnerability of the mood system to stress varies widely from person to person. The greater the vulnerability, the less stress that will be required to kick-start the depressive process. What follows is a detailed look at the damage caused by depression in the brain.

Mood Departments

Depression causes mayhem in both mood departments, especially to the key sections that regulate memory, stress, behaviour and pleasure.

Frontal Mood Department

Malfunctioning of this department usually involves the prefrontal cortex. In depression, this leads to the following problems:

- Decreased short-term memory and concentration
- Slowed thought processes
- Fatigue
- Low mood
- Pessimism

- Impulsive thoughts of self-harm
- Ruminating or negative thinking

Reduced activity in most sections of the prefrontal cortex, combined with increased activity in others, seems to play a vital role in the arrival of many of the symptoms of depression. The prefrontal cortex in particular plays a major role in negative thinking. Reduced functioning of one section of this department (and the serotonin cable supplying it) also increases the prevalence of suicidal thoughts.

This dysfunction in the prefrontal cortex promotes negative thinking for two reasons:

- Positive, logical thinking depends on activation of the prefrontal cortex in particular
- Negative emotional thoughts originating from the stress box are not overruled. This is because some parts of this box have the function of dampening down such thoughts. In depression, the normal functioning of these parts of the box is impaired. This allows the stress box to pour out these negative emotional thoughts.

One prominent theory of depression is that it begins in the frontal prefrontal cortex (particularly on the left side). Neuro-imaging and post-mortem studies have demonstrated increased activity in those sections at the base of this box (involved in the creation of mood) and reduced activity in those at the apex (involved in the cognitive control of mood). A key section of the prefrontal cortex involved in depression is one called 'Area 25'. This area, along with other sections of the prefrontal cortex, seems to play a major role in the creation of mood.

Area 25 appears to be over-active in all forms of major depression, and at the heart of the breakdown of information between the emotional and logical mood departments. Structurally, it is positioned at the junction between these two departments. For this reason, some experts call it a 'gateway'. It is activated (or opened) under normal conditions when we are sad, but in depression this activation becomes chronic. This seems to allow a torrent of negative emotions from the stress box to overwhelm the logical brain, creating the negative thinking that is so prevalent in depression.

At present, doubt exists as to whether this is the actual biological source of depression (which would be a major breakthrough), or, more likely, a consequence of it. A great deal of research into this question is under way. Whatever the role of Area 25, it is obviously well placed on the neural mood circuit to influence, for better or worse, the pain that the illness brings into people's lives.

It has also been shown that, in chronic depression, reductions in actual physical size and structure of the box itself can affect various parts of the prefrontal cortex. In one study (involving familial depression and bipolar mood disorder), for example, a segment of Area 24 (bordering on Area 25) was shown to be reduced in size by 20 to 40 percent. (Subsequent research has suggested that these structural changes are due to a decrease in the number of glial support cells and a reduction in the number of connections between the neurons in this box.) Why this occurs remains uncertain.

Other research into depression has shown varying shortages of neurons, connections between neurons, and in particular glial support cells in various other sections of the prefrontal cortex, particularly Areas 9, 10, 24 and 47. Many researchers wonder whether the shortage of glial cells might lie at the heart of this illness.

This hypothesis is borne out by research which showed a reduction of up to 19 percent in Area 24 of these support glial cells in a group of young women following an initial bout of adolescent-onset depression. The same study found the same changes in a group of middle-aged women who had suffered repeated episodes of depression. This suggests that these changes may be present in the individual from the beginning of their life.

Some scientists are of the opinion that genetic and early environmental factors increase the vulnerability of the prefrontal cortex, perhaps by creating an initial shortage of vital glial cells, but more likely by increasing their vulnerability to stress, thus beginning the depressive cycle. How the latter might occur is uncertain: it may be due to an attack on these glial cells by high glucocortisol/

stress peptides released by the stress system. This process could destroy the glial cells, resulting in some of the deficits in brain matter that are observed in depression. As the neurons depend on these glial cells to function, a reduction in their activity, and indeed the possibility of them being destroyed, is inevitable. At present, all of this is speculative, but a great deal of research is pointing in this direction.

If depression does begin its journey in this section of the brain, it may explain why a bout of depression makes further episodes of depression more likely. When depression damages the prefrontal cortex, the box's ability (through structural and possibly glial-cell deficits) to cope with stress in the future is compromised. A benign stress trigger (having to deal with simple work problems, for instance) in forthcoming years, which would not have been a problem before the first bout of depression, may be too much for the damaged prefrontal cortex to cope with, and the dysfunctional stress response which precipitates depression will be set in motion.

Limbic Mood Department

When it comes to the majority of depressive symptoms, this department has the finger of blame pointed squarely at it. When the limbic mood department is not operating properly, the following disabling results may ensue:

- Low mood
- Anxiety
- Sleep difficulties
- Poor memory and concentration
- Reduced self-esteem
- Anhedonia (lack of feelings of joy or pleasure)
- Fatigue
- Reduced motivation
- Reduced sexual drive
- Appetite and weight changes
- Disturbance in normal biological rhythms
- Negative thinking

Key Departments
THE MEMORY BOX, THE STRESS BOX AND THE PLEASURE BOX

1. *The memory box:* Damage to cells in this box interferes with memory. This occurs due to a combination of prevention of new cells being formed and interference with the efficiency of those already present.
2. *The stress box:* Over-activity causes anxiety, a common symptom of depression. It is also responsible for a pessimistic outlook on life, negative thinking, and a reduction in self-esteem. Over-activity also contributes to excessively negative emotional responses to many common everyday occurrences, as seen in many people with depression. The stress box is also the chief organiser of the stress system, which in turn leads to too much glucocorticol being produced. Post-mortem and neuro-imaging studies have revealed once again a shortage of glial cells and an increase in activity of this box, respectively.
3. *The pleasure box:* The lack of responsiveness of this box results in an inability to derive pleasure from activities which would normally provide pleasure.

Mood Cables

The three mood cables, which communicate using serotonin, noradrenalin and dopamine, are normally depleted in varying degrees during depression. This is due to a decrease in both the production of the transmitters and the sensitivity of the receptors they target. The extent of this damage varies from person to person. As these cables connect the mood departments and their individual sections together, it is clear that any disruption to their normal functioning will contribute to difficulties relating to mood. Such disruption causes the following problems:

Serotonin Cable

This is the primary mood cable. Decreased activity results in low mood, anxiety, sleep difficulties, appetite problems and reduced self-esteem. It also leads to suicidal impulses and actions.

Noradrenalin Cable
Damage to this cable results in fatigue, low mood and lack of motivation. It also interferes with concentration.

Dopamine Cable
Dopamine creates a feeling of pleasure. If this cable is not responding appropriately to life events, a person will not enjoy any activities and will not see the point in taking part in them. In some cases, this contributes to fatigue.

Peptide System
This system is highly activated in depression. It helps to perpetuate the vicious cycle of the stress response and depressive episodes.

Adrenal Stress Gland
In depression, the activation of the stress response is often so prolonged and extreme that the adrenal glands in some cases actually increase in size. This results in further extensive production of glucocortisol, which is unnaturally constant, day and night. It is now clear that these glands are one of the long-sought links between stress and depression.

Glucocortisol Stress Hormone
This hormone is depression's closest comrade. As depression worsens, the level of glucocortisol rises in unison, launching a vicious assault on the mood departments and cables. This causes continuous damage, day and night.

In depression, this hormone is to blame for the following problems:

- Damage to the memory box, interfering with the creation and organisation of memory and reducing the ability to concentrate. It prevents new cells from growing in this box.
- A 200 to 500 percent increase in the risk of heart disease (depending on the

severity of depression), by causing blood platelets to stick together. Prof. Ted Dinan (Professor of Psychiatry at University College Cork) has done a great deal of work on the effects of glucocortisol in this area.

- Reduced defences against illness, by interfering with the white blood cell receptors and their ability to respond to infection. This includes the ability to fight cancerous cells.
- Poor bone formation, leading to osteoporosis (thinning of the bones).
- May increase the chances of developing abdominal obesity and Type 2 diabetes.
- Fatigue.
- May play a role in suicide due to the damage it causes to the serotonin cable and prefrontal cortex.

It is now clear how the Green Flag of normal mood is turned into the Red Flag of depression.

Another useful, indeed revolutionary, way of looking at depression 'within the brain itself' is to view the mood system as a neural 'mood circuit', as discussed in the Green Flag section. Information flows to and fro along this mood circuit between the frontal and limbic mood departments and the mood cable control centres in the brain stem. When this flow is disrupted through malfunctions to any part of this circuit, depression may emerge.

At present, it is felt that the most likely source of such a short-circuit within this loop is a malfunctioning left-sided prefrontal cortex. This allows the emotional limbic mood department to flood the logical brain with negativity and low mood, and sets off the chain of biological effects noted above. Once this neural mood circuit breaks down, all of the symptoms and signs of depression appear.

This mood circuit-breakdown model is also very useful in explaining depression in the elderly. For completely different reasons (such as vascular damage to circuits leading into the left-sided prefrontal cortex, or Parkinson's disease damaging the dopamine control boxes), the same neural mood circuit is disrupted, and once again the signs and symptoms of depression appear. We can now see that this model of depression allows us, for the first time, to explain how this illness can give rise to the same symptoms in both young and old people.

If we were to theorise on the most likely chronology of a bout of depression, it would probably go like this:

1. A period of stress in our lives causes the stress box to kick-start the body's stress system into action by producing stress peptides and glucocortisol in abundance.
2. These substances begin to attack the already vulnerable frontal prefrontal cortex. This in some cases may already have structural changes in place due to glial-cell shortages.
3. The ability of the prefrontal cortex to switch off the stress box is now compromised. Area 25, a key part of the mood circuit, becomes over-active. Negativity pouring out of the emotional limbic brain's stress box begins to overpower the logical brain. Low mood, anxiety, negative thinking and poor self-esteem move in.
4. Another consequence of the stress box being out of control is that more stress peptides and glucocortisol continue to pour out. As the mood cable control boxes (which are rich in glucocortisol receptors) are very sensitive to this barrage, the mood cables begin to become under-active, starting with the serotonin cable and then later the noradrenalin and dopamine cables.
5. Gradual involvement of these cables due to their huge importance in linking the two mood departments and their individual sections together leads to the appearance of many of the vegetative symptoms of depression, such as sleep disturbance, increased or decreased appetite, poor drive, fatigue and poor concentration. These symptoms also consolidate some of the psychological symptoms noted above.
6. Now the whole mood circuit, from the mood control boxes and cables to the emotional limbic brain and the logical frontal brain, is dysfunctional. All the symptoms of depression, both physical and psychological, are present.
7. Due to the constant glucocortisol barrage, the body's platelets, bones and white blood cells may become affected, with the appearance of heart disease, osteoporosis and infections.

Why label depression 'the Red Flag'? Red is a warning colour. Depression does not just affect the mood system, it also warns of damage to many other parts of the body. This includes heart disease, infection, osteoporosis and death by suicide. The lifetime risk of suicide among patients with untreated depression ranges from 2.2% to 15%.

The prefrontal cortex (particularly one key section which we will be examining later in the White Flag) and the serotonin cable that connects with it are extremely influential in suicide. Thoughts of suicide, and the successful completion of the act, are more likely to occur in those who display marked inactivity in the serotonin cable which feeds a particular section of their prefrontal cortex. Identifying these people is a difficult task. In the future, neuro-imaging of this cable, and possibly genetic screening of high-risk families and individuals, may be the most effective non-clinical means of picking out those who are most at risk.

Summary

Depression can have the following adverse effects on the mood system:

1. *Damage to the frontal and limbic mood departments:* This damage will be most extensive in the memory, behaviour, stress and pleasure boxes. Such damage results in low mood, negative thinking, poor memory, anxiety, poor self-esteem, anhedonia (absence of joy) and urges to inflict self-harm.
2. *Damage to the three main mood cables (the serotonin, noradrenalin and dopamine cables)*: This results in reduced motivation, poor concentration, eating problems, sleep difficulties, fatigue and low mood, and the disappearance of pleasure from the person's life.
3. *Overstimulation of the adrenal glands,* producing too much of the stress hormone glucocortisol. This will increase the risk of heart attacks, osteoporosis and general infection.
4. A useful way of looking at depression in the brain itself is to view it as *a dysfunction of the mood circuit.*

Causes of the Red Flag of Depression

The cause of depression has been the subject of intense and acrimonious debate for decades. Many researchers previously attributed it to genetic inheritance. Others emphasised the contribution of family upbringing, social problems and general environment. Modern research has deepened our understanding of the condition. The cause is primarily genetic, with outside environmental triggers also influencing the onset of the illness. A similar example would be type II diabetes, where the underlying malfunction is genetic, with environmental influences such as poor diet and obesity also contributing.

A genetic predisposition towards a malfunctioning of the mood system may, in many cases, be the root cause of depression. As we discussed in the Green Flag section, however, the presence of both positive and negative environmental influences in our lives may hasten or reduce the emergence of depression in our lives. The primary environmental trigger is most likely stress, but poor diet, misuse of alcohol and drugs, and lack of exercise all play an important auxiliary role. As is the case with all diseases, a strong genetic susceptibility means that fewer environmental influences (in this case stress) are required to send the system into difficulty. Where this predisposition is not so strong, a major trigger (or triggers) is needed to start the process.

Genetic Influences

The genes that are present in every cell control the activity of that cell and the brain structure they belong to; the mood departments and cables are no exception to this rule. As previously mentioned, genes form part of a book of instructions, inherited from parents and grandparents, and present from birth.

Exactly what mistakes in this 'book of instructions' result in depression is still the subject of speculation. One gene, called Creb1, has recently been implicated in women from families with a history of recurrent early-onset depression. But in general, depression is polygenetic in nature: that is, many genes are probably involved. For those who are interested, five chromosomes – 4, 5, 11, 18 and 21 – and the X chromosome are under particular scrutiny! Also, environmental influence from the womb to adult life determines how such genes express themselves, complicating the situation further.

People vary in the number of malfunctioning genes they have which predispose them to developing depression (as noted earlier, genetic vulnerability increases when the malfunctioning genes outnumber the protective ones). These malfunctioning genes make the mood system more sensitive to stressful situations. The greater the number of malfunctioning genes, the more likely it is that the Red Flag of depression will present earlier and will have a more chronic course. The smaller the number of malfunctioning genes, the more stress is needed to trigger depression, and the higher the likelihood of fewer episodes of depression occurring. In both cases, however, the same biological malfunctions take place, and the same symptoms manifest themselves. The episodes and symptoms will differ only in terms of severity.

In future, scientists are likely to uncover a complete explanation of the complex blueprint that makes up our brain. This should help to isolate the genes involved in the design of the mood system. Although this may only be science fiction at present, one day it should be possible to generate a 'printout' of our own individual genetic blueprint; this printout will reveal an individual's 'potential genetic risk' of developing this illness. This may lead to various ethical dilemmas, with the increasing invasion of patient rights by large insurance companies and employers to elicit such information posing particular problems. Statutory protections may need to be built in when this day finally arrives.

The Stress Triggers (Environmental Influences)

Research has suggested that stress is the most common environmental trigger of a depressive episode. The most likely explanation for this is that the cells of the mood system are pre-programmed (by genes and early environment) to malfunction when subjected to stress. Possible stress triggers include:

Loss

Loss is a potent initiator of stress. Loss of a mother, father, child, partner, close friend, or even a beloved pet can be a very traumatic experience. For most people, their ability to cope and recover (due to a mixture of their genes and upbringing) via the natural grief process is adequate.

Those with a genetic predisposition towards problems in their mood system may, in such cases, develop the Red Flag of depression. If the loss is of a particularly powerful nature, however, such as a mother losing her child, or a spouse losing a long-time partner, even those who do not have this genetic predisposition may find their defences overrun. The overwhelming stress response that this type of loss produces internally may be enough to trigger a mood disorder.

Loneliness results from a lack of any fulfilling relationship and can be extremely stressful for some people. It can be just as much a feature of isolated rural areas as large anonymous cities. Loneliness may be one driving force behind the growing epidemic of suicide evident in young men. A key risk period is where a young person leaves the security of their family either to begin their studies at college or to take up a new job away from home. Many become isolated in flats or campuses and may find it hard to forge new relationships. If susceptible to depression, some may become quite down.

Loneliness, if it develops, aggravates depression, as there is no one for the sufferer to confide in, and it acts to confirm their thoughts that no one cares about them – or even should do!

The end of a relationship will result in similar problems. Young people are particularly vulnerable when a relationship breaks down, due to their immature mood system's inability to cope with the situation. Loss of a job will be equally devastating for many people. It lowers self-esteem, and there is often a subsequent drop in mood. This is possible in all age groups, but particularly in those aged between forty-five and sixty years old.

Chronic Stress

Modern life is fast-paced, and rarely without its troubles. Pressures that almost all of us experience on a regular basis include those relating to housing, commuting, relationships and finances. The time available for family and relationships is limited and, due to stress, is more likely to involve quarrelling than quality time spent together.

When one or more of the above pressures turns into an impasse, stress can become chronic. An average couple, commuting long distances, trying to cope with childminders and under pressure at work, often struggle to find the time to talk to each other. This lifestyle is in large part a result of excessively high housing prices and the demands of a growing economy. Many couples in this situation feel trapped. If either partner is genetically susceptible to the Red Flag, depression may ensue. Unrealistic self-expectations, as dealt with earlier, are another common stressor. Alcohol, when used to relieve such stress, will accelerate the process.

Bullying, a powerful environmental trigger which can occur at work, at home or at school and can be physical, sexual or emotional in nature, will in very many cases result in chronic stress. The chronic stress, and low self-esteem, it produces can combine, in those who are already at risk, to kick-start a bout of depression. In vulnerable young teenagers, it creates the added risk of potential suicide. In Northern Ireland, many young people have been terrorised by paramilitary groups. This extreme form of bullying has led to many developing depression, and in some tragic cases has resulted in suicide.

Chronic Illness

Long-term illness can often feel like a prison sentence. The lives of many are plagued by pain and immobility. Parkinson's disease, rheumatoid arthritis, stroke, multiple sclerosis and cancer all create huge strain on a person's ability to cope and thereby increase the likelihood of depression – in addition to their direct biological effects on the mood system. Fifty percent of Parkinson's sufferers develop depression, a fact which is often not recognised. Parkinson's causes depression by damaging parts of the mood system, in particular the dopamine cable. Another important cause of depression among the elderly is dementia. A substantial number of people with dementia will develop depression for biological reasons. Alcoholics and drug addicts will also present on some occasions with depression because these illnesses damage sections of the mood system. Finally, illnesses involving an under-active thyroid or over-active adrenal gland can also lead to the Red Flag.

It is worth mentioning in particular the trauma experienced by those who have gone through the ordeal of surgery, chemotherapy or radiotherapy for cancer, and those who are recovering from cardiac surgery. A good example of the former would be women who have treatment for breast cancer. Many become emotionally and physically exhausted – mainly due to prolonged high glucocortisol levels (which attack all three mood cables), which develop as the body tries to deal with the stress of the various treatments used. If the person is genetically susceptible to depression, he or she is at higher risk of developing depression. In my experience, this is one of the most hidden consequences of the battle fought by women who are recovering from breast cancer. Cancer specialists need to be aware of the role of the mood system in this battle, often describing symptoms like fatigue and low mood as a 'normal response'. In reality, the prolonged glucocortisol barrage often overpowers the mood system, and the symptoms of depression appear. The problem is often missed by both the spouse and the medical team looking after the patient, and as a result the condition often remains untreated. Apart from the distress this causes to the patient, who may already be deeply traumatised, it may reduce the body's ability to prevent a recurrence of the disease.

There is also a well-documented link between heart surgery and the potential to develop depression, for the same reasons. So we end up with the unusual scenario where depression increases the risk of developing coronary heart disease, and the treatment for severe cases of the latter increases the risk of developing the Red Flag. The biological machinery of the mood system and the other parts of the body are indeed intimately interwoven.

Those who care for people suffering from chronic illness – dementia being a typical example – are also living under difficult conditions, and can feel trapped. Over a prolonged period of time, their ability to cope with the situation may deteriorate and result in depression – particularly for elderly spouses. Finally, certain drugs used for other medical illnesses, such as high blood pressure and heart disease, and the long-term use of steroids to treat conditions like rheumatoid arthritis and asthma can themselves put stress on the mood system, leading to depression.

Chronic Anxiety

Anxiety (which we will deal with in more detail in the Yellow Flag section) can be a chronic condition, and those who suffer from it are extremely vulnerable to bouts of depression. Sometimes such people, when questioned, may reveal a long history of hidden, underlying anxiety, often going back to their teenage years. This anxiety wears down their biological coping mechanisms, resulting in depression. Some therapists feel that many people with depression, who started with anxiety, end up in a vicious circle of anxiety–depression–anxiety, and so on. Breaking this circle is vital in such cases.

Sexual Identity

For some people (particularly in the fifteen-to-twenty-five age group), confusion about their sexual identity can be a major source of stress. If people have difficulties in forming and maintaining relationships, they may begin to question their own sexual identity. Homosexuals may experience the following problems:

- If they are openly gay, they may suffer harassment, bullying and rejection from their families, friends or workmates.
- If they are hiding their sexual orientation from their family, friends and workmates, they feel trapped in a world of deceit and lies, unable to be honest with themselves and others. This can lead to feelings of loneliness and isolation.

The above problems can place a continuous strain on the person's stress system, leaving them vulnerable to depression and suicide.

Our Past

Our present is forged by our past experiences and decisions, both good and bad. There has been much emphasis on the role that upbringing has on the development of depression. In practice, many people with happy upbringings still go on to develop the Red Flag of depression. Genes and present environmental difficulties are more influential in this group.

A certain percentage of people grow up in particularly difficult situations, and are less able to cope with stress as a result. Members of this group are more likely to develop depression. Such examples include those who:

- grow up in extreme poverty and neglect
- experience severe physical, sexual or emotional abuse. This can haunt the victim for a lifetime, unless they receive help and counselling
- lose a parent at a particularly vulnerable stage of their development
- grow up in a house where addiction was present
- lose a sibling to suicide

Apart from the above exceptions, our past is often not as important as the present: it is in the present where most of our stress triggers arise.

Sex-Hormone Triggers

It has been suggested that sex hormones act as a depressive trigger. Hormones such as oestrogen, progesterone and testosterone play a huge role in development from twelve to eighteen. Hormones are also important in pregnancy and the months following the birth of a baby. Although such hormones do not control the mood apparatus, they are able to interfere with it. In the past, this was assumed to be the cause of post-natal depression, but many experts now believe that the stress of the post-natal period itself may be a more likely origin of such depression.

Alcohol and Substance Abuse

Addiction is extremely destructive. Those suffering from addiction often end up losing everyone and everything close to them, and for this reason alone it is no surprise that depression is a close comrade of addiction. Once again, the greater the genetic predisposition, the more likely an alcoholic is to slide into a bout of depression.

A great deal of interest is emerging in the strong link between alcohol, in particular, and the Red Flag of depression. Many who start by misusing alcohol to 'numb' the symptoms of low mood end up getting 'hooked' on this

91

substance, which in itself is a depressant. The more they abuse it, the more their mood drops. Others who start with alcohol abuse may later develop secondary depression.

In both cases, it is vital to recognise the depression that is lurking under the stormy seas of alcohol abuse. If this does not happen, then the treatment of both conditions may prove to be an impossible challenge. Those who abuse alcohol or drugs, particularly in their teenage years, may also alter the neurochemistry of their brain, predisposing them to subsequent depression. We will deal with this in more detail in the Purple Flag section.

Poor Nutrition

One rarely-discussed environmental trigger is poor diet. It is widely accepted that poor nutrition (along with a lack of physical exercise) lies at the heart of the current obesity, diabetic and coronary heart disease epidemics. Some experts are now beginning to wonder whether depression should be included in this list.

From early childhood, many children are fed a diet in which many of the important ingredients necessary for the smooth running of the developing brain and body are sadly lacking. This puts great internal pressure on the mood system in particular. We need a regular supply of vitamins, essential proteins and fats in our diet to keep it functioning properly. Often, poor dietary habits learned in the home are carried into adulthood, and the vicious circle continues.

Some experts wonder whether poor diet actually causes depression. I prefer to regard it as an important environmental influence which may, when combined with other genetic and environmental factors, help trigger a bout of the Red Flag.

Before leaving the causes of the Red Flag, it is important to examine the stress–mood cycle. The Green Flag/Red Flag models are highly influenced by these stress triggers. As stated previously, the greater the genetic predisposition for the mood cables and departments to malfunction, the less stress is required to turn the Green Flag red.

Some Commonly Asked Questions about the Red Flag of Depression

So far, we have dealt with what depression is, how it presents itself, and how it is caused. Now let's try and answer some common queries about this condition:

How Common is Depression?

At least 10 to 15 percent of the population will experience depression at some stage. In Ireland at any one time, 5 percent of men and 10 percent of women will be experiencing a bout of the Red Flag. Women up to the age of thirty are diagnosed with this illness twice as often as men. It is possible, however, that the number of men suffering from this condition is much higher, and that they do not come forward for help.

The true number of people in Ireland suffering from this illness is unknown, but probably lies between 300,000 and 400,000! What concerns many is the frightening reality that probably only 50 to 60 percent of sufferers will seek professional help – and many of these reluctantly. (Prof. Patrick McKeown of Aware estimates that for every four people in Ireland suffering from depression, only two will seek help, and of these, only one will receive adequate treatment.) The rest suffer in pain and silence. The episodic nature of this illness, combined with the confusion created in the media in relation to treatments and the 'stigma' attached to the condition, encourage many to try and 'stick it out'.

The great work being done by Aware, a depression support and information charity, in highlighting the issue of mental health, in particular depression, and supporting those who come forward for help should be strongly supported by us all. It is time to break the stigma and misinformation surrounding this illness once and for all.

Of particular concern is the increasing prevalence of depression in young people. Lack of recognition of the symptoms of depression in society is leading to many tragically avoidable deaths. There is a growing concern in Ireland, and indeed worldwide, about the increasing incidence of young males suffering from depression who subsequently go on to take their own lives. The Red Flag is by no means limited to this group, however: depression affects both men and women of all ages.

When Does Depression Appear?

Depression can appear at any stage of a person's life, but often occurs for the first time before the age of thirty, and is more likely following periods of great stress. Twenty-five percent of sufferers will first show signs of the illness during their teens. This group is more likely to become chronically depressed and prone to relapse. Another twenty-five percent will have their first bout between eighteen and twenty-five. Others will develop depression later, either post-natally or in response to stress. The elderly are also vulnerable to depression, although it is often misdiagnosed and dismissed as 'old age'.

How long will a period of depression last?

Most episodes of untreated depression will last between six and twelve months. This may seem like a short period of time, but it is a very long time for the person who is depressed. The brain and the body will desperately try to bring the malfunctioning mood apparatus back into balance before this. Frequently, however, the body's defences are fighting a losing battle with both the illness itself and external stress triggers.

If they are successfully treated, most sufferers will make an early improvement in six weeks, and will experience a remission of most symptoms within eight weeks and full recovery within nine to twelve months.

How Often Will an Individual Suffer a Bout of Depression?

It is estimated that 75 percent of those who suffer from a significant bout of depression will undergo between one and four depressive episodes in their lifetime. In 75 percent of cases, there will be another episode of this illness within five years of the first one.

It is also felt (probably for biological as well as psychological reasons) that each episode makes further ones more likely, particularly if the condition is not treated. These bouts usually occur after a period of immense stress. This is why it is important for people with depression to develop coping mechanisms to deal with stress.

The remaining 25 percent will experience constant bouts of low mood, which will alternate with periods of feeling relatively 'normal'. In this group, the depression is likely to start in the teenage years, and often needs only the most benign of stress triggers to reactivate it.

Why Treat Depression At All?

This may seem a ridiculously rhetorical question, given what we know of the devastation that depression brings. However, many argue that, if these episodes of low mood are left alone, they will be corrected by the body after six to twelve months, and that therefore there is no need to intervene. Some even argue that depression is a 'normal' life experience. This solution, although partially correct, is wholly unsatisfactory, because the sufferer is often experiencing intense pain. They feel miserable all the time, cannot remember things, are unable to concentrate enough to read, are constantly tired and anxious, have sleep difficulties, are not eating, have no interest in sex, and cannot derive any pleasure from life. It seems barbaric to suggest that they stay as they are. Such an approach will only confirm in their minds that there is nothing that can be done; in some cases, this makes thoughts of suicide more likely.

The symptoms caused by depression result in mayhem in a person's life. If lifestyle changes, drug therapy or psychotherapy can help to alleviate this emotional pain, there seems to me to be no good reason why the person should be left to suffer alone till it subsides. It has also been shown that each episode can increase the chances of a further episode, particularly if the condition is left untreated.

The second factor that highlights the importance of treating depression is that it sometimes results in suicide. As we have seen, for those who suffer from recurrent bouts of depression, the lifetime suicide rate is 15 percent.

Last, but by no means least, depression can cause very serious damage to other organs in the body. Depression, particularly if it is severe, can increase the likelihood of a heart attack by up to five times. This is due to increased levels of glucocortisol; this affects the body's clotting mechanism, making it easier for clotting to occur inside the coronary arteries, eventually blocking them and leading to a heart attack.

Other physical side effects of depression include osteoporosis (thinning of the bones) and an increased risk of infection. There is even the possibility of an increased risk of cancer, as the normal defences which pick up cancer cells in the body may not work as efficiently. Recent research has even linked depression to the later development of Parkinson's disease.

How do I Know if I am Stressed or Depressed?

Stress and depression often present in a similar fashion, due to the overlap of symptoms that exists between them. The stress system (as we saw in the Green Flag section) is intricately interwoven biologically into the mood system, often making the two conditions difficult to separate during diagnosis. Stress also seems to be the catalyst for many of the illnesses which affect the mood system.

The following are the most common warning signs that someone is under prolonged stress:

- *Fatigue:* This is not as extreme as that found in depression, but is usually the first symptom experienced by the person, as they claim to feel 'run down'
- *Apathy or lack of drive:* This is linked to fatigue, as the benefits of a task are outweighed by the effort expended in completing it
- *Loss of pleasure:* Every activity becomes a laborious chore, and it is difficult to relax
- *Sleep difficulties:* Difficulties getting to sleep or staying asleep ('tired but wired')
- *Anxiety:* People who are stressed are more tense, irritable and impulsive
- *Memory and concentration:* These can be impaired by chronic stress

What differentiates stress from depression is the absence of low mood, poor self-esteem, gross negative thinking and suicidal thoughts. The above symptoms of stress are also prevalent in depression, but usually in a more severe form.

Stress symptoms should be a warning to someone that their mood system is getting into trouble. Stress increases levels of glucocortisol, which feed back to damage the prefrontal cortex and mood control boxes and cables. If prolonged stress continues, particularly in those who are vulnerable to the condition, there is a risk of the mood system breaking down, and full-blown depression emerging. There are also the potential risks of chronic stress detailed in the Green Flag section.

If you are suffering from any of the above symptoms, and feel under major stress, it is advisable to visit your doctor and get help. For those who would like to learn more about chronic stress please see another book in my series called *Toxic Stress*.

Of concern to many is whether strict diagnostic scales (which I have purposefully avoided in this book) should be applied by all family doctors to help them distinguish between stress and depression in their patients. Whilst there is merit in this, I personally am uneasy about rigid assessments in primary care (while being in total agreement with their use in the specialist fields).

I would, however, love to see the availability of personal self-assessment mood and stress questionnaires in all doctors' surgeries and possibly in the workplace and in schools, colleges and so on. The person could bring them home and do their own assessment in private. If they felt that they had a problem with either stress or mood, they could then have a chat with their family doctor. For some, this might in itself act as a useful vehicle for expressing how they feel!

Is Depression a Dietary Illness?

Some experts wonder whether a lack of important proteins, fats and vitamins in our daily lives is enough to explain fully the mystery of depression. While I feel that the absence of such things from a person's diet may possibly play a role in the expression and severity of depression, it is highly unlikely that this is the full story: genetic predispositions and other environmental influences play a larger part in this illness. As we have already seen, depression is more to do with structural and functional difficulties within the mood departments and mood circuit. I do feel, however, that diet must play an important part in our journey to recovery from bouts of the Red Flag.

One interesting recent experiment took a group of people recovering from depression who were being treated with modern SSRIs (which, as we will see later, are drugs which boost our serotonin cable) and gave them a diet depleted of a vital vitamin that was necessary to make serotonin. Those who were getting better subsequently relapsed. So clearly, a healthy diet and possibly supplements are vital in the treatment of this illness.

Is Depression Caused by a Chemical Imbalance in the Brain?

One of the concepts relating to mental health that is most firmly embedded in the mind of the layperson (but which is being increasingly challenged in the media) is that depression is basically caused by a shortage of certain brain chemicals, with serotonin being identified as the main culprit.

In reality, this view of depression is extremely limited. Although a reduction in serotonin, noradrenalin and dopamine activity play a role in some of the symptoms associated with the illness, this is only part of a much more complex picture. The involvement of the chemical neurotransmitters mentioned above should firstly be seen as having more to do with the mood cables they service than with any individual chemical. It is the malfunctioning of these cables which gives rise to many of the symptoms of depression. The mood cables themselves become dysfunctional, more as a result of difficulties within the departments they serve than because of problems within the two main mood departments.

As noted earlier, the two big mood departments, together with the adrenal gland and glucocortisol, play equally important roles in the onset of depression. Involvement of the former gives rise to many of the physical and psychological symptoms of depression, and the latter explains many of the associated risks of osteoporosis, heart disease and infections.

Also as noted above, the mood cables and boxes, together with the two mood departments, are part of a neural mood circuit, and it is difficulties within this circuit rather than shortages of brain chemicals per se that lies at the heart of this illness. We are also now aware that there are structural difficulties within the mood departments which remain even when depression has been treated and the functioning of the mood circuit has returned to normal. It is most likely these structural deficits which predispose those at risk to further bouts of depression if stress arrives again in their lives.

So depression should be seen as a multifaceted illness rather than as a simple chemical imbalance. It is also important to note that the real underlying cause of this condition lies in the interaction between genetic and environmental (both past and present) factors and the mood system as a whole, which creates the cascade of symptoms seen in this illness.

This distinction is crucial. For example, if a person with depression feels that all their problems are coming from a simple shortage of serotonin over which they have no control, they may feel that they have no role to play in the management of their own illness. In practice, nothing should be further from the truth.

Depression, like most biological conditions, requires the person to be very much involved in all aspects of their treatment, whether that be in the areas of diet, exercise, counselling, drug therapy or CBT (cognitive behaviour therapy, which, as we will see later, is a psychological therapy aimed at reducing negative thoughts and anxiety in depression), and other psychological therapies.

Another problem with this erroneous view of the Red Flag is that it suggests that only drugs which elevate brain chemicals can solve the problem! We now know that psychological therapies like CBT work more on the frontal mood department than directly on chemical neurotransmitters. In fact, both therapies work on the neural mood circuit, with CBT working from the top down, and drugs from the brain stem up, via the mood cables.

Some feel that the emphasis on chemical imbalance has led to an over-emphasis on the importance of drug therapy. Although this has an extremely important place in the treatment of depression, so too do all the other therapies discussed above. Psychotherapists in particular argue, with some justification, that this preoccupation with chemical imbalances has stopped some people from getting the psychological help they may require.

Is Depression an Inflammatory Illness (i.e. an Attack by the Body's Immune System)?

Depression is seen by many researchers as having many similarities to heart disease, and numerous other common illnesses. The common denominator in many illnesses, including multiple sclerosis, rheumatoid arthritis and coronary heart disease, is clear evidence that the body's immune system is attacking its own structures. Because of this, a great deal of interest is being generated in the possibility that something similar might be going on in depression.

In favour of this theory is the presence of inflammatory markers (called cytokinines) in close proximity to the structures involved in depression. Other indicators are the evidence of excess activity of the stress system, the increased presence of inflammatory markers in the blood of some people with this illness, and, in some cases of depression, an unexplained reduction in the number of glial support cells in various parts of the frontal mood department.

One could ask whether this is evidence of the body attacking itself. For the time being, we can only speculate that the link between stress in our lives and problems within our mood system is probably mediated through the body's stress system. The final answer to this question lies in the future.

Is Depression a Physical, Psychological or Biological Illness, or a Combination of All Three?

A common statement made by many laypeople is that depression is a mental or psychological illness alone. This denies the possibility that it may also have a physical or biological basis. So what is the true situation? In support of the physical-illness argument, it is clear that symptoms such as fatigue, sleep, appetite and drive difficulties, problems with memory and concentration, and increased risks of heart disease and osteoporosis all have a physical basis. The obvious fact that the brain itself is a physical organ and that, as we have already seen, it plays a key role in depression also supports the view that this illness has a physical basis. The presence of structural and functional changes in various parts of the mood system also supports this supposition. Supporting the psychological (i.e. of the mind) basis of depression are the symptoms of low mood, anxiety, poor self-esteem, negative thinking, reduced enjoyment of life, and suicidal thoughts.

As both the physical and psychological symptoms mentioned above have a biological basis, it becomes clear that this illness is due to a combination of all the above. This is crucial in our understanding of the Red Flag. If all of us could grasp this reality, the stigma associated with depression would quickly become ancient history!

Is There a Unified Theory of the Cause of Depression?

Albert Einstein spent his life trying to develop a unified theory of all the laws of physics. So far, like Einstein, those working in the field of mental health have failed to bring together all the genetic, chemical, biological, hormonal and environmental influences into one cohesive model. Each group researching the area stakes a claim to the truth – whether it is the psychologist, the psychiatrist, the geneticist, the neurobiologist, the psychotherapist or the nutritionist! In practice, all are helping to provide parts of the jigsaw puzzle. It is useful, however, to put together what we know to date.

It seems likely that most people who develop depression have a genetic potential to develop this illness. This may involve various genes which, apart from having a key role in the development of our personality, also control or retard the following:

- The manufacture of the crucial neurotransmitters dopamine, noradrenalin and serotonin, and their receptors
- The healthy development of the mood system, particularly the development of the neurons, and in particular of glial support cells in various parts of the prefrontal cortex and the stress box. The latter may turn out to be the key to this illness.
- The response of the mood departments (particularly the behaviour, stress and memory boxes) to stress
- The likelihood of the body's defence system inadvertently attacking the glial support cells

From birth to twenty-five, the expression of these genes is dependent in varying degrees on the environmental influences the person experiences. This is where the psychologist comes in to flesh out many of the potential negative or positive factors, including family upbringing, abuse and addiction. Such influences may affect a person's capability of handling future stresses in life. This is probably mediated through the genes, as discussed above.

In terms of biology, all of the above may create initial structural changes within the mood departments, usually due to a decrease in glial support cells and connections between neurons. This may create a potential for the future functional disruption of the mood circuits when they are exposed to stress.

Whether depression will appear or not in the teenager and adult then becomes dependent on other environmental factors, such as the stresses of life:

- The difficulties of developing from a teenager to a young adult physically, sexually, emotionally and financially
- The difficulties of moving from the security of home to the isolation of college or working away from home
- The joy and pain of relationships
- Learning to cope with loss, particularly of those close to us
- Learning to cope with all the stresses of modern civilisation, from commuting to work difficulties, exam pressures, the arrival of a new baby, relationship breakdowns, and so on
- Learning to cope with loss of a job or severe illness

What is important is that what might seem to be a stress to one person may be seen as a challenge to another, depending on their personality. People who are more anxious or perfectionist by nature seem to be more at risk of depression. It is also worth noting that, in some cases, genetic influences are so strong that it may take only a small amount of stress to trigger an attack. If we add in some other environmental influences, like diet, alcohol and drugs, and exercise, the picture becomes more complete.

The role of nutrition may be more important than researchers originally thought. Suppose that one of the genetic predispositions is to under-manufacture serotonin or dopamine; in this case, a diet lacking in the protein building blocks of these transmitters, and in key vitamins involved in the process, will certainly not help. Maybe this potential weakness is only exposed when the person begins to suffer from a bout of prolonged stress. If the nutritional state of the person was better, the appearance of the symptoms might possibly be delayed, or even in some cases avoided.

So, too, essential fatty acids like Omega 3s are frequently missing in our diet. As these are important for running repairs to the mood system's neurons, a lack of these substances from the diet may help to speed up the appearance of a potential bout of depression. A well-nourished brain cannot but benefit our general mental heath. Only research, however, can confirm or deny the importance of diet in the maintenance of good mental health and the prevention of mental illness.

Lack of physical exercise is another negative environmental influence. Our brain, and in particular our mood system, craves the buzz that exercise brings. If we are not fulfilling this need, maybe we are making the arrival of latent depression more likely. Could this, along with poor diet and alcohol misuse, be the reason why we are seeing such an epidemic of depression in the under-thirty age group?

Lastly, the misuse and abuse of alcohol, and of illegal drugs like cocaine and marijuana (in all age groups, but particularly among the under-twenty-fives, where the mood system is only maturing) is another environmental influence that has a strongly negative impact. These substances exert pressure on the mood system, encouraging the appearance of latent depression and worsening episodes of active depression.

We will be dealing later with the arrival of depression in the elderly, where a different set of factors (particularly a reduction in blood supplies to vital parts of the mood system combined with a natural reduction in the neurons supplying our mood cables) becomes involved.

The key to all of the factors discussed above is that they end up disrupting the neural mood circuit: this seems to be the final common pathway in this illness. So we can see that the arrival (or not) of depression in our lives depends on many different but intermingled factors – genetic, biological, social, nutritional and psychological – coming together. It will take many years of research before we know the whole story!

Treatment of the Red Flag of Depression

One of the most ingrained beliefs held by those with depression (particularly if it is severe) is that nothing can be done to help them and that they are likely to remain in this state indefinitely. The basis for this belief lies in the symptom of negative thinking that is so common in this illness. They come to believe that depression is part of who they are. These beliefs allow the illness to worsen, as the sufferer is reluctant to come forward for treatment; even when they do, they doubt that they will ever feel well again.

A person with depression must first of all grasp the fact that their family doctor, specialist or therapist wants to help them. If they develop this trust, they are already on the road to recovery. Doctors and those close to the person must make a special effort to empathise with and listen to them. This provides a safe and supportive environment that allows them to talk about their illness – which is the first step to recovery. Because depression is a disease, like diabetes and coronary heart disease, for example, common sense dictates that all forms of treatment that act on the illness have an effect on the body's physiology. Many illnesses are managed with a combination of diet, exercise, drug treatment and counselling, and depression is no different.

These are the treatment options that are available for treating depression:

Exercise
The first, and most basic, treatment recommended to those with depression is simply to spend thirty to sixty minutes each day exercising. This alone has a hugely beneficial affect on depression by increasing levels of both dopamine and endorphins in the brain; this eases stress, lifts mood and improves the functioning of the memory box.

Many with this illness find themselves in a 'Catch-22' situation when advised of this treatment. The symptoms the treatment will cure prohibit the treatment itself. They are suffering from fatigue, which makes it difficult for them to do anything which requires effort. They are also suffering from a lack of motivation, and do not want to do any exercise. They must overcome these stumbling blocks, however, as exercise elevates mood, improves the sleep and appetite disturbances associated with depression, and increases energy levels, memory and concentration. They should choose an activity that suits their lifestyle. Any form of exercise – be it walking, swimming, dancing, tennis or football – will provide similar benefits.

Diet

Another 'Catch-22' situation in which someone with depression may find themselves in is poor diet. A healthy diet is important in the prevention and treatment of depression. In some cases, poor diet may have been one of the environmental factors triggering an attack. In many cases during an episode of depression, those with the Red Flag will lose interest in food. This in turn leads to the mood system running short of vital nutrients, with the risk that the depression may worsen. A good diet rich in essential proteins, fats and slow-release carbohydrates, along with B and C vitamins, fits the bill. This helps the mood system to recover and repair itself. Regular meals of fresh meat, fish, vegetables, grains, nuts and fruit will usually supply most of the above list.

It is also advisable to reduce the intake of caffeine and other drinks that have a stimulant effect. Caffeine produces an immediate yet artificial energy – which is desirable for those who are suffering from unrelenting fatigue. It stimulates the stress box, increasing alertness but also anxiety, and leads to a drop in mood when the effects of the drug have worn off. It also interferes with sleep patterns – which may already be disturbed.

Research has revealed the importance of fish in particular in our diet. Fish oils, which are present in fish like mackerel, salmon, tuna, herring and sardines, help to build, maintain and repair the mood system.

Supplements

Alongside a healthy diet, it is advisable that people with low mood take vitamin supplements (especially B vitamins) to ensure complete nutrition. Other supplements that are helpful as part of a treatment plan include Omega 3 fish oils. These help the neurons and mood cables to function.

The general consensus is that all adults need around 500 milligrammes of EPA (Eicosapentaenoic Acid) in particular for normal brain health, but that those with illnesses like depression may need up to 1 gramme of it. This can be provided by two to three portions of oily fish, but in my experience many people who are already struggling with a lack of interest in food will be unable to reach this target. I personally recommend supplements in such cases.

This is particularly important if the diet of the person with depression has been very poor, as is often the case. Several studies have shown that patients taking these supplements experience a reduction in anxiety, sleep difficulties and suicidal thoughts.

Fish oils work in a similar way to many antidepressants. Sections of the mood department reduce in size during severe depression. This is in part due to decline in the number of connections between neurons. Brain scans have shown that the essential fatty acids found in fish oils encourage the re-growth of these connections. This effect has been displayed in depression, bipolar depression and schizophrenia. Fish oils have also been shown to exhibit anti-inflammatory properties, and this may also be of relevance to depression.

For the initial management of depression, some experts recommend a starting dose of 1 to 2 grammes of Omega 3 oils containing a high EPA content, with 500 milligrammes to 1 gramme being adequate as a continuous daily dose. Some may prefer to take these oils in the form of seeds (sesame or sunflower) or seed oils. They must be used with caution if the person is on anticoagulants. You should always check first with your family doctor if taking these oils in large quantities.

The importance of these oils is questioned by some experts, and we probably need much more research in order to prove that they have an important effect in combating depression. My own opinion is that there is insufficient proof that they are enough on their own to treat this illness, but it makes sense at least to replace the basic daily requirement of 500 milligrammes of EPA necessary for the running of the adult brain. I therefore always recommend them as part of an overall package of treatment.

Some experts have also looked at the role of essential amino-acid supplements in the treatment of depression. Amino acids are produced as a byproduct when the body breaks down the proteins we consume. These acids are transported through the blood to all parts of the body, including the brain. Many of the key neurotransmitters are derived from amino acids.

A good example is a neurotransmitter called tyrosine. In the neuron, it is broken down to form dopamine and subsequently noradrenalin. It makes sense that a good supply of this essential amino acid (as of many other amino acids) will help us to manufacture the extra amounts of EPA we need if we are suffering from depression. A detailed discussion of this whole area is not possible in this book, and I would recommend Patrick Holford's interesting book on the subject, *Optimum Nutrition for the Mind*.

Certain neurotransmitters (e.g. dopamine, serotonin and noradrenalin) are manufactured with the help of B vitamins. These vitamins have many other important functions in the brain and mood system, so it is wise to keep their level high, especially when the person's mood is down. (A B-complex supplement, a daily combination of all the B vitamins needed by the body, is recommended.)

If it can be shown that a person with depression has a healthy diet, there may be no need to add such vitamins, but in my experience this is not usually the case; I often suggest that these vitamins be added to the person's diet in the form of supplements. Finally, it is important to note that supplements like the ones dealt with above can never replace a healthy diet, but they are useful as an adjunct to help the body's defences, particularly in combating depression.

Counselling

The simple act of talking about one's depression helps ease the emotional pain associated with the condition. Some people with this illness may have experienced abuse, bereavement, addiction and stormy relationships in their past. They may also have difficulties coping with stress, which may be domestic or work-related.

The aim of counselling is to help the person identify their problem areas and to look at possible solutions that will help them cope. Counselling can be non-directive, where the person is encouraged to articulate their problems and work through them with minimal interference from the counsellor. It may also be confrontational, either on a personal or group level. This is particularly effective in dealing with addiction. Reality therapy targets the specific areas that are causing difficulty and concentrates on specific methods for dealing with them. This approach is used by family doctors on a daily basis.

All these forms of counselling have their value. When carried out by professionally trained counsellors, they are of great assistance. Counselling should be the first choice for those who are suffering from stress and initial mild depression where obvious stress triggers are present. I do worry, however, about the proliferation of 'counsellors' with little formal training around the country, and feel that it is very important that the proper supervisory structures are in place, to ensure that people in trouble receive help from properly trained personnel.

How can counselling help fight depression? It probably works biologically in a similar way to psychotherapy – by activating the logical prefrontal cortex, which in turn calms down the emotional stress box. In mild cases of depression, this may be sufficient to improve the mood- circuit dysfunction and lift mood.

In moderate to severe cases of depression, the role of counselling becomes complementary to the use of drug therapy. This approach may prove more successful if it takes place four to six weeks after the person has started drug treatment, as he or she will then feel well enough to talk about their problems.

Psychological Treatments

There is often confusion between the role of the counsellor and that of the psychologist. The counsellor helps a person to deal with life's problems; the psychologist changes a person's dysfunctional thought processes and uses the individual's self-perception to modify their behaviour and help transform negative thoughts into positive ones.

There are many ways in which the psychologist can help when a person's mood system is in trouble:

(a) Relaxation Therapy
Exercises to calm the mind and body can help a person to become more

relaxed and peaceful within, reducing the over-activity of their stress system and thereby easing the pressure on the body's mood system. This is particularly effective in anxiety disorders, and in depression with associated anxiety.

(b) Psychotherapy

There are a number of forms of psychotherapy that are commonly used in treating depression:

1. *Psychoanalysis*, the oldest type of psychotherapy, works on the principle that the source of the person's depression may in some cases lie buried deep in their unconscious. This usually involves unresolved conflicts from childhood. Sometimes these conflicts may relate back to periods of physical or sexual abuse, or other very traumatic experiences. By bringing these back to the surface, the person can deal with them explicitly, and this in turn will eliminate their depression by neutralising the cause.

   Although this form of (usually non-directional) therapy has its place, it has generally fallen out of favour. There are many potential dangers in opening up people's past lives to such an extent, and this approach has been shown to be less effective than the other psychological therapies mentioned below.

2. *'Interpersonal therapy' (IPT)*: This form of psychotherapy, which has proved to be of great help to many, is based on the concept that those suffering from depression may be experiencing difficulties with key relationships from either the past or, more often, the present. This can be a 'Catch-22' situation, where depression itself can cause difficulties in important relationships, often due to lack of understanding of the condition, and the stress of such conflicts may exacerbate the depression itself.

   It has been shown that helping a person to learn new ways of handling such relationships, and in some cases to come to terms with previous relationships, can help to lift mood. This approach is used daily by GPs, but more formal work with a psychologist may be necessary. In the case of the latter, a set number (generally between ten and fifteen) of directed sessions is the ideal.

Biologically, IPT probably works by putting the frontal prefrontal cortex (the thinking part of the mood system) back in control over the stress box, where most of the negative memories reside. Recent neuro-imaging studies suggest that IPT and CBT stimulate the same brain areas.

This form of therapy, when utilised properly, reduces the risk of future episodes of depression. It will not suit, and may not be necessary for, everyone, however.

3. *Cognitive Behaviour Therapy (CBT):* This is currently the most popular choice for treating depression, anxiety and addiction. The theory behind CBT is based on the concept that, over time, many people with anxiety and depression develop persistent negative thoughts, and that this in turn leads to destructive behaviour patterns.

In CBT, the psychologist or therapist highlights the negative and dysfunctional thoughts the person experiences (with concomitant negative behaviour patterns) when feeling depressed or anxious. By challenging these erroneous attitudes and explanations, and rationalising them, the person's thoughts (and behaviour) become more logical and positive.

This technique owes much to the pioneering work of Aaron Beck, whose book on the subject was a major breakthrough in how to deal with the negative thinking associated with depression. He noted that, while many people with depression who were treated with drugs improved in relation to their physical symptoms, they continued to struggle with the psychological symptoms. In particular, their view of themselves, their present and the future was overshadowed by a black cloud of negative thought and perceptions. Beck felt that this barrage of negative thoughts fostered and maintained the person's depression.

Beck worked out a system of training therapists to work with people whose thoughts had been distorted by the Red Flag of depression. The end result in many cases was an improvement in the thinking and behaviour of those who worked with such counsellors. This concept was also found to be of help in challenging the hopelessness found in those at higher risk of suicide. It has proved to be a very useful tool in the treatment of depression.

Another parallel form of CBT was created by the psychologist Albert

Ellis. This was called Rational Emotional Behaviour Therapy (REBT), and in many ways it superseded Beck's approach. Instead of challenging the erroneous negative thought, this form of therapy encouraged the person to look at the emotions these thoughts evoked. This in turn helped them to alter their behaviour.

The best way to explain the difference between the two approaches is to examine the following example. Imagine that Peter, on his way home from work, is passed by a friend, John, who is late, and is rushing home to attend a birthday party for his partner, Mary. Under normal circumstances, Peter would chuckle to himself 'I must pull John's leg at a later date that he is either too busy, or too much in love, to notice his friends.'

But let's assume that Peter is suffering from the Red Flag of depression. His reaction to the same event produces the following response: 'John just ignored me on purpose. He obviously feels that I am not worth stopping to talk to. I must be a boring, useless person if that is the case.'

He then goes home, where the negative thoughts run riot. 'I must really be an awful person if even close friends avoid me. I must avoid John in future, as this encounter made me feel so bad. But maybe John is right and I am really not worth spending time with. The world would be a better place without me.'

Beck's approach to the above case would be to encourage Peter to challenge the initial negative thought, the emotions it provoked, and the subsequent conclusions: 'Did John really choose to pass you by or is that just your perception? What emotions did the event provoke? Were those emotional feelings uncomfortable? Is your decision to avoid John a way of avoiding such emotions?'

Ellis's approach would be to encourage Peter to examine why this encounter bothered him at all. He would help him to rationalise his emotional responses to the situation: 'Why does it bother you at all whether John stopped to talk? How and why did you feel so upset that John didn't notice you? Are you really such an awful person as you think you are? Can you give concrete examples to prove conclusively that you are so awful? Is the root of the problem that you don't fully accept yourself unconditionally as a human person without demanding impossible standards from yourself? Once you accept the latter, it won't matter whether or not John bothers to greet you in the street.'

By rationalising Peter's responses to the event, this approach challenges him to alter both his behaviour and his future interpretation of similar situations. The REBT approach (the core of which is unconditional self-acceptance) would also help him to understand the difference between the logical and the emotional brain.

Both approaches are extremely useful in many cases, with the latter more commonly being used to treat depression and anxiety, and the former to treat panic attacks.

A recent adjunct to the above CBT therapies, which have been the mainstay of therapeutic approaches to depression for more than thirty years is dialectical behaviour therapy (DBT). This was created by the American psychologist Marsha Linehan as an approach to dealing with people with borderline personality disorders (which we will deal with later in the White Flag section) who were involved in self-harm behaviour. Over the last ten years, this approach is being increasingly used to treat a number of other illnesses, such as addiction and depression.

The core of this form of therapy is the recognition that some patients are so distressed that the usual forms of CBT are not going to be effective unless the distress is both accepted and dealt with first. DBT is often associated with the term 'mindfulness', which is one of the main planks (along with learning new ways of dealing with interpersonal difficulties, coping with life's crises and managing distressing emotional states) of this form of therapy.

Mindfulness, developed from Buddhist meditation, involves developing techniques to stay with experiences (both feelings and actions) in the present moment (sometimes called 'self-soothing'). If ever there was a generation that needs to become more aware of the present moment, it is the current one!

This form of therapy is felt to be of particular help to those suffering from mental (and indeed physical) pain. Instead of trying to run away or avoid these moments, those in this state are taught, with the help of med-itation and breathing exercises, to absorb and live with them. In Ireland, a key proponent of this approach is Dr Tony Bates, a leading psychologist who is well known for his writings on depression. At the 3TS conference on suicide in 2004, he explained that: 'Mindfulness encourages an attitude of acceptance and kindness towards your experience instead of one of self-criticism. It offers you a way to be with your bodily sensations, your feelings and thoughts without being overwhelmed by them.' He went on to add: 'Mindfulness meditation is essentially about taking time to be in touch with yourself, so you may feel embodied and grounded, instead of disconnected and alienated.' For those who would like to read Tony's beau-tifully written lecture on this subject, I refer them to 'Conversations that keep us alive.'

In the past, most therapists belonged to either the Beck or Ellis (and more recently the Linehan) 'camp' in terms of how they treated patients. Nowadays, most have a much more fluid approach, switching comfortably from one form of CBT to another, depending on the illness and person-ality of the person. A useful way of explaining how CBT and IPT work on a physiological level in depression is to return to the concept of the mood system being composed of an emotional (controlled by the limbic mood department) and a rational, controlling department (the frontal mood department). CBT, through its effects on the mood circuit, helps the person utilise their frontal prefrontal cortex (probably by strengthening inter-neuron connections) to overrule the negative and irrational emo-tional thoughts originating from the limbic system, particularly the stress box. This fosters a sense of control in the person with depression, which is huge step on the road toward their recovery and helps them develop effective long- term coping mechanisms. In eliminating negative thinking and low self-esteem, it reduces the relapse rate among those with chronic depression

Some neuro-imaging studies have shown that, in cases where CBT is successful, activity in the prefrontal cortex initially increases but then, as the person improves, reduces. The memory box was shown to become more active. This suggests that a great deal of intensive cognitive activity occurs as the patient tries to address their negative thoughts. The memory box works harder to consolidate the memories of these cognitive changes. As the person improves, they don't have to use their logical prefrontal cortex as much, and activity there reduces. This is the opposite of what happens during drug treatment!

Needless to say, given the seriousness of the conditions being dealt with, these therapies should only be carried out by trained professionals (psychologists, psychiatric nurses, counsellors, or family doctors trained in CBT).

It is felt that CBT is best suited to those with mild to moderate depression, those who do not want or are unable to take drug therapy, those who are prepared to become fully involved in their own treatment, those with a history of recurrent bouts of depression (to try and reduce relapses), and those who are combating suicidal and impulsive thoughts.

The disadvantage of CBT is the amount of time it can take to produce lasting changes in the mood system compared to drug treatment. It is also not available to most patients in Ireland, due to the great shortage of psychologists and trained CBT therapists within the public-health system, and the high cost of treatment within the private sector. It also involves a time (and motivation) commitment from the patient which is often not possible. Without the latter, CBT will be doomed to failure.

While some GPs are starting to study and apply CBT, it can be difficult for them to find the time in a busy practice to deal with the large number of patients who require it. The system needs more therapists who are trained in this area. This would reduce the need for drug therapy, speed up the treatment of depression, and reduce relapses.

The advantages of CBT are the absence of the side effects that are associated with drug treatment, the practicality of the approach in dealing with the person's present state rather than an in-depth analysis of the past (with the former often being more acceptable to patients), its effectiveness in reducing relapse rates of depression, and the clearly defined nature of the course of treatment.

My personal opinion is that CBT concepts would be of use to many with depression and that we need to look at new ways of reaching these people. I feel from experience that a combination of drug therapy and CBT is the ideal approach, as it tackles the mood circuit dysfunctions at two different levels in the brain and both speeds up recovery and reduces relapses. In the absence of proper health funding, the best way to achieve this ideal may be through a combination of training GPs and possibly working through self-help groups.

4. *Other psychological therapies:* There are a number of other approaches that have also been found to be helpful. Of these, 'problem-solving' is one of the most useful. Problem-solving has been shown to be a major difficulty for many with depression, and in particular is very common amongst those who self-harm. Improving these skills has been shown greatly to assist those with the Red Flag and to be a valuable preventative measure in those identified as being at risk of suicide. As always, getting such help (apart from useful advice from the more experienced family doctor) is the problem.

Drug Treatment

The most common – and most controversial – form of treatment for depression involves medication. Some maintain that antidepressants are simply placebos, and work by tricking the mind into believing it is getting better. Others compare their use to that of taking paracetamol for a headache: it deals with the symptoms but not the causes. Some believe that they are addictive. Users of antidepressants often complain that the drugs make them feel numb, eliminating some of the symptoms of depression but also leaving them unable to experience happiness. Another common argument against the drugs is that they are having no discernible impact on suicide rates, and that in some cases they may be increasing the risks of a suicidal act.

With such controversy surrounding their use, should these drugs be prescribed at all? Most experts would reply that they are simply one of a number of useful tools available in the management of this illness. Many of the actual users of these drugs (who should know better than anyone!) value antidepressants, but also understand the limits of these drugs. They are not a miracle cure on their own, but they do often enable the person to function and, when used with the above therapies, frequently yield positive results. They do have their disadvantages, but their ability to help a person 'get back to normal' is often invaluable.

Interesting trials have been carried out to compare and contrast psychological (CBT) and drug therapies, using them both individually and together. These trials have shown that both forms of treatment offer advantages and disadvantages. Drug treatment was shown to work faster but, after four months, both approaches were shown to be effective. On finishing individual courses of both, those that had used CBT, in particular, seemed to have a lower relapse rate.

The conclusion was that the use of both, in many cases, maximised the patient's chances of recovery. This view is shared by many modern CBT therapists and is supported by the neuro-imaging data. If symptoms like fatigue and concentration are improved, it is easier for the latter to help the person to change their negative thoughts and behaviour.

In chronic depression, CBT should be utilised to reduce the need for long-term drug treatment. In severe depression, it is often necessary to combine drug treatment with CBT to keep the person well.

How Do Antidepressants Work?

All current prescribed antidepressant drugs operate in a similar manner. Neurons communicate by releasing chemical messengers (neuro-transmitters) into the gaps (synapses) between the adjoining cells (see the Green Flag). These messengers cross the gap, activate receptors in the adjacent cell, and are then re-absorbed back into the original cell.

Much of what we think, feel and do is partially mediated by these neuro-transmitters.

Low levels of serotonin, noradrenalin and dopamine have been implicated in depression. Scientists discovered that drugs which blocked the absorption of these transmitters back into the original cell increased these low levels, and subsequently helped alleviate the depression. They also found that drugs that affected the re-uptake of serotonin and noradrenalin were the most effective.

What has baffled researchers since then is that, although these drugs initially increased the levels of these neurotransmitters in the synapses, within twenty-four hours this effect seemed to stop, and relieving the symptoms of depression then took between two and four weeks. This latter delay suggested that other mechanisms had to be involved. A great deal of research has been done to try to clarify this process, and we still do not know the full story. Here, however, is one possible explanation that has been put forward:

- Antidepressants block the re-uptake of the serotonin/noradrenalin back into the neuron which released them in the first place.
- The level of the neurotransmitter tries to rise, but is initially held in check by a normal feedback mechanism which stops this neuron from releasing more into the synapse.
- This delay lasts about two weeks, but eventually the feedback mechanism weakens and levels of the neurotransmitter increase.
- The gradual rise in the neurotransmitter within the synapse then instructs serotonin/noradrenalin receptors to pass information into the nucleus of the cells, where the DNA/genes reside.
- The DNA/genes then issue instructions to encourage neurons to re-grow connections between them. This is particularly beneficial in depression, because it repairs the behaviour and memory boxes. The most likely mechanism for this is encouraging the manufacture of a crucial enzyme within the neuron called BDNF, which encourages the neuron to improve its connections with other neurons. This effect is probably mediated through the neurotransmitter glutamate.
- The DNA/genes also alter receptor function and other key neuron activities. The final result is that the neurons of the mood system are now interacting much more efficiently, and the mood cables and departments start to function better.
- It is also likely that the growth of new connections takes much longer to consolidate, which may explain why those who stop treatment before this process is completed are more likely to relapse.

- In this scenario, a neuron would need at least two to four weeks to begin these alterations, and much longer to 'bed in' these changes.

What Happens Within the Mood System When These Drugs are Taken?

The most likely sequence is as follows:

- The mood cables (serotonin/noradrenalin cables in particular) are stimulated, initially (within two weeks) by the increased amounts of no-radrenalin and serotonin that have become available within synapses. When these cables activate, they calm down the stress box and Area 25, leading to many of the symptoms of depression – such as fatigue, lack of concentration, and eating/sleeping disturbances – gradually disappearing.
- The mood departments (particularly the frontal prefrontal cortex) start to heal, at a gradual rate, due to neuronal changes directly caused by the antidepressant, and stimulation of the mood cables/circuit. This leads to an increase in positive thinking, self-esteem and memory, and a reduction in suicidal impulses and anxiety.
- The above changes help to calm the stress box further, and this box sends messengers to the adrenal glands instructing them to produce less gluco-cortisol. When the normal daytime and nighttime levels of glucocortisol are restored, blood platelets, bones and the immune system start to recover. This reduces the risk of heart disease, osteoporosis and infection.
- The vicious biological circle of the Red Flag is reversed, and the Green Flag reappears.

It is also worth examining what happens with regard to neuroimaging when this process occurs. The key findings are: an increase in activity of the mood control boxes/cables, a reduction in activity of the stress box, a dampening down of activity in Area 25, a gradual rise in activity of some key sections of the prefrontal cortex (and a reduction in others), and an increase in activity in the memory box . An interesting way of comparing the neurobiological effects of both drug therapy and CBT is to regard the former as working from the bottom of the brain upwards, and the latter from the top downwards. Because the two mood departments are, as we have seen, really part of a two-way loop/ neural mood circuit, both therapies often end up with similar results. This is the beauty of understanding the flag model of the mood system. It also suggests that combining both may be the ideal way of treating this illness.

It is also interesting to reflect on the reasons why there is a difference in the speed at which drug therapy lifts many of the symptoms of depression when compared with CBT and interpersonal therapy. The former acts initially on the mood cable/boxes and, through them, on the stress box. Since, as we have already discussed, many of the vegetative symptoms, such as fatigue and problems relating to sleep, appetite, mood, concentration, drive and so on stem from problems within these cables, it makes sense that a therapy that activates them leads to an early lifting of these negative effects.

It has also been shown that Area 25 normalises much faster with this form of therapy. The effect of drug therapy on psychological symptoms of depression, like negative thinking, comes later. This is due to the normalising of the mood circuit finally improving these symptoms.

In comparison, CBT/IPT works by activating the logical prefrontal cortex. This in turn begins slowly to calm down the circuits leading to the stress box and, by gradually normalising them, leads to a secondary improvement in the vegetative symptoms noted above. This takes much longer. People with symptoms like fatigue and poor concentration often find it difficult to engage with this form of therapy.

Types of Antidepressants
Antidepressants can be separated into two groups, old and new:

Older Antidepressants
These drugs, which were introduced in the 1950s, revolutionised the treatment of depression. The most renowned group are the tricyclics, so called because there are three circles within their chemical structure. They act primarily on the serotonin, dopamine and noradrenalin mood cables.

They prove effective in most cases of depression but can have undesirable side-effects, including sedation, dry mouth, blurred vision, difficulty passing urine, and impotence. Furthermore, some are extremely toxic, and often fatal, when taken in overdose.

This is obviously a serious problem because, although they are effective in severe depression, the person who is unwell may be suicidal: prescribing them a drug like this in effect gives them a means to kill themselves. Side effects like sedation can often simply replace the depressive symptoms, making it difficult for them to function normally. Many have to stop taking these drugs due to the side effects, despite the fact that the medication is working. Nevertheless, they were the drug of choice for decades in treating depression, and have cured millions of patients. To this day, I have patients who respond much better to these older drugs than to more modern ones – although this is the exception.

Two common tricyclics are:

1. *Amitriptyline:* This is the most well known and most widely prescribed tricyclic. It is extremely effective in restoring the mood system to normal. But sedation, and a very high risk of fatality if taken in overdose, makes it a dangerous drug to prescribe, particularly if suicidal thoughts are present.
2. *Imipramine:* This is very similar to amitriptyline but has less of a sedative effect.

A second group of drugs used in the past were called the MAOIs. These drugs worked by blocking the natural breakdown of noradrenalin and dopamine at nerve endings. This build-up of neurotransmitters helped many with depression, but some of these drugs also interacted in the gut with common foodstuffs like cheese, sometimes producing a life-threatening increase in blood pressure. Due to their effect on the dopamine cable, they were particularly useful in improving symptoms of fatigue and loss of pleasure. Their use waned due to the seriousness of the potential serious side effects, however.

Newer Antidepressants

In 1988, depressive drug treatment was revolutionised with the arrival of SSRIs: selective serotonin re-uptake inhibitors. Their primary target is the serotonin mood cable; most SSRIs also target other mood cables to a lesser extent, with the exception of Citalopram and Escitalopram, which are exclusively selective to the serotonin cable. The first SSRI drug to be released was Prozac. This drug prohibits the re-uptake of serotonin. It demonstrated similar efficacy to tricyclics, but offered two major advantages. Firstly, it is safe in overdose, and secondly it has fewer side effects. The introduction of Prozac was followed by many similar serotonin mood cable antidepressants, which were modified to be more effective. Another major landmark in depressive drug treatment was the development of drugs that specifically prevented the re-uptake of noradrenalin.

It was hoped that these modern groups of drugs would turn out to be the 'miracle cure' for depression. Up to 30 percent of patients do not respond to them, however. They are also not without side effects. Nausea, tremor, anxiety, headaches and sexual dysfunction are commonly reported.

These drugs are not recommended for routine use, without specialist approval, for under-eighteens, as it is thought that, in some cases, they increase the risk of suicide in these individuals.

As a general guide, SSRIs are more useful than older antidepressants in treating mild to moderate depression, with the exception of Lexapro (Escitalopram), which has proven efficacy in the severly depressed. SSRIs are particularly useful if anxiety, sleep and appetite difficulties are present. Drugs that target the noradrenalin cable may be more useful in severe depression, where extreme fatigue and poor drive may be major problems. Despite their fairly numerous disadvantages, these drugs continue to transform the lives of people suffering from depression.

Here are some of the common modern antidepressants in use:

1. *Fluoxetine (Prozac):* This drug has proved a very effective and safe drug in the treatment of depression, anxiety and eating disorders over the past fifteen years. Some find that it has a very positive effect on their outlook on life. This has led to a growing debate (particularly in the USA) as to whether the drug is sometimes being used for the wrong reasons. This drug has been used in the under-eighteen age group usually under the care of a specialist.

2. *Escitalopram (Lexapro):* This drug is the most recent addition to the SSRI group and is different to the other SSRIs as it is a serontonin dual-acting agent, effective in all types of depression. It is now the drug of choice for the treatment of depression and anxiety. It has a favourable side-effect profile, with occasional nausea in the first week, but reduced sexual dysfunction compared to other SSRIs. It is generally fast-acting, well-tolerated, and effective in restoring normal mood and calming anxiety.

3. *Paroxetine (Seroxat):* This drug, which was a follow-up to Prozac, was initially greeted favourably. It then received a great of bad press because of its sexual and withdrawal-related side effects. Severe dizziness and disorientation can occur when the drug is stopped, so care is needed to do this very slowly. Concern has also arisen about its use in younger age groups (where some feel it may lead to an increase in suicidal thoughts), and in pregnant mothers, where it should be avoided.

4. *Venflaxine (Efexor):* Unlike the three previously mentioned drugs, this drug targets both the serotonin cable and (at high doses) the noradrenalin cable. It is effective in treating depression in those with poor drive or motivation. It has similar side effects to the SSRIs in low doses, but sweating, constipation and headaches can be additional problems, particularly in higher doses. Its effects on the noradrenalin system in higher doses also require careful monitoring in the elderly and in those with cardiac problems.

5. *Mirtazapine (Zispin):* This drug also targets the serotonin and noradrenalin cables. It is a very useful medication, but side effects like weight gain can be a problem. It is often used as a second-line drug where sleep difficulties and weight loss are a problem. One of the advantages of this drug is an absence of sexual side effects.

6. *Duloxetine (Cymbalta):* This is similar in type to Effexor. It is claimed that the side-effect profile of this drug, especially concerning sexual dysfunction, is more favourable. It will take some time, however, before this claim can be borne out in clinical practice.

7. *Vortioxetine (Brintellix):* This drug targets the serotonin mood cable in a similar manner to the SSRI's but also other key receptors which are more

targeted. It is purported to be effective in improving cognition as well as mood. Its main side effect is initial nausea.

This is only a sample of the many drugs of this type.

The biggest advancement that these drugs have brought is the ability of the general practitioner to treat depression without the need for referral to a specialist. Nowadays, only serious or resistant cases need to be referred. This has helped to demystify depression as an illness.

Complementary Therapies

Complementary therapies (which accept the relevance of traditional therapies like drug treatment and psychotherapy but hope to assist or complement them) are frequently favoured over alternative therapies (some of which reject the role of traditional medicine completely and suggest alternative approaches) because they do not encourage the abandonment of conventional medicine completely – a dangerous approach to take when a patient has severe depression or is suicidal. There is much to learn from complementary medicine. Firstly, it takes a holistic view of the person, looking at their body, mind and spirit. Secondly, it provides more weapons in the growing arsenal of treatments for depression. Thirdly, it encourages the person to play an active role in their own treatment and recovery. Finally, it brings in other cultural influences, which can be helpful. Complementary therapy should only take place under the guidance of a trained professional. It should also, in my opinion, be exposed to the same rigorous controls as conventional medicine. Complementary therapies used to treat depression include the following:

Massage

Massage is one of the most well-established forms of complementary treatment. The healing power of touch is thought to reduce stress and depression. Various forms of massage are available, including aromatherapy massage (where selected aromatherapy oils are blended together and used in the massage), sports massage and Indian head massage (a massage which concentrates solely on the head and scalp). Massage helps the mood system by calming the stress box, which in turn reduces levels of stress peptides and glucocortisol. Regular massage is often suggested to those suffering from depression as part of their treatment.

Reflexology

Reflexology is an Eastern therapy based on the concept of energy flow. Certain points on the feet and hands are thought to be connected to various channels of energy that flow through the body. By pressing and massaging these points, energy blockages can be released, and symptoms can be relieved. Some find this treatment effective in releasing stress.

Relaxation Exercises

Relaxation exercises include yoga, pilates and meditation. Yoga and pilates combine stretching with the development of correct posture and breathing. Meditation involves deep concentration to clear the mind and block out all distractions. These ancient 'workouts' have a beneficial effect on many areas of the body, and are particularly helpful for calming the stress box. They probably lead to a reduction of stress peptides and glucocortisol. All of these therapies share a similar goal: by surrounding the mind in peace and quiet, the mood system is given time and energy to heal. Some find meditation particularly helpful in managing anxiety, as it teaches the person to eliminate the worries that plague them.

Acupuncture

This has been used in the East for thousands of years. It is based on the Chinese principle that the whole body is mapped out by invisible energy lines. According to this approach, illnesses such as stress and depression originate when energy lines become blocked. Acupuncture involves using needles on particular energy points around the body, called acupoints. Neuro-imaging studies show decreased activity in the limbic mood system, particularly in the memory and hormone control boxes. Other studies have revealed an increase in activity in the serotonin cable, as well as in the level of brain endorphins, all of which contribute to a lifting of mood.

Herbal Treatments

There is a bewildering array of herbal remedies available for the treatment of anxiety and depression. Naturopaths are trained medical specialists who prescribe herbal treatments as part of a treatment regime. Herbal remedies can be just as effective as prescription drugs but they can also have similar side effects, and should be used with equal caution. It is therefore reasonable to suggest that herbal remedies undergo the same rigorous testing procedures as prescription drugs before being released on to the market. If this was the case, doctors would feel more comfortable about prescribing them.

The most widely known herbal treatment (particularly in Europe) for depression is St John's wort, derived from the plant *Hypericum*. This has mild-to-moderate mood-enhancing properties and mimics the action of SSRI drugs. If taken with SSRIs, the person may experience the serotonin syndrome (a range of unpleasant side effects, such as confusion, agitation, nausea, muscle spasms, difficulties with balance, high blood pressure and, in severe cases, seizures and coma, resulting from too much serotonin in the body). On its own, it seems to be free of many of the side effects associated with the SSRIs. If you are on prescribed medication, you should check with your doctor before taking any herbal remedies.

Dawn Simulators

These are very effective in the treatment of seasonal affective disorder, or SAD, which is discussed further in Chapter 2 below. This device is plugged into a bedroom lamp, and gradually increases the amount of light available before the person wakes up. This tricks the body into believing that it is summertime, and helps the mood system to fight the effects of SAD. This is a good example of the way in which a complementary therapy can be used to treat a mood disorder.

All of the above treatments are available for those with depression. The other more serious forms of intervention, such as psychological and drug therapy, are usually initiated by the family doctor or a specialist.

Each person is individual. What works for one person may not work for another. It is important to remember that all treatments take time, and that patience is vital.

Treatment of Depression: The Doctor's Dilemma

There has been widespread concern regarding the increase in the prescription of antidepressants in recent years. Such concerns range from depression being over-diagnosed, to the drugs merely working as placebos, to whether or not they have a lasting effect on depression.

Depression affects a large number of people. Experts estimate that, contrary to the concern some have about 'over-diagnosis', many cases in fact go undetected. The Irish College of General Practice often talks about the 'pyramid' of illness. For illnesses like heart disease or diabetes, they feel that only 5 percent of those suffering from such illnesses are seen and treated by a specialist, 40 percent or so are diagnosed and in some cases treated by their family doctor, and the rest remain undiagnosed or are self-medicating. (Of those who are receiving help for mental illnesses, around 85 percent are treated by the family doctor.) If this is so, it is likely that we are not over-diagnosing depression but, rather, missing many cases! If we accept Prof. McKeown's figures of only two out of every four cases coming forward for help, and one in four getting adequate treatment, we still have a lot to do!

Due to the shortage of trained psychologists and suitably qualified CBT therapists in Ireland and indeed in many other parts of the world, psychological treatments are not easily accessible or affordable to many people who are suffering from depression. In these cases, especially when the patient is in great distress, the doctor has no choice but to recommend drug treatment as the first option. Those with moderate to severe depression may have been struggling with crippling symptoms for quite some time before coming for help. They naturally want to get better quickly.

Since referral to a psychologist or therapist within the health-care system can involve a considerable delay (if this option is available at all!), the doctor must prescribe medication to prevent the condition worsening. Where the GP is trained in CBT techniques, this is of help, but time pressures often limit the level of assistance he or she can offer in this area.

Doctors can also provide the patient with a complete array of treatment options. Diet, exercise, supplements, relaxation techniques, and temporary abstinence from alcohol are all practical steps that the person can implement themselves. Counselling can help the person to cope with stress or relationship problems. In many cases of mild depression, this may be all that is required.

Sometimes, as in moderate to severe depression, the person is so low and exhausted that only an antidepressant can bring them up to a functional level, as they may be too tired to try anything else. Medication is not a 'quick fix' and will not magic away life's problems. It is, however, of great help in many cases in reducing the crippling physical and psychological symptoms associated with depression, allowing the person time and space to review all aspects of their lives, including their thinking patterns.

If CBT and other psychological treatments were freely available and the person could afford them, the need for longer periods of drug therapy might be substantially reduced. To ignore completely the benefits of drug therapy would in my opinion be naive and dangerous, however. The ideal situation would be a combination of both, as part of a holistic package. Above all, the person must be allowed to have an input into their own treatment. They must take their life back into their own hands.

Many doctors would like to have CBT freely available to all suitable patients, not just to those who are able to afford it. Money spent by the Department of Health in this area (in both training therapists and providing easy access to them for all Irish GPs) might swiftly reduce the need in some cases for drug treatment, and actually save money in the long run. It is also worth listening to the CBT therapists themselves, who feel that many patients benefit from drug therapy to start with as it assists them in reaching a functioning level where they can become more actively involved. Otherwise, it can be difficult for the patient to find the energy and motivation necessary for successful CBT therapy.

We would also benefit from money being spent on educating people about the importance of mental health, and the need for proper nutrition and supplements, and exercise. Finally, it might be time for the health authorities to fund self-help groups to investigate the possibility of bringing CBT help to their members.

Some Commonly Asked Questions about the Management of Depression

The long-standing ignorance and misconceptions that surround depression has made people reluctant to talk about it. In my experience, these are the most commonly asked questions about depression:

What Will Happen If I Go To See My Doctor Complaining Of Symptoms Of This Illness?
Many who suffer from this illness are unsure about how to approach their GP and struggle to put into words how they are feeling. They may not attribute their symptoms to depression, and may ask about some other illness instead.

The simplest thing is to tell your GP that you feel down and despondent. You should not be afraid to do this: there is no shame in it. Your doctor will then start to ask you a number of questions relating to fatigue, sleep, memory, mood, anxiety, and thoughts of harming yourself. He or she will probably ask about the medical history of your family.

He may ask questions unrelated to depression, or carry out a blood test, in order to eliminate the possibility of other illnesses. He may inquire about your weekly intake of alcohol. Once he is satisfied that you are suffering from depression, he will go on to discuss the possible causes, and the treatment options that are available to you.

Your diet, exercise, and use of supplements may be discussed. He will probably advise you to reduce or cease your alcohol intake. In the case of recent bereavement or relationship difficulties, counselling may be suggested as the next step. If, however, extreme fatigue, poor concentration, sleeping difficulties, and acts or thoughts of self-harm are evident, the doctor will probably consider drug treatment or psychological therapy.

You may be considered to be a patient who requires urgent referral to a specialist. This is likely if you are suicidal, or if the doctor is unsure about your diagnosis. The doctor or specialist might recommend that you go into hospital for a while so that you can avail of twenty-four-hour care until you feel better. This is particularly the case with patients who are suicidal, as there will be health professionals present to help them deal with suicidal thoughts, and keep an eye on them. However, most people can be successfully treated by their GP.

If your doctor decides on drug treatment, he will probably prescribe you one of the modern SSRIs. He will then review you after four to eight weeks to assess whether the medication has relieved your symptoms. If he deems it necessary, he will increase the dose until a satisfactory response has been obtained. You will probably have to take this medication for six to eight months, to ensure that your illness is properly treated.

When you feel well enough, the GP may, if he feels it appropriate, refer you to a counsellor or psychologist for a course of CBT. If you are reluctant to take antidepressants, or if they have proved ineffective in the past, your doctor may well recommend this method of treatment. Unfortunately, this can depend on the availability of such services. You should feel much better after six to eight weeks of drug treatment, and it is at this point that you need to make the necessary changes in your life to ensure that you remain this way. You may decide to move from a stressful job to a less stressful one, to cut down on your working week, to spend more time relaxing with your family, or to examine your financial situation and organise your spending to minimise stress. You may re-evaluate your weekly intake of alcohol and decide to incorporate regular exercise, a balanced diet, and supplements into your life.

When you reach the end of your course of medication (providing that you feel that you are back to normal), the doctor will slowly wean you off it. He will then advise you to make an appointment to see him immediately if any of the symptoms return.

Common Questions About Psychological Treatment
How Long Does a Course of CBT Take?
CBT usually involves eight to ten sessions (although sometimes much fewer), working with either a trained psychologist or therapist, or more rarely a psychiatrist who specialises in CBT. Each session lasts for about an hour.

What About the Cost and Availability of These Treatments?

The difficulty with CBT and other psychological treatments is that there is a huge shortage of trained professionals in this area. As a result, there are long waiting lists in the public system. Normally, you will be referred to a psychologist by a psychiatrist. If you cannot afford to pay privately, you could be waiting for a considerable period to see a psychologist. To go through the private system is a costly affair (around €80 to €100 per session), and beyond the financial means of many.

What About Psychotherapy?

Sometimes a person with depression, particularly if it is chronic, will not respond to drug treatment or CBT. There may be unresolved childhood difficulties like abuse, violence or addiction. There is a need to return to these painful memories and deal with them before the person can move on. This can be a lengthy and distressing process. We described it earlier as 'psychoanalytical psychotherapy'. Some believe that this is the only way to treat depression. There is no doubt that the physiologies of some people's brains are directly affected by adverse life experiences: in such cases, this form of psychotherapy can be of great help.

Much of the time, however, the depressive trigger does not lie in the person's past, but in an obvious stress trigger in the present. Psychotherapy in this form as a treatment for depression, although extremely useful in some cases, must therefore be put into perspective: some studies suggest that CBT in particular may be more useful as a general psychological tool for the treatment of this illness.

Although there is a great deal of truth in this approach, it ignores the abnormalities present in the brain, often at an early stage of adulthood, of some people with this illness. If depression was purely the result of problems occurring during childhood, or was due to some other unresolved issues or conflicts, one must ask why many people with very traumatic backgrounds do not develop depression, while others with quite peaceful backgrounds do. This view also ignores the effects of our present environment on the genes of the mood system.

Interpersonal psychotherapy (which explores the effects of past and present relationships in the creation and maintenance of depression, and the effects of the latter on present relationships) is a much more useful psychological therapy. For reasons that have already been discussed, relationships can be a problem, both in the present and the past. Improving such dynamics can be of great help. The same problem exists here as with regard to CBT counsellors: a lack of personnel. A recent positive development is a trial that involves providing counsellors to GPs to help with this form of therapy. If this could be extended to all GPs, it would be of great help.

How Long Before These Treatments Show Results?

Depression is usually alleviated within four months of beginning psychological treatments like CBT/IPT. Drug treatment starts to work faster, usually within two to six weeks, but after the first four months both forms of treatment are equally effective. CBT is effective in reducing the rate of relapse in depression, so the results are in some cases more long-lasting. These treatments, by helping people to change their thinking and behaviour, teach them how to cope with life. Many experts feel that a sensible combination of drug treatment and CBT would be the ideal scenario.

Common Questions About Drug Treatment

Why Should I Take Drug Treatment At All?

Depression is an illness, bouts of which normally last between six and twelve months. Without intervention, the body would eventually repair the damage that has been inflicted on the brain and revert back to normal mood. However, depression can be so distressing and disruptive that restoring normal mood through some form of intervention is the only logical course of action. Secondly, the lifetime risk of suicide can be up to 15 percent in this illness. Thirdly, depression opens the body up to other diseases, such as coronary heart disease and osteoporosis.

Many people are apprehensive about using drug treatment for depression. If drug treatment is used appropriately, however, it is invaluable in relieving the symptoms of depression and allowing the person to function normally.

Although these drugs can have some side effects, their short-term benefits usually outweigh these negative aspects. The primary advantage of drug treatments is that it is the fastest method of relieving the symptoms of depression. The ideal form of treatment involves a mixture of pharmacological and psychological treatments: this gives the person the best of both worlds and maximises their chances of success.

Are Antidepressants Addictive?

This fear dates back a time when tranquillizers like Valium and Librium were widely prescribed. These drugs were often used to treat anxiety and were extremely addictive. This stigma spread to all other psychiatric drugs. In reality, whatever other side effects they may have, antidepressants are generally not considered to be addictive. They simply restore normal mood, and are usually taken for a specific period of time.

Only in a small number of chronic cases will it be necessary for people to take antidepressants for long periods. This does not mean that the person is addicted to them; rather, they function better on them. Upon discontinuing these drugs, users will not experience the cravings associated with withdrawal from an addictive substance.

Most people will simply take the prescribed course of treatment, and withdraw from the medication slowly over a period of time (giving the neurons in the brain time to readjust to the absence of the drugs). Sudden removal of antidepressants will result in symptoms of dizziness and light-headedness. This is often mistaken for evidence of addiction, but clearly this is not the case.

There has been a lot of bad press, with Prozac in particular, concerning addiction. It became an over-prescribed 'wonder drug' in America, and was often used to boost low self-esteem and make people more assertive, rather than being used simply to treat depression. This clouded the issue. In reality, Prozac is not addictive (if the correct parameters of addiction are applied) and is an easy drug to come off, with almost no withdrawal problems.

Many mistake the reappearance of symptoms of depression as a sign that they are addicted to the drug. This causes great confusion amongst those who may need drug treatment but are put off seeking such treatment by a lack of clarity in the media about the use of these drugs. The antidepressant Seroxat is another example of such media misinformation. It received controversial publicity because when people suddenly stopped taking this drug, they felt extremely dizzy. Many people took this as an indication that the drug is addictive. Once again, although this side effect is a great nuisance, it does not necessarily constitute a symptom of addiction.

Are Antidepressants Simply Placebos?

A placebo is a tablet with no active ingredients, normally given to a person during scientific research into a drug, to test what happens if the person simply 'thinks' they are getting better. The tablet will look identical to the one that is being tested. By comparing this effect with the effects on those who have taken the actual drug, researchers can find out if the drug is making any difference. Some maintain that all antidepressants work as placebos by making the person believe they are getting better, and that the brain responds by elevating mood. Many psychoanalytical psychotherapists quote this fact and dismiss such drugs as 'expensive, drug-company-driven products'. I have had to treat some patients who were attending such therapists and whose depression was gradually deteriorating despite such intervention.

Many people hear this argument from a media that is sometimes in thrall to alternative-medicine approaches – 'anything other than drug therapy' – and this can lead to confusion and uncertainty. Let's examine the scientific data.

The placebo effect does indeed complicate matters. A certain number of participants in any study, who have taken the placebo, usually report that they get better. We must therefore be cautious in interpreting the results of all drug trials. A percentage of those who 'responded' to the pill (and indeed to all therapies) include those who experienced the placebo effect and those experiencing a placebo and real effect simultaneously. So it is difficult to extrapolate from the results. In general, the more severe the depression, the less the placebo effect is likely to be of relevance.

The situation is particularly complicated in the case of depression, as believing that you are going to get better is one of the steps towards recovery. For this reason, the placebo effect may be larger in antidepressants rather than in other drugs, due to positive thinking. However, the fact that drug therapy seems to take effect in many cases by the end of the second month, whereas CBT, which is an excellent psychological therapy, can take up to four months, would suggest that drug therapy is having more than a simple placebo effect. It would also suggest that the placebo effect for CBT works along different neurobiological pathways.

How Long Does It Take For These Drugs To Work?

It takes two to four weeks for an antidepressant to start relieving the symptoms of depression. Some patients may note an improvement in symptoms such as anxiety after ten to twelve days, but most people will need six to eight weeks of treatment before they feel 'normal' again. When this happens, symptoms such as fatigue, anxiety, forgetfulness, reduced concentration, low self-esteem and low drive are alleviated. The person will have regained a positive outlook on the future.

How Long Will I Have To Take These Drugs?

For the vast majority of people, courses of treatment will last from six to nine months. The general consensus is that it is advisable to take these drugs for a minimum of six months from the time you feel well. Since this is normally two to three months, the usual recommended period is about six to nine months. After this, the majority of people can be slowly weaned off the antidepressants. This will usually be sufficient, but for about 20 to 25 percent of patients, drug treatment may have to continue for longer periods, and may sometimes (usually following specialist advice) be permanent. CBT, along with lifestyle changes and a healthy approach towards alcohol, greatly reduces the need for such long-term treatment in this group.

Why Does It Take Six To Nine Months Of Treatment?

The body seems to need around six to nine months of treatment to restore its physiology. It is unknown why this is the case. The most likely reason is that it takes a long time for positive internal biological changes to occur in the cells of malfunctioning neurons in the behaviour and memory boxes, and indeed in the whole mood system. After this time, the body's mood system is functionally (if not structurally) healed, and when the person comes off these drugs they will remain well. How long the person remains healthy will depend on how they deal with the stress triggers that caused the depression, learn new ways of challenging negative thoughts, perhaps embrace ideas like mindfulness or yoga, learn to treat alcohol with respect, and improve their diet and exercise routine. A healthy, relaxed, physically fit body, together with a well-nourished brain, are the enemies of depression.

What Will Happen If I Stop Taking The Antidepressants Too Quickly?

Patients often stop taking their medication as soon as they feel better. The danger time for this is between two and three months. At this stage, they feel much better, and – usually because they feel 'guilty' about taking the medication, a feeling which is often exacerbated by media hysteria about the use of antidepressants – decide to cease taking them. This is a major mistake, and the person usually does not remain well for long. Such a situation is very frustrating for doctor and patient alike. It is very important when a person starts a course of drug treatment to make a conscious decision to finish the course, regardless of how well they feel after the first two months.

What Side Effects Can I Expect?

With the older drugs, sedation, dry mouth and blurred vision are common complaints. With the newer SSRIs, initial nausea (due to initial activation of serotonin receptors in the gut), sweating, tremors of the hands, and heavier periods in the case of females (through their effects on blood platelets) are all commonly reported side effects. (Nausea can be counteracted by taking the over-the-counter medication Motilium.) They often disappear after a while as the body adapts to the medication. By keeping in regular contact with your family doctor, such side effects can be monitored, and adjustments can be made if necessary.

What About Sexual Side Effects?

Many people taking medication for depression suffer from a loss of libido, impotence, and delayed or abnormal orgasm. For some, this may not be a great problem, as they had no sex drive due to their depression anyway. However, after several months of treatment, people will generally start to feel better and will regain their interest in sex. It is then that any sexual side effects caused by these drugs may become an issue. Many people find these side effects so frustrating that they stop their medication. For the following six months of treatment, the following difficulties may be experienced:

(a) *Men may have difficulty producing or sustaining an erection.* This can be remedied for the remainder of the course of drugs by supplementing with Viagra or Cialis. Others may experience difficulties with ejaculation. This is more difficult to treat. Some experts suggest ceasing medication at weekends, but there are risks involved, so consult your family doctor first.
(b) *Some women may have difficulty achieving orgasm.* This symptom seems to vary from person to person, and some will learn to overcome it with relaxation exercises.

These sexual side effects can occur because the drugs, as well as targeting the serotonin receptors that regulate mood, act on other serotonin receptors in the brain which regulate sexual activity. These problems will disappear within a week of stopping the medication. Upon finding this out, most people will agree to finish the course. The sexual side effects for some are a small price to pay for keeping depression at bay; others cannot tolerate them and stop taking their medication. In the latter cases, CBT should be considered as an alternative, along with the usual lifestyle changes. The hope is that future drug treatments will eliminate these side effects.

Do Antidepressants Increase an Individual's Risk of Committing Suicide?
This has become an increasing concern, particularly with the widespread use of SSRIs. Initially, the concern was to do with the use of these antidepressants in the under-eighteen group; recently, this has been broadened to their use in general. This concern relates to the tendency of these drugs in some cases

initially to increase agitation in some people, with an increase in suicidal thoughts.

The current expert view on the use of antidepressants in the under-eighteen group is that in some cases there is an increased risk of suicidal thoughts and actions, hostility and impulsiveness. Because of this, it is felt that the use of these drugs should be confined to specialists. Even under specialist care, there should be strict supervision.

But what can we say about the use of antidepressants by adults? All antidepressants may increase the chance of suicidal thoughts being actualised, as the person's energy and drive improve at a faster rate than their mood. This has always been identified as a potential risk.

The question being asked about SSRIs in particular is whether the drugs themselves are prompting the creation of suicidal thoughts. The general feeling is that only a very small number of those treated with these drugs will experience intense agitation or thoughts of self-harm as a direct result of taking them. Careful monitoring in the first two months should reduce any such risks, along with early identification of those who seem to be generally more at risk of self-harm. Personally, I have come across this problem only occasionally in practice, and in general feel that the SSRIs reduce the risk of suicide. Some international trials suggest that SSRIs actually reduce the risks of suicide, because they encourage increased activity in the serotonin cable. It is also important to note that depression itself creates impulsive suicidal thoughts and actions. Eliminating all antidepressants would deny help to many who are at risk from the dangers of depression, and would seem unwise.

The widely accepted current view is that the risk of suicide associated with antidepressants is not sufficient for patients to stop using these drugs. Until some more expert scientific data appears to change this situation, these drugs will continue (quite sensibly, in my opinion) to be prescribed.

Can Mild Depression Be Treated Without Drugs?

Many people ask this question; the answer to it is an unequivocal yes! For many people, a change in lifestyle, in the form of exercise, proper diet and supplements, and a good look at major stress factors, may be enough to turn things around. This may be helped by counselling and interpersonal therapy in some cases. Another common error is to mistake chronic stress for depression. We have already dealt with the signs of the former. It is only if these measures do not work, or if the depression becomes more severe, that drug treatment may be recommended.

Is It True That SSRIs Are More Useful For The Treatment Of Mild To Moderate Depression?

This is true. Research has shown that SSRIs seem to play an especially useful role in the treatment of mild to moderately severe depression, particularly if sleep or weight is a problem. The SSRIs are also of particular help in those with anxiety and depression, in younger age groups (the under-forties) and in the elderly (due to the fact that they are associated with fewer side effects).

Drugs which stimulate the noradrenalin cable seem to have a more powerful effect on those with severe depression. (In general terms, the more severe the depression, the more important noradrenalin and dopamine depletion probably are.)

Some experts feel that SSRIs are prescribed too liberally. My own opinion is that, if used sensibly, they can play a useful role in many cases, as long as all the lifestyle changes that we have already dealt with are also being made. They are not, and never will be, the answer to life's many and varied problems, however! They are simply one of a useful group of therapeutic options available to help those who are suffering from a bout of the Red Flag.

What Happens When The Course Of Antidepressants Comes To An End?

Abrupt discontinuation of the newer drugs (apart from Prozac) will, as we have already explained, produce symptoms such as giddiness, dizziness, nausea and lack of coordination. When it is time for your doctor to end the course of treatment, he will plan a gradual reduction of the drug, reducing the dosage from its current level to zero over a period of four to six weeks. If treatment is reduced gradually in this way, the patient should experience no withdrawal symptoms. By then, the patient will hopefully be feeling much better. Once their mood has improved, further changes can be made in their life to tackle the initial stress triggers and lifestyle choices that may have been the cause of the illness.

Are There Any New Drugs Or Other Treatment Options For Depression On The Horizon?

I am happy to say that there seem to be many exciting new drug options coming in the next five years and beyond. As a family doctor, I feel that there are many drawbacks to the drugs that are currently available. We are grateful for and continue to use them, as they help treat many of the distressing symptoms of depression, but most doctors look forward to the possibility of newer and better options.

Much of the work is being done into drugs which might dampen down the stress peptide/glucocortisol barrage which seems to lie at the heart of the biological malfunctioning in depression. We talked earlier about CRH (one of the stress peptides), which is, along with a number of other substances (including one called substance P) being examined with a view to tackling depression from a different angle. Some of these drugs are now in the pipeline.

One other exciting area is research into the role of dopamine in depression. Many people with this illness describe how current drug treatments numb their pain and help to reduce many of the physical symptoms of depression, but do nothing to help restore their sense of joy and pleasure in life. Some go further, and say that some SSRIs in particular numb their feelings completely. This is an issue that many psychiatrists and family doctors do not in my opinion understand or engage with to a sufficient extent. It is clearly of great importance to the sufferer, however.

The reason that these modern drugs are unable to improve this distressing symptom is due, in the main, to their relative ineffectiveness in directly stimulating the dopamine cable into action. Any effects on this cable are usually secondary in nature. This is because their main effect is on the serotonin cable, and even here their action is not very targeted. Drugs which affect the noradrenalin cable also suffer from similar limitations in relation to the dopamine cable.

Paradoxically, some of the older type drugs, such as the tricyclics and in particular the MAOIs, were probably more effective in targeting all the cables, including the dopamine cable, than some of the newer drugs, particularly the SSRIs. As we discussed earlier, however, the side effects associated with these drugs, especially MAOIs, greatly limited their general use. This was a pity, as the MAOIs in particular were very effective in stimulating the dopamine cable into life, with a subsequent lift in the patient's feelings of joy and pleasure. The main concern was their capacity to interact with parts of the diet to produce potentially life-threatening increases in blood pressure.

Research into treatment for Parkinson's disease has thrown up an interesting drug called selegiline (Eldepryl), however. As we have already seen, half of those with this illness also suffer from depression. This is not surprising, as a lack of dopamine is common to both. It was discovered that, in smaller amounts (between 10 and 20 milligrammes), this drug (which is at present being used to help those with Parkinson's) was effective in helping those whose depression seemed to involve the dopamine and noradrenalin cables in particular. The classical example of this type of depression is atypical depression, which we will discuss in the next chapter.

Selegiline is available now, particularly in the USA, for treatment of depression and has helped many of those who suffer from both extreme fatigue and the dark emptiness to which a life without joy or pleasure can give rise. This drug has the major additional benefit of not interfering with the sexual life of the person who is being treated.

There has also been interest in drugs which affect melatonin. This is an important hormone released by the brain at night-time, as sunlight diminishes in the evening, causing us to feel tired and sleepy. Its levels are low in the daytime and high at night. If we have to remain awake when it is in our system, we can become irritable, fatigued and very moody (which explains why shift workers often struggle with these symptoms). It also explains why depression worsens in the winter months, when people have higher melatonin levels and lower serotonin levels. It has been shown that serotonin and melatonin are intimately linked, with the latter being manufactured from the former. Some studies have revealed higher levels of melatonin in major depression, so obviously it is also being affected by dysfunction in the mood circuit. A drug called Agomelatonine (which acts on both the serotonin and melatonin receptors) has been shown to assist in resetting sleep patterns in depression but seems to be less effective as an antidepressant in itself. Other future areas of research may involve examining the causes and consequences of glial-cell shortages on the survival of neurons within key structures like the prefrontal cortex. In the long run, this may prove to be the best long-term treatment for depression. There is recent interest in the effects of a general anaesthetic called Ketamine which has been found to assist mood and reduce suicide risks. It was found to be addictive so the search is on to isolate the mood improving part of this drug and isolate it from the addictive components.

One important finding involves the recognition of the importance of Area 25 of the prefrontal cortex in depression. A great deal of this work in this area has been done by the pioneering research scientist Helen Mayberg. She demonstrated that Area 25 seems to be over-active in most cases of severe depression and that, irrespective of the type of therapy used, activity in this area reduces if the depression is successfully treated. Because of this constant finding, many wonder if studying this area will lead to a major breakthrough in the treatment of depression.

One consequence of the interest in Area 25 has been the exciting (although hugely expensive) treatment option in the case of very serious depression not responding to any form of drug or psychological treatment. This form of treatment, known as 'deep brain stimulation', is similar to the treatment of intractable Parkinson's disease. It involves the surgical implantation of a battery-powered electrode into Area 25 of the brain of individuals affected by intractable depression. The electrode is then connected to a small battery placed under the collarbone. The electrode then sends out a constant low-voltage charge to the surrounding area. The person has the capacity to switch the device on or off. The results have been profound, and in some cases immediate.

This form of therapy is at a very experimental stage, but initial results look very promising, and this treatment may in the future play a role in very extreme cases of depression. Of great interest to many was the finding, made by Mayberg, that stimulating this area produced the same neuro-imaging changes as CBT and drug therapy combined!

Another interesting area of research is examining the way in which genetic differences between people with depression, relating to how they will respond to various forms of drug treatment. Hopefully, this will in time help medical professionals to 'target' the correct treatment option for each individual. We may also be helped by neuro-imaging studies to decide who would be best treated by drugs, versus psychological therapy.

There are many other areas where further research into this distressing illness may throw up new drug treatments or other options which will hopefully improve the quality of life for many without creating problems in the form of unwanted side effects. For the present, we must make the best use of what is available, in the knowledge that better therapies are on the way.

Is There Any Way Of Using Neuro-Imaging To Decide Which Patients Using Particular Drugs Or CBT Will Or Will Not Respond To Therapy?

A great deal of excellent work by Helen Mayberg has started to reshape the way in which we view depression. She has been at the forefront of the circuit concept and work into the importance of Area 25 and has done research where patients with depression were scanned before and after treatment. She has identified some key findings:

- That those who showed more activity than others in Area 24 prior to treatment with drug therapy and CBT were more likely to respond to both, and vice versa. Obviously, if Area 24 is very under-active, the mood circuit dysfunction is more severe, and therefore harder to treat.
- That CBT and psychotherapy worked on the prefrontal cortex first, with the other changes in the limbic mood department, brain stem and mood control boxes responding as the mood circuit settled down.
- That it was possible to pick out patterns which made it more likely that changing therapies was less likely to be successful.

This is obviously a new and very exciting area of research, but we have a long way to go before we have worked out the whole picture. Nonetheless, in the future such mechanisms may prove to be of great help in 'targeting' specific therapies for resistant depression.

Others Affected by the Red Flag (The Carers)

The Red Flag causes a great of pain and suffering not only to those with depression but also to those who are close to them. The former may be angry because they hate themselves, and they may project this anger on to those around them. Often their silence, apparent laziness (due to extreme fatigue) and self-absorption, amongst other things, can be the cause of quarrels and disputes within the home.

This negative environment is fuelled by a lack of recognition of the symptoms of the Red Flag by both the person with depression and those close to them. The person with depression may blame those close to them for causing the problem. In fact, they are upset that their loved ones do not observe or appreciate the pain they are in. This hostility offends family members, who withdraw further, increasing the depressed person's sense of unworthiness, and lowering levels of mood and self- esteem further.

In reality, a person who is depressed is often not capable of communicating their problems to those who are close to them. This is partly because the ignorance which surrounds depression often takes away the family's ability to empathise with the sufferer, and to help them. It is important for those close to some who is suffering from depression to understand both the symptoms of and the various treatments for depression. A depressed person is greatly encouraged when they discover that they are suffering from an illness, and that it can be treated. This gives them the ability to say: 'This is how I feel, and I am not ashamed of it any more, because I know now that I have an illness. I am not weak, I am sick.' For the carer, knowledge of this illness educates them as to why things are the way they are: why their loved one is being hostile and pushing them away. It also plays a role in teaching them how they can help.

Depression occurs essentially because of a lack of communication in the brain, and is often accompanied by a similar lack of communication and understanding in society. If we can finally talk about this illness and what can be done to cure it, those suffering from it will finally realise that 'It doesn't have to be this way', and their loved ones will echo this epiphany.

2: SPECIAL SUB-GROUPS OF DEPRESSION

The previous chapter dealt with uncomplicated unipolar depression; patients in this group are generally treated by a GP, with occasional help from specialists in the field. The remainder, whose illness is more complicated in nature and difficult to treat, require intervention from a psychologist or a psychiatrist, or both.

Depression in the Under-Eighteens

This is a unique group which has to be dealt with in a completely different way from their adult counterparts. The first crucial difference is that the body and brain of a child is in a gradual and constant state of transformation, which will eventually lead to the full formation of an adult body and brain.

A huge reorganisation of the brain takes place between the ages of twelve and eighteen. The production of sex hormones, and the immaturity of the frontal-lobe prefrontal cortex, makes this a time a neurologically vulnerable one. The Red Flag of depression often initially emerges during this phase.

The young person has to endure many new stresses, which may include peer pressure, sexual discovery, physical changes to their body, increased independence, and the need to make decisions about their future. Combine this with alcohol and recreational drug use, and a breeding ground for depression is formed. Other illnesses, such as schizophrenia, may also begin to emerge at this time.

Not only are the mood departments underdeveloped in this group, but so too are the mood cables. This may explain why drug treatment is less effective

– as well as being occasionally dangerous – and not routinely recommended in under-eighteens, although it can in some cases play a vital role.

This is an important group to focus on, because of the increased risk of suicide in males in particular. Nonetheless, it is important to note that more females than males in this group suffer from depression.

It is useful, in terms of symptoms, to divide this under-eighteen age group into two sub-groups, as follows:

Depression Among the Under-Twelves

Although depression is not common in this group, suicide by children younger than twelve is not unheard-of. Members of this group will not complain of the symptoms of depression like an adult; the illness is more likely to manifest itself as an irritable, angry, apathetic and generally disruptive disposition. The individual also lacks interest in all activities. Features of anxiety, such as recurrent abdominal pain, headaches and limb pain, may also be present.

Depression in the Twelve-To-Eighteen Age Group

According to Prof. McKeown, community studies have shown that between 10 and 20 percent of adolescents will develop major depression, and there is evidence that the incidence is increasing. He also noted that having a parent with depression, particularly if it is recurrent, is the single most important risk factor for depression among adolescents. In the twelve-to-fifteen age group, the symptoms are closer to those documented above.

As teenagers approach the age of fifteen, symptoms of depression will start to resemble those found among adults. Common triggers include image obsession in girls and acne in boys. These individuals are inclined to look at themselves in a negative and critical manner.

A major risk factor during these years is separation or divorce in the family, and youngsters at this age are also acutely sensitive to peer pressure and bullying. They are also just starting to learn about their sexuality. Young girls feel under pressure to look like models from as early as the age of twelve; young boys feel that they must achieve and assert themselves, with the 'six-pack' physique almost mandatory. If they do not reach the goals that society has set out for them, they feel like failures, and their self-esteem may drop to a dangerously low level.

All these stresses and difficulties can combine to put a great deal of strain on the young person's stress system. Those who are genetically susceptible to depression become most vulnerable to the illness at this stage; alcohol and drug misuse exacerbate the problem. Some experts go further and wonder whether heavy alcohol or drug misuse may directly change the neurochemistry of the developing brain, thereby increasing the risks of depression and suicide.

It is advisable for parents to go through the Red Flag checklist for warning signs in their children; don't wait for them to come to you. Watch for withdrawal or isolation from groups, relationship problems, sexual-identity issues and alcohol misuse. Where there is a family history of depression, suicide or alcoholism, not picking up on these clues can prove to be a fatal oversight.

A major controversial issue is who should treat this group, and how they should do so. The physiology of this group, as well as the numerous influences on the maturing process from twelve to eighteen, means that the only person who is qualified to treat these teenagers is a psychiatrist. These individuals' mood departments and mood cables are too immature to risk routine drug treatment: it is not known what effect these drugs may have on the brain's development at this age. Many concerns have been raised about the possibility that the use of antidepressants of all types (although the modern SSRIs, especially Prozac, are the only ones that are generally used) in this age group may lead to an increase in suicidal thoughts and actions.

The present expert view is that, although these drugs can in some cases lead to increased agitation, suicidal thoughts and even suicide itself, their sensible use by experienced child and adolescent psychiatrists as part of an overall treatment package may, in severe cases of depression, reduce the danger of suicide. In mild to moderate depression, however, the consensus is that other therapies, such as CBT and family therapy, are more than adequate.

The modern approach to treatment involves a multi-disciplinary team consisting of a psychiatrist, a psychologist, a social worker and an educational expert to assess the child's problems in different areas and to isolate the possible environmental and psychological causes of their depression. Once these causes have been discovered, they must be dealt with by the team. In more severe cases, this approach may include the child psychiatrist prescribing drug therapy.

This makes the child's environment favourable and free from stress, and this in turn helps the mood system to repair itself and continue to develop normally. The difficulty with this approach is that it requires time, money, resources and organisation: in many parts of the country at the moment, this service is just not possible. Another problem is the lack of child psychologists.

Of great concern to many family doctors, parents and those working with at-risk adolescents between the ages of sixteen and eighteen is the apparently nonsensical situation that only those under sixteen are eligible to be referred to such teams. Another concern is the lack of inpatient beds for high-risk young people.

The diagnosis and treatment of depression in this group is vital. Firstly, it is important to identify those who may be at risk from suicide. Secondly, this illness, if left untreated at this stage, when the mood system is forming, may in some cases continue for the duration of the person's life.

Many people spend decades suffering from depression, and remain undiagnosed and untreated until their thirties or forties. It has been shown that those who develop the Red Flag in their teens are more likely to suffer from recurrent bouts of depression later on.

If the multi-disciplinary approach can be so successful, why not apply it to the over-eighteen group? In adults, the mood system is fully formed. The mood cables and departments are operating normally. Many of the issues which affect this group become resolved as they approach twenty-five years of age.

Diet is crucial in the under-eighteen age group. The growing brain needs a diet rich in essential vitamins and nutrients and high in fish oils, which are easily available in the form of omega 3 from oily fish or other sources or in the form of supplements. Exercise is also important: apart from helping the young person's mood system, it reduces the incidence of obesity and diabetes.

Depression in the Elderly

There are also some key differences at the other end of the spectrum. The picture of depression in the elderly (defined as those over sixty-five) may be complicated by the presence of multiple other illnesses. For example, there is a high rate of depression among those recovering from heart attacks and cancer – two diseases that are common in this age bracket. Depression itself, as we saw earlier, can also increase the risk of both of these illnesses! So there is a huge overlap between our mood system and the other conditions that are common to the aging process. There are two subgroups of the elderly suffering from this illness: those who have suffered from depression for the duration of their lives, and those who have become depressed for the first time over the age of sixty to sixty-five. The causes of depression are completely different for the two groups.

The first group may have suffered from bouts of depression since their early teens, and nothing has really changed by the time they reach the age of sixty to sixty-five. The stresses may take a different form: personal loss, loneliness, alcohol misuse and addiction, financial difficulties, and the loss of a job. The physiology of their depression remains unchanged, however, and by extension their possible treatment remains unchanged too: drug treatment, psychological help or counselling.

The second group, however, may have suffered damage to their mood system because of a stroke, either small and silent, or large and paralysing. Out of the whole mood system, vascular damage to the connections leading to the frontal mood department (particularly the prefrontal cortex) and the dopamine control box on the left side of the brain seem to be the most common. The end result of this damage can be depression. Aging in general also leads to a gradual reduction in both the number of neurons and in the blood supply to the brain, and this too may be a contributory factor. The mood cables themselves (the serotonin and dopamine cables in particular, and to a lesser extent the noradrenalin cable) begin to shrink as we get older, and this may also explain the high rate of depression in this group.

Two elderly groups that are particularly at risk of depression are those who suffer from dementia and those who have Parkinson's disease. Both of these illnesses occur as a result of abnormal degenerative and vascular changes in the ageing brain. In Parkinson's disease, for example, a shortage of dopamine (which also causes difficulties with balance and movement) and serotonin in the mood cables they supply may lead to the appearance of this illness. Due to these unwanted biological changes, there is a high rate (up to 50 percent), in both of these illnesses, of the Red Flag of depression appearing.

Vascular damage to the mood sections mentioned above is of great relevance, as it helps to explain the sudden emergence of depression in those who never before suffered from it. This is an obvious target for prevention, as treating illnesses like high blood pressure, eliminating high cholesterol and smoking, and using drugs like aspirin may reduce the risks of developing depression, as well as of suffering major strokes.

The real problem is the difficulties associated with the diagnosis of depression among the elderly. Too often, elderly people are dismissed as 'cranky' or 'senile', when a closer examination will reveal depression's classic calling cards. In general, the symptoms of depression are similar in both the young and the elderly: a lack of enjoyment in life, memory difficulties in particular (often confused with dementia), apathy, anxiety, and a preoccupation with minor ailments are often key findings in the elderly. Such people will often experience a substantial improvement in their quality of life when an antidepressant is prescribed.

The isolation of many elderly people is an important environmental factor for depression, as is the loss of a long-time partner. Another important factor is alcohol misuse and abuse. The lack of physical contact in many cases compounds the above factors. These social factors accelerate the arrival of depression in those who are biologically vulnerable to it.

Treatment of both types of depression in the elderly will usually involve drug therapy, and this therapy will typically be prescribed for longer periods than in younger people. SSRIs, because of their lack of cardiac side effects, are the drugs of choice. Elderly people should receive lower doses, and the maxim of 'start low and go slow' applies. Psychological therapies like CBT are also of help, but are frequently unavailable. Exercise is of great help, if it can be done.

The role of alcohol, as always, needs to be carefully examined. Suicide (particularly in Asian countries such as China, where over-sixty-fives make up the bulk of suicides) remains a high risk in some cases.

Other ways of treating depression in this age group include:

1. Ensuring that the elderly person's diet is sufficient in the vitamins and nutrients which the mood system requires.
2. Exercise and supplements like B vitamins and omega 3 fish oils can be of great help. Massage and reflexology can also play a role.
3. Where there is social isolation, it can be extremely helpful for the elderly person to acquire a pet. The attention and affection which a pet bestows on its owner can have a beneficial affect on the person's mood system.
4. Encouraging elderly people to socialise in modern, well-run day-care centres. This makes them feel less isolated. In such centres, they can have conversations, eat together, and take part in activities such as painting, artwork and pottery.
5. Encouraging, if possible, regular contact with children and young teenagers.
6. Family members should not be afraid to demonstrate affection by physically embracing the elderly person. Many older people are starved of this type of emotional contact. For those who have become isolated through depression, this can be a particularly nourishing experience.

All of these factors can contribute to the health of the elderly person's mood system. Another factor which exacerbates the problem of depression in the elderly is the way they are treated by society. They have become increasingly isolated and alienated from the modern world. Elderly people need love, warmth and physical touch, and deserve to be treated with dignity.

Finally, it is interesting to note that, in the elderly group, the physical changes that affect the brain and predispose them to the appearance of depression give rise to similar symptoms as those appearing in the fifteen-to-thirty-five age group. This is a powerful example of the importance of the brain in this illness at all stages of our lives.

Post-natal Depression

It is common for women to feel down and weepy from day three to day four following the delivery of a child. This low mood may last for days or weeks, but usually dissipates without any intervention. It happens due to a combination of 'coming down' from the high of having a baby, the body's sex hormones reorganising themselves after the delivery, and the stress of looking after the needs of the newborn baby. Most women, having gone through this phase, return to normal within a short period of time. Some women are slower to come out of this phase, however, and remain depressed.

It is likely that pregnancy, and the period of time after it, can in some people activate a latent genetic disposition towards depression. The symptoms of post-natal depression are identical to those of the Red Flag. Any lack of bonding with the new child occurring as a result of depression is extremely upsetting for the mother and is obviously not healthy for the child.

As with normal depression, the aim of treatment is to restore mood-system functioning within six to eight weeks. This can often be achieved quite effectively with the use of antidepressants and psychological therapy. Post-natal depression is normally dealt with by the family doctor. The time span of treatment is very similar to ordinary depression. Indeed, some experts maintain that post-natal depression is no different from ordinary depression and that the birth, together with the stress of the post-natal period, is simply a trigger for it.

One in every thousand cases of pregnancy-related depression will take the form of psychotic depression. In such cases, the woman suffers from serious delusions, often involving harming either the baby or themselves. This is a critical and dangerous situation and should be dealt with only by a specialist, in a hospital environment. It is extremely traumatic for the family involved. Most of these cases will respond to treatment, and the woman's life will return to normal. There is always the risk, however, of suicide, and, infrequently, infanticide.

Women with post-natal depression are also trying to cope with caring for a new baby. Some wait for three to six months before coming to their GP for help. If you experiencing any of the symptoms of depression, do not be afraid to come to your family doctor to discuss them. Your doctor will be able to assess the severity of the problem; antidepressants may not be necessary.

Mothers in other parts of the world have a much lower incidence of post-natal depression. One possible explanation is that mothers in the Western World are often lacking in the omega 3 oils (in particular DHA) which the baby desperately needs, particularly in the final stages of its development. When the baby has been born, the mother may suffer from a deficiency of omega 3 oils, and this may be a factor in the development of post-natal depression. Perhaps all mothers should be advised to supplement their diet with these oils for the last three months of their pregnancy and for the three to six months following the birth of the baby! Once again, only further research can throw more light on this area.

Another interesting, and almost completely overlooked, area is the effect of the arrival of a newborn baby on the emotional life of the father! It is felt by some experts that the high-stress phase experienced by the father in the first year of the infant's life may lead to many young males developing depression (which usually remains hidden). We could learn a great deal from a large research project looking at the mood status of such males. One wonders whether it is the stress rather than the hormonal changes that make both men and women vulnerable to developing the Red Flag during this phase.

Atypical Depression

Some patients will present with low mood but also with unusual symptoms which do not feature on the Red Flag checklist. These are:

- Hypersomnia (sleeping too much)
- Hyperphagia (eating too much)
- Overwhelming fatigue, often termed 'leaden paralysis'
- An ability to be cheered up for short durations by positive life events
- Long-term sensitivity to rejection

- Avoidant personality

This type of depression may be far more common than is currently believed. Some experts estimate that up to 25 percent of depressives may fall into this group. Others wonder whether we should really treat this form of depression as a special entity at all! It is thought to be associated with reduced activity of the noradrenalin and in particular the dopamine cable; this may explain the symptoms of fatigue and over-eating.

Atypical depression is often undetected, and these patients can be misdiagnosed as typical depressives. They are not likely to respond to SSRIs, however: drugs which affect the other two mood cables have a better chance of success.

A drug called Bupropion or Zyban, which is used in America for this form of depression, is also used here in Ireland to help smokers with their addiction. Earlier, we mentioned the drug selegiline (Eldepryl). This works on both the dopamine and the noradrenalin cables and will in my opinion offer much to those who suffer from atypical depression. CBT and psychotherapy can also be helpful in some cases, but many patients will need drug therapy as well as exercise-based behaviour therapy to ease the extreme fatigue in particular.

Severe Depression

Severe or profound depression occurs when there is a complete breakdown of the Red Flag mood structures and cables, often as a result of prolonged stress. A person with severe depression will present in a zombie-like state, with total depletion of their noradrenalin, dopamine and serotonin cables, causing visible difficulties in movement, thought and speech.

They suffer extreme fatigue because they rarely sleep. In some cases, delusions can occur. Any action becomes almost impossible. They do not hear what people are saying, because they are unable to focus on it. Thought processes are extremely delayed; the world appears to be moving in slow motion; the passage of time is just pain, nothing else.

The total depletion of the serotonin cable puts suicide at the top of the agenda for these people. Sometimes, only their catatonic state prevents this suicidal urge from becoming a reality: it will take too much effort. Their dopamine system is also totally depleted, so their world is black, devoid of anything worthwhile.

Members of this group are clearly in serious difficulty: apart from being completely unable to function in the normal world, they are at great risk of suicide and other impulsive acts of self-harm. They are no danger to anyone but themselves, but the danger they pose to themselves is lethal. Those belonging to this group are very sick, and should be immediately admitted to hospital. They may not respond to drug treatment at all. There has been such a depletion of the three main mood neurotransmitters – serotonin, noradrenalin and dopamine – and such extensive damage to the mood departments that these drugs cannot block the re-uptake of neurotransmitters, as they are not being released in sufficient amounts into the synapses.

Psychiatrists may decide that only ECT (electro-convulsive therapy) will be of any benefit. This is usually a last resort, and is carried out under general anaesthetic to protect the patient. ECT was the original treatment for severe depression, before the advent of antidepressants. An electric current is passed into one side of the brain to artificially activate the mood cables and departments. An appropriate analogy is that of a car with a flat battery. If it is attached to an active battery, the flat battery is reactivated by a charge from the active one, and the car begins to come back to life. ECT is normally given in a course of three treatments per week for a maximum of six to twelve sessions, depending on how quickly the person responds.

This process may seem scary and barbaric to many patients and their families, and remains a very controversial practice. In some cases, however, it remains the only form of treatment left, and seems to be effective. Often within a week, the person's mood system appears to kick back into life.

It is still uncertain exactly how ECT works. Many are of the opinion that it has a pronounced effect on the dopamine and noradrenalin cables. It has also been shown, through neuro-imaging, that ECT, like drug therapy, seems to act from the bottom of the mood system, activating the mood control boxes, and that Area 25 is also calmed. Some neuro-imaging studies have also shown no serious side effects. ECT is usually combined with drug treatment, which then takes over when ECT has brought the mood system back to life.

This form of treatment is only used in a tiny proportion of cases of the most severe depression. Maybe in an ideal world, deep-brain stimulation, as previously described, might be a good alternative. The psychotherapist may in particular object to the use of ECT, but what is the alternative when all other forms of therapy, including psychoanalysis, CBT/IPT and drug therapy, have failed?

A more advanced form of ECT treatment that is currently under investigation is trans-cranial magnetic stimulation. This involves a magnet stimulating the brain electrically, in the same way as ECT does; it is particularly aimed at the frontal mood department. Initial research into this treatment is promising: it does not require an anaesthetic and was initially thought to be as effective as ECT. Recent research, however, has dampened down initial enthusiasm, bringing into questioning whether it will prove to be of as much assistance as was formerly thought.

One danger in the area of severe depression is that, when the person starts to get better, they may become less sluggish and therefore more likely to act on suicidal urges. As a result, they are often safer in a controlled hospital environment until their condition has improved.

Resistant Depression

This is another interesting group that the family doctor will refer to a psychiatrist. Up to 25 percent of cases of depression will not respond to treatment. It is not fully understood why some people are more resistant to treatment than others. There are, however, some common trends running through this group:

- *The diagnosis may be wrong.* Certain illnesses, such as Bipolar Type 2 depression, and schizophrenia, can be difficult to diagnose. Many people suffering from these illnesses are misdiagnosed with normal depression. This may render their treatment ineffective, as bipolar mood disorder, in particular, may not respond to antidepressants. Another possibility is atypical depression, which will not respond to SSRIs.

- *The person may not have dealt with underlying issues,* such as bereavement, loss or abuse. In this case, the stress system may be overwhelming the mood system to such an extent that treatment does not work successfully.
- *The person may be confining themselves to a single form of treatment,* be it medication or therapy. For some, only a combination of drug and psychological treatment will treat their depression successfully. The real problem is the inaccessibility of the latter to the vast majority of patients!
- *Non-compliance.* Some people stop taking their medication, or take it only infrequently.
- *The dose of antidepressant is too low.* This is a common occurrence, in my experience.
- *The wrong antidepressant is being used.* Some types of antidepressants work on the noradrenalin cable, and others work on the serotonin cable. If one of these types of drugs does not work, then the other group should be prescribed.
- *The patient is abusing alcohol* or other substances to combat their feelings of depression. This is quite a common occurrence. Alcohol is a depressant, and will limit the success of whatever treatment the individual is on; this can be dangerous if combined with drug treatment.

When depression is not proving responsive to any treatment, the GP will usually refer the person to a psychiatrist, who may make the following changes to treatment:

- Review the diagnosis
- Use psychological therapy such as CBT or psychotherapy, depending on the nature and causes of the depression
- Review the type of medication or dosage
- Prescribe a mood-stabilising drug. Lithium, which has been used for years in dealing with bipolar mood disorder, is sometimes used in cases of resistant simple depression. Another group of drugs which have been used with great success are anti-convulsants, which are traditionally used to treat epilepsy. Common examples include Tegretol, Epilim and Lamictal. They can

be used with or without antidepressants.

If you have been suffering from depression, and treatment has not alleviated the symptoms of your illness, there are a number of areas you can address. These include:

- *Diet:* Are you eating a healthy, balanced diet?
- *Exercise:* Do you include exercise as part of your treatment plan?
- *Alcohol:* Are you using alcohol to block out the depression? Are you mixing drug treatment with alcohol?
- *Relaxation:* Are you taking time out every day to relax?
- *Stress:* What makes you stressed? How can you reduce this stress?
- *Drug treatment:* Are you taking your medication as instructed and finishing the course?
- *Psychological treatment:* Are you open to accepting help in this area? If you are, are you turning up for your sessions?
- *Keeping an open mind with regard to your treatment:* If you are currently using only psychological treatment, and it is not helping, are you open to the possibility of drug treatment also, or vice versa?

Seasonal Affective Disorder (SAD)

Another variant of depression is a condition called seasonal affective disorder. It is well known that people become more depressed during the long nights of winter than during the long days of summer. It is known that around 25 percent of those with unipolar depression may deteriorate during the winter.

For some people, particularly in more northern climates, the darkness of wintertime creates a unique depression. People with SAD develop all the symptoms of depression, as well as a craving for food, with accompanying weight gain. Some experts feel that darkness encourages the brain to produce a neurotransmitter called melatonin. This has the general function of helping us to sleep at night. Light, on the other hand, encourages the production of serotonin. There is an important neural connection between the eyes and a part of the hormone control box which, as we discussed earlier, controls all our body rhythms/biological clocks. As daylight arrives every morning, it penetrates through our closed eyelids and activates this pathway (leading to increased serotonin cable activity in this box), stimulating us to wake up. When darkness falls, this neural pattern is reversed, and the brain produces melatonin to encourage us to sleep.

In real life, artificial daylight (through our narrow-spectrum light bulbs) combats much of this natural pattern, in comparison to the world of our ancestors. Despite this, melatonin and serotonin are intimately interwoven into the normal circadian rhythms of our lives.

SAD seems to be caused by an excessive production of the former, and in particular a lack of the latter. Of great importance is the seasonal difference in production of serotonin, with higher levels in the summer and lower ones in the winter. It may be the case that this exposes a general shortage of serotonin in people with this condition. This may explain why they recover during the bright summer months and slip back into trouble in the winter. This seasonal difference may also apply to the 25 percent of people with normal depression whose condition deteriorates in the dark winter months.

It is also felt that a shortage of serotonin in the hormone control box in particular leads to a craving for carbohydrates, with resulting weight gain, during SAD episodes. This probably happens to us all during the dark months of winter but is a particular problem in those who suffer from depression.

It is of note that melatonin is manufactured from serotonin! Numerous studies have been done trying to link melatonin and biological circadian rhythms, in order to explain this illness, but they have been inconclusive so far. At present, the role of serotonin seems to be more important than that of melatonin. SAD is almost certainly genetic. It is believed that the disorder is linked to problems with specific serotonin receptors (probably 5HT1A, 5HT2C and 5HT7).

Apart from difficulties within the serotonin system, it has also been shown that there are many similarities between SAD and atypical depression (so much so that some experts now feel that SAD should be considered as a sub-type of atypical depression) in that the noradrenalin and dopamine cables seem to be under-active during episodes, explaining the extreme lassitude, reduced motivation and libido, and hypersomnia so often seen in those with this illness.

Efforts have been made to treat this condition by exposing the person to bright lights for several hours, particularly in the morning. An effective way of treating this condition is to use a dawn simulator. The sufferer has a light installed in their room; this light starts to illuminate about half an hour before the person wakes up in the morning. The light simulates natural sunlight, and its intensity gradually increases, mimicking what would happen if the sun were rising at that time. This form of treatment is also sometimes effective in treating normal depression. I would highly recommend an American model, the 'Rise and Shine' bedside lamp, with its full-spectrum light bulb, for those who would like to try this form of therapy. It can be purchased online at www. verilux.com. (In Europe, it must be used with a 110-watt step-down voltage converter, which can be found in any good electrical store.) Research is continuing into dawn simulators, but they remain a more affordable and more practical treatment than moving to a country with a sunnier climate!

3: BIPOLAR MOOD DISORDER

Bipolar mood disorder, which forms a special sub-group of depression is often confused with unipolar depression. People also refer to it as 'manic depression' and often view it as a form of madness; in fact, it is neither. Because it has been linked to high-profile creative people such as Spike Milligan, it has also been associated with genius. This illness is now better known as bipolar mood disorder, a term which describes it more accurately.

While the depression component of this illness is almost identical to that in unipolar depression, the mania component is its antithesis. In unipolar depression, the mood will swing from normal to low and back again, but will rarely become elevated. When looking at bipolar mood disorder, think of the North and South Poles, the two most extreme points on the Earth. Depression is down at the South Pole, and mania is up in the North. Normal mood resides in the middle, on the Equator. Sufferers experience not only depression but also its polar opposite.

Bipolar mood disorder differs in many ways from simple depression: in its causes, genetics, presentation and treatment. There are, however, a number of areas where the two illnesses overlap.

Symptoms of Bipolar Mood Disorder

Bipolar mood disorder can be divided into two main groups:

Bipolar disorder, type one
Here, the person will have suffered at least one manic episode, usually associated

with a period of low mood or depression. They suffer the usual symptoms of depression, which have already been dealt with, including:

- Low mood
- Sleep difficulties
- Fatigue
- Low self-esteem
- Anxiety
- Suicidal thoughts

Mania is the opposite of depression. It is defined as a distinct period of abnormally and persistently elevated mood lasting at least one week, and which sometimes requires hospitalisation. During this period of elevated mood, the person may display the following:

- Extremely inflated self-esteem and mood
- Decreased need for sleep
- Talkativeness, and speech will often rhyme like poetry
- Racing thoughts and ideas
- High creativity
- Inexhaustible optimism
- Energy and enthusiasm
- Anger upon being challenged
- Indiscreet behaviour, with very poor judgement
- Insensitivity to the feelings of others
- Impairment of social function, particularly with regard to everyday activities
- Involvement in pleasurable activities with no regard for the consequences, such as spending sprees, shoplifting, reckless driving, excessive sexual activity or impulsive behaviour

This change in mood usually causes difficulties in close personal relationships, and may result in the person becoming a risk to themselves or others. On occasion, the person may suffer from grandiose delusions ('I'm the Pope!') or hallucinations; this is why bipolar mood disorder is often misdiagnosed as schizophrenia.

A very unpleasant form of bipolar disorder, type one, is dysphoric mania. This is where the person gets a bout of depression during an episode of severe mania: instead of the person feeling 'on top of the world', they become extremely distressed, irritable and agitated, with racing and suicidal thoughts. This condition, which is also called mixed mania, probably constitutes up to 30 to 40 percent of cases of mania. It is more common in women, and is associated with a high risk of suicide and a higher rate of familial depression than uncomplicated mania. This condition will usually require hospitalisation (and occasionally, in very serious cases, ECT) and may be more difficult to treat successfully. It can be a very distressing condition for both the person and their family. It can also be present in a lesser form as dysphoric hypomania, where depression is present during an episode of hypomania (see below).

Bipolar Disorder, Type Two

Here, the person suffers mainly from bouts of depression, interspersed with periods of hypomania. Hypomania is a distinct period of euphoria lasting at least four days. During this period of elevated mood, the symptoms of mania emerge, although they are not particularly obvious, usually do not cause major difficulties in the person's ability to cope with normal activities (in fact, many feel that they cope better during such phases), and seldom require hospitalisation. The person will rarely suffer from delusions or hallucinations. A person with hypomania will have periods where they experience the following:

- A sudden increase in energy levels
- Racing thoughts
- Increased talkativeness
- Decreased need for sleep
- Irritability and annoyance if confronted
- Feeling on top of the world

Bipolar disorder, type two, may have a different biological source (possibly closer to that of unipolar depression) from bipolar disorder, type one, although this is an area where research is ongoing.

The main differences between the above symptoms and those of normal depression are the major fluctuations in mood, which are usually not seen in the Red Flag of unipolar depression. This suggests that something completely different is happening neurologically.

It is also important to note that low mood, normal mood and elevated mood are present at different times in the life of the bipolar depressive. There are huge variations in this illness from person to person. Bouts of low mood usually outweigh the highs by about three to one. A small number of people may get about four bouts or more of mania per year, which can cause chaos in the lives of themselves and those around them.

The Course of Bipolar Illness

Bipolar illness usually appears in the teenage years; even when it is observed, it is often misdiagnosed as normal depression. It is only when the elevated mood periods are either admitted to by the individual or noticed by others that a new diagnosis emerges. Bouts of low mood, periods of normality, and occasional bouts of elevated mood merge to create the distinct pattern of this illness.

Unfortunately, there is often a substantial delay in diagnosis, due to the erratic nature of the illness. This can be further complicated by the concomitant presence of the Purple Flag of addiction. Some people with bipolar disorder may (through a combination of not presenting early enough and a delay in accurate diagnosis) have their illness remain undetected for up to ten years. In fact, only one in four bipolar depressives are diagnosed within three years of the onset of the illness. Most are labelled as normal depressives and treated accordingly – women in particular, as they are more likely than men to present with symptoms of depression.

This illness is not as common as unipolar depression, and it affects both men and women in equal numbers. The incidence of bipolar type one is around 1 percent of the population, and bipolar type two probably between 1 and 2 percent. Some experts feel that the true incidence of this illness may be substantially higher. It seems to be more common in urban than in rural areas.

The main difficulty with bipolar illness is the disruption it can cause to the social, working and relationship life of the sufferer. The condition is associated with a high rate of suicide. Between 20 and 50 percent of those who remain un-detected or untreated will attempt suicide. At least 10 to 15 percent of people with this illness will succeed in taking their own lives.

There is also a strong link (in both the depressed and elated phases) to alco-hol and substance abuse. The latter in particular is a major problem, with some placing the lifetime occurrence of alcohol and substance abuse in this group as high as 60 percent! Alcohol and substance abuse can sometimes be the trig-gering factors, particularly if drugs like marijuana or cocaine are used. Up to a third of those who suffer from this illness may struggle to function inde-pendently. Holding down jobs and establishing emotionally stable, permanent relationships becomes very difficult for many of them. Correct diagnosis and appropriate treatment can transform the lives of these people.

Over their lifetime, a bipolar sufferer will typically suffer eight to ten epi-sodes of mood swings. Untreated episodes of mania may last from four to six months. In practice, the symptoms of mania are so severe that help is usually received quite quickly, so episodes may last only weeks. Episodes of hypoma-nia are generally much more subtle and are of shorter duration, so they often go undetected.

Bouts of depression, if untreated, last up to nine months in people with biploar illness. One of the difficulties is that a patient who is treated with anti-depressants may develop a subsequent bout of hypomania or mania as a result of the medication. A particular concern is where a person with dysphoric hy-pomania presents with appears at first glance to be simple depression, and is treated with antidepressants. The antidepressants can make them more agi-tated, and suicidal thoughts and actions may increase. The risk of suicide is greatest in the early stages of this illness (which is why early diagnosis is vital), and more often occurs in the depression or mixed-mania phases. Another problem is that patients sometimes do not respond to antidepressants at all in bipolar disorder.

There can be a delay of four to ten years between the first and second episode of bipolar disorder. Following this, the length of time between episodes will gradually begin to shorten. In some cases, the severity of the illness, especially if untreated, will worsen. In terms of the probability of recurrence, some estimate it at 50 percent for the first year, 70 percent by the fourth year, and 90 percent by the fifth year.

The Biology of Bipolar Illness

Bipolar disorder is a very different illness from depression. Despite intensive and exciting research in this area, there is still no working model as to how this illness occurs. This is what is known to date:

The Mood Departments

Both the frontal and limbic system mood departments are involved in this illness. Recent research has focused on the role of the prefrontal cortex and the stress box, and has reported the following:

- A decrease in activity of the left frontal prefrontal cortex in the depression phase of this illness
- An increase in activity of the right frontal mood department in the manic phase of this illness
- A reduction in size in some sections of the prefrontal cortex: in one study already discussed, a particular section (Area 24) shrunk by up to 40 percent
- An increase in activity in the stress box
- A reduction in volume in the following: the stress box, the pleasure box and, as noted above, various parts of the prefrontal cortex, with a corresponding reduction in the number of neurons, neuronal connections and glial support cells

The Mood Cables

These were the focus of attention for many years but research findings have proved insufficient in explaining the disorder. Findings to date include:

- The noradrenalin mood cable is over-active in mania (explaining the reduced need for sleep and the unlimited energy seen in this group) and under active in the depression phase of this illness (explaining the usual depression symptoms of fatigue, difficulties with sleep, poor concentration and lack of drive).

- The serotonin cable is under-active during the depression phase. This explains why suicide thoughts and attempts are more common during this phase of the illness.
- The dopamine cable is more active in the manic phase. This may explain the tendency to seek pleasurable activities. It is under-active in the depression phase.

The Neurotransmitters And Receptors
A great deal of research has looked at the role of other neurotransmitters in bipolar disorders. The main findings are:

- A reduction of GABA, the brain's calming neurotransmitter
- An increase in intercellular G-proteins during mania, and a decrease during the depression phase

What are G-proteins? Some of the receptors activated by neurotransmitters, glutamate and serotonin in particular, release these proteins, which travel from the cell membrane to the genes in the centre of the cell. This in turn may lead to inter-cellular changes, probably involving BDNF, which we dealt with earlier in the Red Flag. We still do not understand the role of the glial support cells in this process. The malfunction of this process may explain the volatility of cells of the mood system in bipolar depression.

The Stress System
There is an increase in glucocortisol levels in both the low and high phases of this illness. The same risks that unipolar depression carries regarding heart disease, osteoporosis and a weakening of the immune system are also present with bipolar depression. The above finding lead to the following conclusions:

- The depression phase of this illness is almost identical to that of normal depression.
- The manic phase of this illness remains a mystery. The most likely explanation is that there are problems at cell-membrane level which make the cells of the mood system more vulnerable to becoming hyper-stimulated. The role of G-proteins, glutamate and glial support cells, in particular, may in the future be shown to play an important role in this process.
- Some speculate that changes may happen in the womb, as the brain's mood system is developing, resulting in the emergence of this disorder when pruning of the brain begins in the twelve-to-twenty-five age group.
- It is quite likely that stress may trigger mood changes, through the usual mechanisms.

Summary

Bipolar mood disorder causes the following changes in the mood system:

1. Decreased activity in the left prefrontal cortex during the depression phase of the illness, and an increase in activity of the right prefrontal cortex during periods of elevated mood. The former explains the high rate of suicide among people with bipolar mood disorders.
2. Bipolar disorder affects the three main mood cables. The serotonin and noradrenalin cables are under-active during the depression phase of this illness. This gives rise to all the normal symptoms of depression. During the manic phase, the dopamine and noradrenalin cable are over-active. This explains the drive towards pleasurable activities during this phase, as well as the boundless energy and lack of need for sleep

Causes of Bipolar Disorder

It is widely accepted that bipolar disorder has an even stronger genetic foundation than normal depression. Between 8 and 9 percent of those with first-degree relations who have bipolar disorder will develop depression.

It has proved difficult to isolate the genes responsible for this illness. Initially, there was only one gene thought to be at fault, but recent research suggests that a number of different genes are involved. (For those who are interested, chromosomes 1, 4, 6, 14, 16 and 21 have been under scrutiny in this regard.) This would explain the wide variety of forms of presentation of this illness, and the fact that, although this illness is quite different from simple depression, there is a marked pattern of both illnesses developing in relatives of people who have this disorder.

It is more difficult to ascertain how stress triggers affect this illness. Stress and anxiety disorders are often linked to bipolar disorder. Presumably the stress system, including glucocorticol, is involved in kick-starting mood swings. The problem is that the understanding of the biological pathways is at present so limited that it is hard to quantify the role that stress triggers may play.

Treatment of Bipolar Disorder

Bipolar disorder is dealt with exclusively by a specialist, as it can be extremely difficult to stabilise the swings in mood. The mood, whether up or down, has to be brought back to a normal level and maintained there. The first, and often most difficult, step in treatment is diagnosis.

Bipolar disorder continually flies under the radar of even the most highly trained professionals. An episode of high mood, a bout of severe depression, or an attempted suicide often leads to the diagnosis. Severe episodes of either high or low mood may require a visit to hospital to help stabilise the person. Occasionally in severe depression ECT is required, and sometimes in severe mania high doses of tranquillizers may be needed to sedate the patient and bring their mood down to a normal level.

Most cases of bipolar disorder will be prescribed drugs by a psychiatrist, who may request the assistance of a psychologist. It is difficult to treat depression in people with bipolar disorder, as they often either do not respond to any form of treatment or respond too much, and drift into mania. As has already been stated, high mood is usually counteracted with tranquillizers. The tranquillizer Zyprexa (olanzapine) is commonly used to stabilise elevated mood. Such drugs, while very useful in treating bipolar disorders, do have significant side effects, including weight gain.

Flagging the Problem

Lithium has changed the lives of many people with bipolar disorder. This drug is very effective in treating the manic phase of the illness and, more importantly, is able to stabilise mood swings. Many will show a dramatic response to this drug in just one to two weeks. Lithium probably works at cell-membrane level (possibly on the G-protein messenger system), calming down cells which have become too agitated (and increasing their chances of survival), thereby helping sufferers to lead normal lives. Many now feel that this drug is the only one which is not only neuroprotective (i.e. encourages the production of internal cellular enzymes, which improve the neurons' survival) but which also increases the volume of key areas like Area 24.

The use of Lithium has to be carefully monitored through regular blood checks; it can cause some side effects, such as tremors and weight gain, but is usually well tolerated. Its use is nearly always initiated by the specialist, but is often monitored by the GP. Occasionally, the specialist may combine its use with antidepressants or may seek to stabilise low mood with antidepressants first, and then start the patient on a course of Lithium. Unfortunately, up to one third of patients do not respond to this drug.

The major problem with Lithium is that patients often miss the euphoria of the manic stage of this illness, or may feel that they simply do not need the drug. In both cases, patients may stop taking it, and the massive mood swings return. They may also cease taking it due to associated weight gain. Lithium also cannot be used during pregnancy, as it can cause foetal abnormalities.

Following the success of this drug came the discovery that some anti-convulsion drugs might mimic the action of Lithium. They achieve this by stabilising the cells of the mood system (probably by acting on cell membrane glutamate receptors). They may be used in the prevention of hypomania, mania or depression, either in conjunction with Lithium or on their own. The two main anticonvulsants used are Lamictal and Epilim:

- *Lamictal:* This is useful in preventing the depression episodes in bipolar type two disorders. It can be used on its own, together with antidepressants, and occasionally with Lithium. It can also be used safely during pregnancy.

- *Epilim:* This is useful in preventing the mania phases of bipolar disorder. Its main side effect is weight gain. There is also increasing concern about potential foetal abnormalities, so this drug should be avoided in women of child-bearing age.

Stress triggers relating to bipolar disorders are handled in the same way as in normal depression. But the key to this illness lies in the use of mood stabilisers. There is also a great need for further research into possible drug treatments for this illness, with the aim of improving the quality of life of bipolar sufferers.

Bipolar disorder is a complex mood disorder: it is difficult to diagnose and understand, and, in terms of treatment, is a challenge to both the specialist and the patient. Due to the high suicide rate associated with this disorder, however, and the degree of destruction it can wreak on people's lives, it is important that treatment takes place. This chapter will hopefully be of help to anyone who suffers from this disorder, or who has a family member or friend who suffers from it. Just as it is very important to be able to spot the warning signs of depression, such as low mood, it is also important to note that, on occasions, these warning signs can also be accompanied by elevated mood. If this pattern is observed, it is very important for the person to get help from their family doctor, and then from a psychiatrist. Bipolar disorder is highly influenced by genetics. As in the case of unipolar depression, all of us have a responsibility to try to understand the condition and help those who suffer from it in any way we can.

PART THREE

The Yellow Flag:
Anxiety

1: ACUTE AND CHRONIC ANXIETY DISORDERS

Anxiety is a universal phenomenon, occurring in response to a situation which demands our absolute attention, usually when we feel threatened. These situations are usually temporary, and so is the anxiety that prepares the body to tackle them. Anxiety is best described as an uncomfortable state of hyper-alertness due to fear.

When it increases to a certain level, however, anxiety becomes an illness. For the people affected, anxiety is constant, out of proportion, disabling and exhausting. It controls what they can and cannot do in their lives and, more often than not, makes them too tired to do anything.

Anxiety disorders are very common: at least 5 percent of people will suffer from such a disorder at some stage in their lives. Unfortunately, just as in the Red Flag of depression, the Yellow Flag of anxiety often remains hidden. The two most common anxiety-related illnesses are panic disorder and phobias.

Panic Disorder

Episodes of this disorder are referred to as panic attacks and are common problems, presenting to both A&E departments and family doctors at all hours of the day and night. Such an episode is a short period of extreme anxiety which can occur at any time. The person may experience some or all of the following symptoms:

- A feeling that they are going to die

- Profuse sweating
- Palpitations (fast heartbeat)
- Dry mouth
- Weakness
- Headache
- Chest pain
- Hyperventilation (rapid, shallow breathing)
- Trembling or shaking
- Fear of losing control or 'going mad'
- Dizziness
- Sensation of choking

When these symptoms occur suddenly and simultaneously, they are terrifying for the sufferer. The attack, depending on how the person handles it, may last from a few minutes to several hours. Attacks are usually not prompted by any particular outside stress, and the person may be involved in their normal daily activities when they occur.

Someone encountering an episode like this for the first time will appear to be extremely ill to friends and loved ones, and they often are admitted to a casualty department for an ECG or chest X-rays, as many lay people assume that they are having a heart attack or a stroke. It is often very difficult to convince the person that they are in fact physically quite healthy. They often attend their doctor the following day, seeking assurance that all is well.

Panic attacks are completely unpredictable, and consequently often affect the person at the most inappropriate times and places. This leads to a constant fear and dread amongst those with the condition that another episode will occur at an inopportune moment. For instance, a panic attack may take place in a crowded area; this may lead to the individual being afraid of entering such an area again, in case an attack recurs. Fear of such episodes – the so-called fear of fears – can thus become nearly as great a problem as the panic attacks themselves.

This disorder will often appear for the first time in a person's teenage years or early twenties. For genetic reasons, women are more prone to developing the illness. Panic attacks often appear out of nowhere; if they are allowed to proceed in a normal manner, the attack will usually plateau in about twenty minutes. If the person takes avoidant action, such as using tranquillizers or alcohol, or attending A&E, however, the attack may last for much longer. Attacks may occur weekly or monthly, and on occasions more often.

The initial episode may follow a period of intense stress or pressure, but after this the illness takes on a life of its own. Without treatment, this chronic and unpredictable pattern of attacks will continue indefinitely, interspersed with a continuous apprehension as to when such attacks will strike again. The tragedy is that a few sessions of treatment can in many cases quickly banish them for good, but sufferers who are unaware of this fact may never come forward for help.

Panic attacks are often experienced in association with other illnesses of the mood system. These illnesses include addiction (particularly in alcoholics), depression and chronic anxiety.

Phobias

Few people are without fear. Many people will suffer from an irrational fear of a place, crowd, object, animal or insect. There are numerous documented exotic examples of such random fears. The most well known one is agoraphobia, which is a fear of either open spaces or large crowds. An agoraphobic may be afraid to leave not only their house but even their room. Phobias affect a large number of people – more often women than men – and are frequently never discussed by the sufferer. Other common phobias are fears of heights, mice and spiders. A person who encounters the object of their phobia may experience the following symptoms:

- Sweating
- Palpitations
- Shortness of breath due to hyperventilation
- Weakness
- A strong desire to escape
- Dry mouth

Removing oneself from the situation is a common reaction, and one which provides immediate relief. This approach does not solve the problem permanently, however. The person may later encounter their phobia in the middle of a supermarket, for instance, and want to just drop everything and run. As a result, the life of a phobic can be very restricted.

Because of their irrational nature, phobias are often very embarrassing to the sufferer. They feel helpless, as they have no control over their body and mind when the phobia is encountered, and may as a result try to hide the problem.

A particularly crippling phobia is social phobia, where a person dreads meeting other people. Such people are painfully shy. Suicide rates are higher in this group than among people with any of the other anxiety disorders. The probable reason for this is that they cannot ease their burden by sharing it with anyone: the company of others is the source of the problem. This phobia usually begins in the teenage years.

Chronic Anxiety Disorders

There are two forms of chronic anxiety: general anxiety disorder (GAD) and obsessive compulsive disorder (OCD).

General Anxiety Disorder

While we may find it relaxing to watch ducks gliding serenely across a pond, we fail to see the frantic paddling that is taking place beneath the surface. When we observe a GAD sufferer, we can be fooled by their calm temperament and fail to notice the panic they are feeling underneath. GAD sufferers may experience feelings of intense anxiety, foreboding and excessive worry about their health, their family and their job, and often have a sense of impending disaster. This illness is associated with other symptoms, such as:

- Mental and physical fatigue
- Poor concentration
- Mind going blank in common social and domestic situations

- Difficulties with memory
- Restlessness
- Sleep difficulties, and nightmares
- Indecisiveness
- Regularly avoiding situations in everyday life due to fatigue and worrying about their ability to cope

The sufferer is also very vulnerable to bouts of acute anxiety, with the following physical symptoms:

- Tension headaches
- Constant sighing
- Palpitations
- Stomach cramps and disturbance
- Loss of appetite, with associated weight loss

Severe stress, particularly in relation to loss or major health or financial concerns, will lead to bouts of extreme inner anxiety. In such cases, all of the normal symptoms of GAD are magnified, with the person becoming quickly exhausted.

Many people with general anxiety disorder (who are often perfectionists) learn to conceal their condition well, to the extent that even close friends and loved ones may not be aware of the problem, or the degree to which the person is struggling with their daily life. The sufferer may not even realise they are suffering from anxiety. They will, however, identify the fatigue and the difficulties in concentration, among other symptoms.

People who suffer from GAD will go through periods where they cope reasonably well. Any form of sustained stress will bring their mood system down again, however. During these periods, their apprehension and worrying will intensify, they will feel fatigued, and they will experience difficulties concentrating and sleeping. Often people reach the conclusion that they are simply not coping, or are stressed out.

Two-thirds of those who suffer from GAD will also suffer at least one bout of the Red Flag of depression at least once in their lives. Many use alcohol as an escape from the inner turmoil and intensity they experience – with the obvious associated problems. The condition can present at any stage of life but most often appears first in the mid teens and early adulthood. Women are twice as likely to suffer from this disorder as men. The illness often remains unrecognised and undiagnosed until the person is in their thirties or forties, particularly in women. As the stresses in life start to take their toll, the person, if untreated, may find the symptoms worsening with age. This deterioration will usually continue for life until help is sought.

Obsessive Compulsive Disorder

This form of anxiety has become increasingly recognised in the past ten years and it is now regarded as a separate illness, unique from the other forms of anxiety. OCD results in constant unwanted irrational and obsessive thoughts, accompanied by compulsive actions to satisfy the urges these thoughts are producing. These incessant thoughts and compulsions (which the person often tries to suppress or avoid) will cause major interference with the person's family and working relationships, not to mention their own psychological state. The obsessive thoughts use up the person's mental energy by causing extreme feelings of anxiety. The resulting tension is only relieved by 'doing what the thoughts demand', but this is incredibly tiring, as the thoughts are never-ending. Such obsessive thoughts may relate to:

- Fears about health, particularly personal health
- Fears of contaminating themselves
- Fears of harming themselves
- Sexual and religious obsessions
- Constant fears that something terrible is going to happen

Examples of compulsive actions are:

- Cleaning
- Checking

- Counting
- Repeating
- Arranging

What separates a person with OCD from someone who is simply very neat, or a 'clean freak', is repetition. They will check the light switch, or the lock on the front door, three or four, or even up to ten or more, times in a row, knowing full well that the situation has not changed since they last checked, but feeling an overpowering urge to check again anyway. They experience a sense of relief and security when they re-check something, but this is only temporary, and the urge returns again. Paradoxically, the more they check something, the stronger the urge to check it again becomes. It is like an addiction, where carrying out the act reduces the cravings for a while, but in the long run intensifies them.

The condition usually starts in the young adult, but many experts believe that, due to lack of knowledge or awareness of the condition, its existence may go unrecognised for up to ten years before diagnosis. The pattern of this illness can be very difficult, both for the person themselves and also for those who live with them. The individual usually faces a lifelong battle with their obsessive thoughts and compulsive behaviour. Men with OCD will usually start to act compulsively earlier in their teens, and women may present with the condition much later. Men tend to worry more about checking things, and women more about cleanliness. There are powerful biological causes of this behaviour. Sufferers usually have an above-average IQ.

People who have lived with an OCD sufferer often find it impossible to get through to them emotionally, so relationships within this group are regularly troubled. The constant battle with obsessive thoughts and acts causes exhaustion on the part of the sufferer or those close to them, as it takes up a great deal of their time and energy. They know that their behaviour is stupid and irrational but are powerless to stop it.

The fear is that the Yellow Flag may turn into the Red Flag of depression. Some estimate that up to a third of those with OCD will experience a major bout of depression in their lifetime.

Biology of the Yellow Flag

What is the difference between stress and anxiety? With stress, the threat is immediate, whether it is acute (such as sitting an important exam) or chronic (dealing with financial problems due to unemployment). In anxiety, however, the body's internal stress system is constantly activated, despite the lack of an external threat. Since stress is a response to an actual external event, and anxiety is a response to an internal, imagined one, the fear that fuels anxiety can be constant and potentially long-lasting. Anxiety is the result of the emotional brain or mind taking over control from the logical brain. It is the power of the former that makes the condition so hard to treat.

The stress box in the limbic mood department (the emotional brain) controls the stress response and acts as a storage area for the emotions associated with bad memories, thereby helping to produce negative thoughts. We have already seen how, under normal conditions, the flow of information from the stress box to the prefrontal cortex is much greater than the reverse. So emotions such as fear will always tend to overrule our logical brain. When the stress box becomes hyper-stimulated, trouble will inevitably loom.

Over-activity of the stress box is present in most anxiety disorders. A combination of genetic and early environmental factors causes subtle changes in this box, making it hyper-sensitive from the early to mid teens onwards. It is not only the stress box that is involved in anxiety, however: the rest of the mood system also plays a part.

(A) Mood Departments
The Frontal Mood Department
The prefrontal cortex plays a role in sometimes inadvertently triggering the stress box to over-act, and in other cases failing to shut off inappropriate responses from the latter.

The Limbic Mood Department
In anxiety, the stress box incorrectly activates the whole stress system. It sends

instructions to the adrenal gland, activating it. Over-activity in this box leads to the irrational fears and worries seen in some forms of anxiety.

The Adrenal Gland

In acute anxiety, the adrenal glands release adrenalin and noradrenalin in response to instructions from the stress box. When elevated, these produce the following symptoms:

- Dry mouth
- Profuse sweating
- Headaches
- Hyperventilation
- Stomach upset
- Palpitations

In chronic anxiety, the adrenal glands release glucocortisol.

Glucocortisol

This works with the stress box to produce the symptoms of chronic anxiety. When levels of glucocortisol are elevated, the person will experience some or all of the following symptom:

- Fatigue
- Poor concentration
- Difficulties with memory
- Sleep problems
- Anhedonia (inability to experience pleasure)

(B) Mood Cables

The two main cables activated by anxiety are the noradrenalin and serotonin cables. The noradrenalin cable is highly active in bouts of acute anxiety but may eventually become depleted in chronic anxiety, leading to fatigue and poor concentration. The serotonin cable is under-active in some cases of chronic anxiety.

When all this knowledge is compiled, a model of anxiety can be formed:

- The prefrontal cortex mistakenly activates the stress box.
- The stress box, which is already predisposed to be hyperactive, completely over-reacts.
- This causes the stress peptides to flood the brain and activates the no-radrenalin cable.
- It also causes the adrenal gland to pour out noradrenalin, adrenalin and glucocortisol.
- In acute anxiety, this gland mainly releases noradrenalin and adrenalin.
- In chronic anxiety, it mainly releases glucocortisol.

Most of the symptoms of anxiety are caused by the above mechanisms.

Acute Anxiety Disorders

In phobias and panic attacks, the body's stress response is called upon by the stress box. The stress peptides and noradrenalin mood cable activate, and the adrenal glands release copious amounts of adrenalin and noradrenalin. The latter gives rise to symptoms that may include sweating, dry mouth, palpitations and weakness. This combination leads to the commonly expressed statement: 'I thought I was going to die!' When this activity recedes, the body disposes of the excess adrenalin and noradrenalin, and the system returns to normal.

If this is the case, what causes the 'fear of fears' that is evident in panic disorders? This is where a person remains constantly on high alert, fearing another panic attack. The memory box is the most likely culprit here, coordinating with the stress box to keep the fear of fears alive.

Chronic Anxiety Disorders

In GAD, there is continuous stimulation of the stress box, adrenal glands and noradrenalin mood cable, and a constant flow of stress peptides and gluco-cortisol. All of these factors result in fatigue, poor concentration, difficulties with memory, sleep problems and other symptoms that have already been mentioned.

Constant worrying and a feeling of impending doom originate from the stress box, where negative memories are stored. In GAD, the stress box replays these memories over and over and projects them on to the future. Normally, this is prevented by the prefrontal cortex, but in GAD the stress box runs amok.

OCD is a unique illness because it is biologically distinct from the other anxiety disorders. There are operational difficulties between parts of the frontal mood department and other sections of the brain. The secondary stress symptoms of OCD are mediated through the stress system, but the source of the illness is completely different.

Summary

Anxiety can cause the following problems in the mood system:

1. Over-activity of the stress box in the limbic mood department. This leads to worrying, apprehension and a sense of impending doom.
2. Disruption of the noradrenalin mood cable. This results in poor concentration and fatigue.
3. Over-stimulation of the adrenal stress gland, leading to an excess of adrenalin, noradrenalin and glucocortisol in the body. This causes the palpitations, hyperventilation, sweating, dry mouth and stomach cramps often seen in acute anxiety, and the fatigue and poor concentration seen in chronic anxiety.

2: CAUSES OF ANXIETY DISORDERS

Scientific research over the past two decades has identified major anxiety as an illness rather than a personality trait. Genes, upbringing and environmental factors all contribute to the development of this illness. The biological model suggests that the stress box, through a combination of genetic predispositions and environmental factors, malfunctions when it is put under stress. It becomes hypersensitive to any stimulation, and this results in the symptoms of anxiety. This model is corroborated by psychological research, which suggests that many anxiety illnesses begin with difficulties or major stress periods in childhood. Genetic vulnerability to such stress periods during development may be a crucial factor. The final result is a stress box that is predisposed to hyperactivity in the presence of even apparently innocuous stress triggers. What follows is an assessment of the genetic and environmental influences on the development of these illnesses:

1. *Panic attacks and phobias:* There is a moderate genetic component to these illnesses, particularly for panic attacks. Environmental factors also contribute.

2. *GAD:* There is a moderate genetic vulnerability. (Almost 20 percent of first-degree relatives of people with GAD also have the condition, compared with 3 to 4 percent of those who do not.) It also seems that GAD and unipolar depression share similar neurological mechanisms. Why one person with such a vulnerability develops GAD and another develops depression is not known. Once again, environment plays a crucial role.

3. *OCD:* There is a moderate genetic vulnerability. Environmental triggers also play a role.

Environmental Factors

Recent neurological research into anxiety supports observations by psychologists that people at a certain time in their upbringing experience some major stress or loss which seems to act on susceptible genes to change the way in which their stress box and its pathways will respond in the person's adult life. By the time the person reaches their mid-teens or early twenties, their stress system is predisposed to malfunction, forging a lifelong battle with anxiety. What are these early stress triggers? They include:

- Loss of a parent or sibling at a crucial stage of development as a child or adolescent
- Emotional, physical or sexual abuse
- Being reared in an authoritarian household
- Coming from an addictive parental background
- A major trauma in the life of the developing child
- A very stressful or frightening episode at a vulnerable stage of development

3: TREATMENTS FOR ANXIETY DISORDERS

Many of the treatment options suitable for depression are also suitable for anxiety. Bouts of depression may last between six and twelve months, whereas anxiety disorders, if untreated, may be present for life. Treatment options for anxiety include:

1. *Exercise:* This tackles many of the symptoms of anxiety. The chemicals it releases calm the stress box, aid memory and concentration, reduce the effects of external stress influences, and generally encourage the person to take a more positive approach to life.
2. *Diet:* Many people with anxiety will go through periods of not eating properly. It is very important to have a healthy, balanced diet. Caffeine and other stimulant-rich drinks should be avoided, as they promote anxiety by activating the stress system. GAD sufferers can become dependent on caffeine to alleviate the symptoms of fatigue. This is counterproductive, as it will interfere further with sleep and increase anxiety, both of which will in turn increase fatigue.
3. *Supplements:* Omega 3 fish oils in particular may help to alleviate some of the symptoms of chronic anxiety, particularly fatigue.
4. *Counselling:* This is helpful in dealing with outside stress factors (rather than with anxiety itself), especially relationship problems, bereavement and addiction problems.
5. *Psychological therapies:* The psychologist is the expert when it comes to dealing with anxiety disorders. Nowadays, many counsellors and

psychiatric nurses are also trained in CBT techniques, as are an increasing number of family doctors.

The following therapies psychological therapies are commonly used:

(a) *CBT:* In the section on the Red Flag, we dealt with the various types of CBT, its neurobiological impact and its role in treating depression. CBT is also extremely useful in helping people to overcome panic attacks and deal with their phobias, and in reducing the symptoms of GAD. Here, the person's thinking and behaviour, both of which are negative and fearful, are challenged, and new coping skills are introduced.

CBT can be of enormous help in dealing with panic attacks in particular, often banishing them for good after a few sessions. At the end of this section, I include simple but very effective advice on how you can get rid of panic attacks for good using simple CBT techniques.

(b) *Relaxation exercises:* Relaxation of both body and mind are of great help in dealing with anxiety. If people can consciously ignore their stress system by relaxing their body and mind, they break the cycle of stress and worry, take back control of their lives and are better able to deal with acute anxiety and GAD.

(c) *Psychotherapy:* This seems to be the least effective psychological means of helping people to cope with anxiety. For some whose anxiety is rooted in a traumatic past, however, it may be of great help.

Before we leave this section, let's look at how CBT can help in preventing panic attacks. Before looking at such techniques, we must once again separate the role of the emotional brain or mind (the limbic system) from the logical brain or mind (the frontal cortex). The former often exerts a dominant effect over the latter. Let's look at some simple examples:

1. Imagine that you are walking down a dark alley which is poorly lit. You suddenly hear a loud noise. You instantly freeze, your heart starts to race, you feel goose pimples all over, your mouth goes dry, your stomach churns,

and you rapidly turn to face the source of the noise. Then, out of the darkness springs a cat, and you start to relax, as you have logically located the cause of the noise.

The emotional brain was the first to respond to the sound. Without thinking, the stress system swung into action, and the logical brain took over later. This happens biologically because, if danger is sensed, the brain alerts the stress box first, so that we react instinctively, before identifying the source of the threat logically, through other pathways.

As we continue up the dark alley, even though we logically know that the cause of the sound was a cat, most of us will stay in a state of high alert, instinctively quickening our pace and looking into shadowy areas despite ourselves. In short, we are unable to shake off our sense of unease until we reach the apparent safety of a well-lit area. All of this happens because our emotional mind overpowers our logical one. We know that there is no danger but cannot stop our emotions from taking over.

2. If I tell you: 'Close your eyes and don't think about bird droppings landing on your hair and face' despite your every effort to stop this image coming into your mind, your emotional brain will take over and you will be unable to do so. Once again, the emotional brain overrules the commands of the logical brain or mind.

3. Imagine your favourite football team being beaten by a last-minute goal. You will feel completely devastated. Although logically it makes no difference whether the goal was scored in the first or last minute of the game, the latter scenario makes us feel most upset. Once again, our emotional rather than our logical mind is in charge.

This is not to denigrate the importance of the emotional side of our lives. Life without emotion would be a colourless, drab place. Indeed, all of us constantly switch between the logical and the emotional during our daily lives: a healthy balance between both is vital. With these general concepts in mind, let's move on to examine in more detail what happens during a panic attack, and ways of dealing with them.

Let's imagine three different scenarios where a panic attack begins. In the first, we are sitting at home watching TV; in the second, we are in the middle of a busy office meeting; in the third, we are in the middle of a busy supermarket about to start the weekly shop. Although all three situations are different, the pattern of how the panic attack begins and progresses is quite similar.

- *Stage One:* We begin to feel the first symptoms of anxiety developing. We start to notice our heart pounding and our breathing becoming faster; we may start sweating and begin to feel weak. There is usually no obvious cause for this anxiety, but it acts as the initial trigger for the attack.
- *Stage Two:* Because there is no logical cause for the appearance of these symptoms, the person begins to assume that there must be a serious reason for how they feel. They may imagine that they are in the process of developing a major medical disaster, such as a heart attack or stroke, or that they are about to collapse and die. They may also become embarrassed that they are going crazy, or that those around them will see the state they are in.
- *Stage Three:* The feelings above further increase the anxiety symptoms, creating a desire to get rid of the cause of these feelings – namely anxiety, the initial trigger.
- *Stage Four:* This causes anxiety levels to rise further, by activating the body's internal stress system and finally kick-starting a full-blown panic attack. Here the heart races, we feel weak and faint, our stomach churns, we find it hard to breathe, and we experience an overwhelming sense of doom and disaster. The natural length of time it takes for the body to stop this panic episode is twenty minutes. If we did nothing at all, the attack would settle down and everything would return to normal.
- *Stage Five:* The real problem occurs when our natural sense of worry and desire to bring the attack to an end leads to so-called 'avoidant behaviour'. Common examples are using tranquillizers or alcohol; rushing off to the nearest A&E department, usually at the prompting of a well-meaning relative, friend or member of the public; trying hard to control our breathing during a panic attack; or running away from the site where the attack occurred. If such avoidant behaviour is undertaken, the panic attack may last for several hours.

The key to all of the above is that the emotional brain or mind is ruling the roost. Our more logical brain has been silenced. In order to defeat panic attacks, we now have to put the latter back in charge.

Firstly, we have to eliminate all avoidant behaviour. The enemy must be faced head-on: running away merely prolongs the problem.

Secondly, we must never try to stop a panic attack when it is in progress, rather go with the flow (swim with the current rather than against it) and wait for it to settle naturally (as it always will) within about twenty minutes. The key to doing this is to accept that these symptoms, although unpleasant, will never do us any real harm. As I often say to patients: 'Emotions can sometimes be uncomfortable, but they are not dangerous'. Rather than trying to stop them, we should actually try to bring them on so that the problem can be addressed. Surprisingly, it is quite difficult to do this.

Thirdly, and most importantly, we have to return to Stage Two above. We have to start challenging the false perception that the physical feelings (such as palpitations and sweating) brought on by the initial symptoms of anxiety are indeed the precursor to something more serious happening. Although my heart is racing, have I ever had a heart attack during a panic episode? Of course the answer is no. Although I may feel as though I am going to collapse and die, has this ever happened? Once again, the answer is obviously no! Just because my breathing becomes shallow and fast, have I ever stopped breathing? The answer is once again no.

This is the key to eliminating panic attacks for good. If we learn to accept these feelings of anxiety as being a nuisance but not dangerous, then we stop becoming so anxious to get rid of them and start to dismiss them. This, in turn, reduces the build-up of anxiety that is necessary to trigger a full-blown panic episode. When our logical mind/brain regains control in this way, panic attacks become a thing of the past.

To summarise, in order to eliminate panic attacks, we must firstly stop all avoidant behaviour, never try to stop an episode if it does occur, and finally, and most importantly, logically challenge and remove once and for all the concept that the initial anxiety symptoms which can trigger an attack are in any way dangerous to our health physically or mentally. This all sounds too easy, but in practice it works amazingly well. Try it and see!

One final note of caution: sometimes panic attacks may be associated with other conditions, such as depression, alcohol/substance abuse, or general anxiety. Be honest with yourself. If you feel that any of these are present, go and have a chat with your family doctor. He will assess your symptoms and suggest further help. If you are unsure, reading the chapters on the various flags should clarify the situation. In general, the first step is always to deal with the panic attacks and then to move on to treating the accompanying illness.

If you continue to have difficulties with panic attacks, you should ask your family doctor for help. If he has the necessary skills, he may be able to help; if not, he can refer you to a cognitive therapist. For most people, if they apply the above simple principles their panic attacks will become a thing of the past.

Drug Treatment

Drug treatment has a place in treatment of the Yellow Flag, but most experts feel that it should only be used in conjunction with all the other treatment options. If combined with CBT and relaxation exercises, drug treatment can be of great help. In the past, however, the use of anxiolytic drugs (medications such as tranquillizers, used to calm down the symptoms of anxiety) did more harm than good.

Tranquillizers

These drugs combat anxiety by using the GABA receptors to relax the stress box: in effect, they force the brain to relax and stop worrying. They rapidly reduce all symptoms, and this makes them popular with anxiety sufferers.

The main group of these drugs are the Benzodiazepams. They were initially heralded as a revolution in the treatment and understanding of anxiety disorders in the late 1960s and early 1970s. They were potent annihilators of the acute anxiety symptoms seen in panic attacks, and allowed people with GAD to live without constant worry and fear.

They worked a little too well, however. The feelings of relaxation and pleasure induced by them created a generation of Valium, Librium, Xanax and

Lexotane addicts. Tolerance to these drugs develops quickly and, as with any addictive substance, doctors had to keep increasing the dose to achieve the same effect. As doctors tried to wean patients off their addiction, the symptoms of anxiety were replaced by more serious physical and psychological problems. They also cause drowsiness and impair concentration. The drugs are very attractive to alcoholics and drug addicts.

As a result, the cure for anxiety ended up becoming a substance of widespread misuse and abuse. To this day, doctors still have certain patients who are addicted to these drugs, and have been for decades. A further complication is that sudden withdrawal of these drugs in such people may lead to convulsions.

Nowadays, drugs such as Xanax and Lexotane are used by doctors on a very restricted basis. If used correctly for short periods, while other forms of treatment are being utilised, they can be very helpful.

In short, these drugs are still useful, but the way in which they are prescribed must be carefully monitored, and their use stopped as soon as possible.

Antidepressants

The genetic and biological pathways of depression and GAD are quite similar. It is therefore not surprising that antidepressants have been found to be of help in both acute and chronic anxiety.

The main drugs used nowadays are the SSRIs. These drugs have all been shown to decrease anxiety. When activity is increased in the serotonin mood cable by these drugs, the stress box and stress pathways are calmed. In practice, they are used regularly for short periods, together with CBT, to deal with panic disorders. They are also used in some cases of GAD and OCD for longer periods, sometimes for life.

In the case of long-term treatment, there is the issue of side effects, particularly sexual ones. As a result, psychological treatment should always be seriously considered in such cases, to try to reduce the need for such drugs.

Complementary Therapies

Several complementary therapies can be very helpful in the treatment of anxiety disorders, as part of an overall treatment package. These include massage, meditation, yoga, pilates, reflexology and certain herbal treatments. Relaxation therapies such as yoga and meditation can be beneficial in calming the mind and body – something which is obviously particularly important in the area of anxiety.

Biologically, they seem to work by calming the stress box, and thus reducing levels of glucocortisol. As certain anxiety disorders, such as GAD, can last a lifetime, it is especially important that the person look holistically at their own treatment and lifestyle. Those who suffer from such illnesses also need to learn to manage the stress in their lives more efficiently.

Common Questions About the Yellow Flag

Why Treat It At All?

People who suffer from these illnesses dread getting up in the morning to face the world. Those with acute anxiety constantly fear another attack, and have difficulty dealing with these attacks when they arrive. Those with GAD will suffer from constant apprehension and worry. They will also struggle with fatigue, poor memory and concentration, and sleep difficulties, all interspersed with bouts of acute anxiety. Many live lives of quiet despair, always feeling a failure, unable to cope with any stress, and getting over one worry only to be faced immediately with another.

If untreated, many people with GAD will struggle to hold down jobs or may use alcohol as an escape, with negative consequences. They will sometimes misuse tranquillizers or alcohol in order to cope and will always remain at risk of developing a bout of depression at some stage in their lives, particularly after a period of severe stress. Similarly with OCD, many who do not get help are strangled in their attempts to lead normal lives. Obsessive thoughts and actions become their lives, and everything else is secondary:

the actions must be carried out first. Once again, their ability to form and maintain relationships, hold down jobs and cope with stress is severely compromised.

Another practical reason for treating anxiety when it is combined with stress is that it affects the general health of the body. We have talked earlier about the effects of acute stress on blood pressure and the heart. We have also looked at the effects of chronic stress on heart disease and osteoporosis. GAD, as it follows the same pathways as chronic stress, may also lead to similar increased risks and, especially in the presence of outside stress, may lead to the immune system itself becoming impaired. This makes it more likely that, if the condition goes untreated, people with GAD may suffer from more viral and bacterial illnesses than other people.

How Long Will Treatment Last?

Assuming that the usual lifestyle changes, such as revising diet, taking exercise and supplements, and avoiding misuse of alcohol and caffeine have been looked at, the usual treatment package may involve drug or psychological therapy, or both. The length of treatment will depend on the type of anxiety disorder and its severity:

(a) *Acute anxiety:* Panic disorders and phobias can be treated in most cases with a few sessions of CBT. The former can sometimes be handled with as little as two to three sessions, particularly if the disorder in question is uncomplicated. Drug treatment in the form of tranquillizers should be avoided due to the risk of developing dependence.

(b) *Chronic anxiety:* GAD is a lifelong illness. Relaxation exercises and CBT with a therapist can lead to a definite reduction in symptoms, however. The length of time for this treatment will vary depending on the severity of the condition.

If drugs are used, particularly the SSRIs, there is usually a trade-off between side effects, particularly sexual ones, and the efficacy of the drugs over a long period of time. Ideally, drug treatment should be combined with the above psychological therapies and withdrawn, if at all possible, when such therapies start to yield results.

In OCD, treatment in sufferers may continue for life. The use of drug treatment, particularly SSRIs, and cognitive therapy will vary from person to person, depending on the severity of the illness.

What Are The Side Effects Of Treatment?

The side effects of the SSRIs have been dealt with in the Red Flag. The tranquillizers may cause drowsiness and impaired concentration and should only be used for short periods. If long-term drug treatment is necessary, it is better to switch to an SSRI. Psychological treatment carries few risks when performed by a trained psychologist or therapist. If, however, a person is complaining of severe fatigue and memory loss, it may be better to use an SSRI first to try to restore normal mood, energy and behaviour before therapy can be really effective.

What Will Happen When I Go To The Doctor?

Many people worry that their family doctor will be dismissive and condescending when they admit to their irrational fears. This prevents many people from getting the help they need. Instead, just tell him how you feel. This will allow him to assess you, both physically and mentally. He will ask you a number of questions to clarify which type of anxiety disorder you may be suffering from. Sometimes, he may feel that the symptoms are more to do with stress than anxiety, and will discuss methods of dealing with this.

If he is satisfied with the diagnosis, he will firstly discuss with you the various lifestyle changes detailed above. He may also recommend a referral to a psychologist or trained CBT therapist, if one is available, or to a psychiatrist with CBT training. If appropriate, he may recommend drug treatment.

In general, acute anxiety is best dealt with by the psychologist or CBT therapist, and chronic anxiety through a combination of psychological therapy and drug therapy, to combat the symptoms of severe fatigue and poor concentration associated with severe panic attacks.

Above all, remember that the Yellow Flag of anxiety is an illness, not a weakness or a personality defect. You are neither mad nor insane. Quite the opposite, in fact: many people with these illnesses are often very sensitive and intuitive people. Your condition was created by an interaction between your genes and early environmental influences; you did not bring this upon yourself, and treatment is readily available.

PART FOUR

The Purple Flag:
Addiction

1: THE CAUSES, SYMPTOMS AND BIOLOGY OF ADDICTION

The ability to feel pleasure motivates us to live a full and active life. Going for a drink, eating out in a restaurant, having sex, and placing a bet on the races are all examples of normal enjoyable activities. Despite the variety of pleasurable activities available to us, the stimulation of a single mood cable makes them all 'pleasurable'. When one constantly engages in any one of these activities to the detriment of everything else in one's life, however, the outcome ceases to be pleasurable. Eating to excess results in obesity, and drinking alcohol in excess gives rise to violence, vomiting and sometimes poisoning. In fact, the use of any drug in large quantities gives rise to a range of family, social and personal problems.

When a person feels compelled to engage constantly in a certain activity, to the neglect of everything else in their life, they can be said to be suffering from addiction. This is the term used to describe a physical or psychological dependence on either a substance or an activity; it is a worldwide problem.

Research carried out over the last five years has revealed a dramatic change in the understanding of what is happening in the body when a person is addicted. This research is badly needed, as the cost of addiction is borne not just by the medical services but by the families of addicts as well.

This chapter explains addiction, the biological factors associated with it, and the treatment methods that are available. The following chapter will focus on specific areas of addiction, which include alcohol, nicotine, gambling, drugs and food.

The Ubiquitous Addictions

Smoking and alcohol are the most common addictions. Smoking in particular is highly addictive; the habit is usually begun in the mid teens. Alcohol, a depressant drug, is consumed to excess by many people, but about 10 percent of adult male and 5 percent of female drinkers will develop a serious dependence on it. Gambling is a hidden but prevalent addiction that is not as obvious as the first two.

The next most common addiction is drug addiction. This can take many forms. Some drugs, such as amphetamines, ecstasy and cocaine, are stimulatory; others, such as tranquillizers and cannabis, are depressants. Hallucinogens include LSD and magic mushrooms. Finally, there are the opiates, such as heroin. While drug use is fairly common among people in the fifteen-to-thirty-five age group, the actual number of addicts is not as high as the media would lead us to believe. Dublin city is a good example of this. There are approximately ten thousand heroin addicts living in Dublin. As this group is responsible for a great deal of crime, and is quite noticeable because many heroin addicts are homeless, it is understandable that it receives most of our attention. The problems associated with illegal drug use pale in comparison to the misery and social problems caused by alcohol in Ireland, however. Prescription drugs like Valium and sleeping tablets are also a major source of abuse, food addiction is widely under-recognised, and other forms of addiction, including shopping addiction, computer-games addiction and sex addiction, are also serious problems.

Two concepts that are commonly used when discussing addiction are tolerance and dependency. Tolerance refers to the diminishing pleasure derived from a substance through its constant use. (The corollary of this is the necessity to increase usage to maintain the pleasurable feelings.) Dependency relates to the unpleasant physical and psychological effects experienced when the drug or activity is withdrawn.

An interesting feature of addiction is that many addicts have more than one vice. This is known as cross addiction. Examples of this are an alcoholic who smokes, a gambler who drinks excessively, or an alcoholic who is addicted to prescription drugs. Addicts may succeed in stopping one addiction, only to switch to another (e.g. they stop drinking and start using tranquillizers instead). Many people who try to stop abusing alcohol will start to smoke even more. Even food addiction is often used as a substitute for alcohol or nicotine addiction. There is a biological explanation for this: all of these activities share the same brain pathways.

The Symptoms Of Addiction

Despite the diversity of addictions, the symptoms of addiction are fairly universal. Firstly, the substance being abused will be more important to an addict than anything else in their lives, be it family, friends or work. Secondly, they are usually fine as long as their addiction is being fed. If they are deprived of the substance or activity, they suffer physical (sweating, vomiting and tremors) and psychological (tension, anxiety, depression and suicidal tendencies) effects. The longer they engage in their addiction, the more they need to consume just to feel normal, let alone feel good. As a result, their addiction starts to take over their lives: unless they do it all the time, they feel terrible. Lastly, addiction damages the physical well-being of its victims, resulting in illnesses of the heart, lungs, liver and brain, and psychiatric illnesses such as anxiety, depression and schizophrenia.

The Biology Of Addiction

All addicts behave in a similar manner, and this fact is known to any health professional working in the field. It is therefore little surprise that the latest research reveals that all addiction behaves in a similar biological manner.

One of the main boxes in the limbic-mood department is the pleasure box. It has been known for years that the dopamine mood cable is involved in the process by which we experience pleasure. During normal activities such as eating, having sex, drinking and taking part in a sporting activity, the dopamine cable activates, as does the pleasure box itself. Without this activation, our capacity to enjoy the good things in life would be seriously compromised. So from this point of view, the activation of the dopamine cable is vital.

We as humans have for millennia found ways of artificially stimulating this cable to produce profound pleasure, however. To achieve this, some people misuse alcohol and other related substances; others may begin to gamble, shop, overeat or play computer games to an excessive degree. In those who are genetically or environmentally at risk of addiction, however, this persistent hyper-stimulation of the dopamine cable starts to cause subtle chemical and molecular changes in the neurons which make up the pleasure box.

When the person becomes seriously addicted, these changes become more permanent. These aberrations cause the addict to crave the substance and become dependent on it. They also require the addict to use more and more of the substance in order to achieve satisfaction.

The biological composite of addiction is explained in the Purple Flag model below. Purple is the colour of debauchery, which is why I have chosen it to depict addiction.

Although the other mood cables (particularly the serotonin cable) and departments may be directly affected by alcohol and other drugs, it is the excessive stimulation of the dopamine cable and changes to the pleasure box which create the illness that is addiction. Experts are also looking at the so-called 'reward circuit' between the stress, behaviour and pleasure boxes (a part of the mood circuit we dealt with earlier) as being crucial in relation to the behaviour patterns related to this illness. The chemical changes which cause the malfunctions in the pleasure box are the same for all addictions. This is a very exciting discovery, as it may lead in the future to the development of drugs that are capable of treating all forms of addiction. Once again, understanding the biology of our flag system may lead to a re-evaluation of how we treat addiction. Unfortunately, it may take many years to reach this point.

For the present, turning the Purple Flag of addiction back to green is probably the most difficult challenge of all.

Course of the Purple Flag

Many addictions, like smoking, alcohol and illegal drugs, begin in the teenage years and early twenties. The process of becoming an addict usually takes a substantial period of time. Alcoholics generally take the longest to develop a problem – often after gradual increased drinking over a period of years. This fact should not go unnoticed as there is a time window present in such cases, which makes early intervention particularly important.

Drug addicts are more variable in the time it takes to develop a serious habit, and this can depend on the drug involved. Cocaine can be addictive from the first administration. Most addicts' lives involve periods where they feed their addiction, with pauses in between. During these pauses, the addict will be restless, will have difficulty sleeping, and may even suffer periods of low mood. Again, depending on the substance involved, the length of these time periods last is highly variable.

Addiction is usually a lifelong illness. With assistance, some will be able to restrain their addictive urges and live a normal life. Although it may be controversial to say so, biologically speaking these people are still addicts – they have just learned how to manage their illness.

The life of many addicts involves recurring bouts of addiction, which can destroy their health and their relationships. Some will die from the direct effects of the addiction on their physical health, and others from the White Flag of suicide. Most will live in unhappiness and loneliness until they reach a point where they seek help from the medical profession, addiction counsellors and their fellow addicts. The addict justifies their actions and delays facing the problem with the mantra: 'I will stop tomorrow'. Unfortunately, for many, tomorrow never comes.

Causes of the Purple Flag

Addiction is now seen by most experts as being caused by a mixture of genetic and environmental factors. Many people can take drugs and alcohol, and in excessive amounts, without becoming addicted. Finding out why this is so is crucial to the understanding and treatment of the illness.

Genetic Predisposition

Although no specific gene has been associated with addiction, many studies suggest that it has a genetic component. Genetic vulnerability varies from person to person and in most cases is polygenetic in type. Even in the case of alcoholics, there are at least two subsets with a different genetic susceptibility in each.

There are two rival theories explaining the relationship between genes and addiction. The first states that genetic predisposition to addiction is a direct one based on malfunctioning genes within the dopamine system. The second theory (favoured by many therapists) is that genes play an indirect role, by creating certain vulnerable personality types. These types are more likely to experiment with pleasurable activities such as drinking and drug use than the norm, making them more vulnerable to addiction. It is quite likely that both of these mechanisms are involved and that only a full decoding of our genes will settle the debate.

Environmental Factors

There is little doubt that environmental triggers play an important role in both the development and the maintenance of addiction. Very young people who start to smoke often move on quickly to abuse alcohol and are more likely to become addicts of some description. It has also been shown that those who start misusing alcohol under the age of fifteen have a much higher risk of developing alcohol dependence. Their brains are only developing at this stage of their lives, so such substances will have powerful effect on the genes which are in charge of the process.

Addicts also often emerge from addictive homes. There seems to be a potent combination of a genetic predisposition to addiction and unhappiness due to growing up in such an environment. In short, addiction breeds addiction.

Those reared in the following circumstances are more at risk of becoming addicts:

- Homes and areas of poverty, neglect, unemployment and crime
- Addictive homes, especially if the mother or father is the addict
- Abusive homes

Those living in the following situations are also at risk:

- Poverty, unemployment, lack of education and crime
- Anxiety or depression which is self-medicated with alcohol or drugs
- High-stress situations

Another important environmental factor is the cultural availability of the potentially addictive substance. In Ireland, for example, the easy availability of alcohol to all age groups, together with the widespread availability of opportunities for gambling makes these two into obvious sources of abuse. If a potential alcoholic lived in Saudi Arabia, for example, where alcohol is prohibited, it would obviously be more difficult for his addiction to actualise.

The Addictive Substances Themselves

The neurons in the brain are not impervious to alteration by addictive substances. The brain is a plastic organ: it adapts to the situations it finds itself in. When alcohol and drugs are abused, the brain reacts by altering its own chemistry to compensate; this is where the problems start.

The substances therefore play an indirect role in the addictive process itself, by forcing the brain to make changes. The more the drugs are abused, the more likely it is that such changes will become permanent. Inevitably, the earlier the brain is exposed to drugs, the more likely it is that such changes will occur. Individual substances vary in their capacity to alter brain chemistry, and also in the speed that they do so. The primary site for such changes is obviously the pleasure box/dopamine system.

A great deal of work is also going on to try to understand how these substances are, in some cases, able to cause permanent neurochemical changes to the behaviour, memory and pleasure boxes which make up the reward circuit noted above. This research may lead to new treatment options. When these three factors are combined, a model of addiction is formed.

It will take time for the whole jigsaw puzzle of addiction to be assembled. Within the next few decades, the complete genetic pathways relating to pleasure will be mapped out. The chemical process going on inside the pleasure box will also reveal the secrets of addiction. This, along with further research into how our neurons are altered by the drugs themselves, should create new ways of shutting down the whole addictive process.

The 'Addiction Castle'

Addiction has a profoundly negative effect on the mental and physical well-being of its victims. As has already been seen, physical damage to the heart, lung, liver, pancreas and brain threatens the general health of the person. Psychological damage includes anxiety, panic attacks, depression and, sometimes, suicide.

The negative effects of addiction do not end there, however. Addicts will also have friends, families and partners, who must share in the misery of addiction. For every addict, there are five to seven people who will be indirectly affected by the addiction. I would like to share with you a concept that I developed a long time ago to help people understand what it is like to be, or to live with, an addict. It is called the 'addiction castle'. This is a concept that has brought the addicts' loved ones to tears (sometimes joined by the addicts themselves) as, for the first time, they begin to understand what is happening to them or their loved one. This castle model works for all addictions.

Andy is an addict. As a result of the effects the addiction has had on his brain, Andy the addict has completely changed his behaviour and has decided to build a stone castle wall around him. He retreats into his lair and firmly closes the castle door behind him. In the middle of his castle, Andy lives in glorious isolation, cutting himself off from all of those around him, and then getting on with the serious work of feeding his addiction.

When Andy the addict enters his castle, the original, real Andy disappears from sight. It is also very lonely inside his castle looking at high stone walls and a closed gate, with only his addiction to keep him company. But Andy remains determined to defend his castle at all costs and has many weapons to make sure that his addiction is preserved.

Outside this castle are all those who care about Andy. They want to interact with Andy, but he is gone out of sight. All they can see are the stone walls, the closed gate and the castle full of weapons, all designed to keep them out.

His loved ones become desperate to reach him. Initially, they ring the bell at the gate, but they get no response. As the situation worsens, they then try charging the gate and the stone wall to try to break a hole in the castle and reach Andy. Then they bounce off the heavy wood and stone and get bruised and hurt in the process. Tragically, love has no boundaries, and this process is repeated over and over again until the loved ones' spirits are broken from crashing into the stone of the addict's castle.

Eventually, somebody wise comes along and puts an arm around them, explaining that it is useless to continue like this and persuading them to withdraw or detach. They explain that only cannons will be able to blow holes through the stone walls. Only these, and overwhelming loneliness, will encourage the addict to open the gate himself and look for help. Many, discouraged by this information and by the battle with the castle wall, will turn around and depart for good, abandoning Andy to his lonely vigil inside this stony retreat.

All addicts surround themselves with a defensive, wall-like castle and firmly shut the gate on those who are close to them. Signs of this wall are selfishness, self-obsession, and a complete denial that they have a responsibility to deal with their own addiction. The castle wall is built to protect the person's addiction at any cost. The weapons used by the addicts inside their castles are lying, cheating, stealing, minimising the significance of their condition, and most of all transferring their own guilt and blame onto those who are closest to them. Statements like 'I only drink because she nags me all the time' are examples of such behaviour.

Outside the wall are the innocent victims of addiction. They desperately want to reach their loved ones, who have closed themselves off in their castle. They get battered and bruised emotionally – and sometimes physically – from encountering the addict's defensive wall. Many feel guilty and responsible for their loved one's addiction: a sure sign that the addict has aimed well with his weapons. The families of those with addiction are often destroyed by this castle.

There are only two ways that Andy can be brought out of his castle. Firstly, Andy himself may get so lonely that he himself opens up the castle wall and comes out looking for help, and to find his loved ones. This rarely happens. The second way is for large cannons to be fired at Andy's castle; these weapons of destruction include the loss of a relationship with a partner or child, the loss of a home, the loss of a job, or severe illness as a result of his addiction.

These cannons, in some cases, can be enough to convince Andy that he must change his behaviour, and he may open up the gate and come out looking for help. Sadly, some addicts will choose to stay in their castle for life. They can die from either the side effects of their addiction, or sometimes they end their own lives as a means of stopping the loneliness and isolation of their life in the castle.

Stages of Insight into the Purple Flag

Another useful approach in helping addicts and alcoholics in particular is to assess their level of insight into their own illness. I call this 'staging'. I classify the addicted into four main stages. Stage 1: 'I have no problem!' Stage 2: 'I occasionally abuse alcohol or drugs, but so does everyone else, so it's not really a problem!' Stage 3: 'I am an addict. I accept that I have a problem but I can handle it myself!' Stage 4: 'Help!'

If the addict is at Stage 1 or 2, they are usually not ready to receive any help. I advise loved ones in these cases to detach themselves physically, emotionally and financially from the addict, if possible. This detachment has two important functions. Firstly, it safeguards the loved ones from future pain and hurt, as it means that they do not have to crash into the 'castle wall'. Secondly, it may force the addict out into the open. Life is no longer easy in his castle. The cannons are attacking his defences. I also refer the loved ones to self-help groups to get help from others who have been hurt by addiction.

If the addict reaches Stage 3, and in particular Stage 4, and the castle gate finally opens, help from doctors, counsellors and addiction self-help groups can start to restore Andy back to his original state. It often takes years, and even a lifetime, for addicts to go from Stage 1 to Stage 4. Many never get beyond Stage 2; others may stay stuck for long periods at Stage 3. In some cases, it can take many years before Andy can finally feel able to open the door and look for help.

Treatment of the Purple Flag

Addiction is still very difficult to treat. There are two main reasons for this. Firstly, the biological changes that have occurred in the pleasure box, over a lifetime of addiction, become consolidated. The addict has been living for a long time with the cravings that these changes have produced. Secondly, the longer the addict has been living in his 'addiction castle', the greater the destruction he has caused both to his own life and to the lives of those around him, through neglect. This damage is difficult to repair, and it can take a lot of work to help the person to change the Purple Flag back to green.

If the addict begins to feel that there is nothing left for him to lose, he is unlikely ever to leave the comfort of his addiction, and will probably remain in his castle for life.

The journey to recovery can only begin when the addict opens up the gates of his castle and looks for help. When the addict begins the difficult road to recovery, he must accept the help of others, in particular other recovered addicts, in the battle towards health. He must also acknowledge the damage that he has done to those around him. The tragedy is that the lives of so many addicts and their loved ones are completely destroyed before they reach this point; death often becomes the final outcome.

Currently, it is very difficult to treat the addict before they reach Stage 3 or 4 of their illness. Therefore, it is not surprising that the success rate in the treatment of addiction, depending on its type, is as low as 25 to 40 percent. This is why research into the underlying causes of the Purple Flag is so important. The modern approach to addiction treatment involves two main steps:

1. Stopping the use of the addictive substance or behaviour
2. Changing the negative behaviour patterns that have developed in the 'addiction castle'

This second step is vital. Many addicts learn to stop their addiction but still have a tendency to remain 'in the castle' in terms of how they behave with friends and family. In order to recover fully, Andy the addict must, through counselling, learn to tear down the walls of his 'addiction castle'. Only then can he fully reintegrate back into a happy and fulfilling life with his loved ones. Only then can the Purple Flag be changed back to green.

The above treatment approach is now very community-based. Firstly, the addict must be dried out, i.e. removed completely from the addictive substance and behaviour. This can generally be achieved by the family doctor, but in some cases admission to hospital may be necessary.

Secondly, the addict must work with specialist counsellors to help break down his castle walls. This will involve accepting the power of the emotional pleasure-driven emotional brain over the more logical one. They also have to learn new coping skills to deal with the problems and difficulties of life without the crutch of their addiction. They must also come to terms with the damage they have inflicted on their loved ones. This involves genuine self-acceptance as well as honesty about their previous behaviour in relation to others. CBT is now being increasingly considered as a treatment option for people suffering from addiction. (One useful approach suggested by modern CBT therapists, and which I have found useful for patients, particularly those with alcohol addiction, is to encourage them to challenge their 'cravings' directly. This involves teaching them that cravings last for only five minutes! If they can learn techniques to beat these short bursts of longing, they can stay out of trouble. I often suggest texting a close friend, alcohol counsellor or AA colleague during such periods. By the time they have finished doing this, the craving has usually settled.)

Thirdly, he must learn to take part in addict self-help groups. Here he can lean on the collective wisdom of those who have spent their lives battling addiction. Most of these groups are founded on some form of spiritual basis, and rely on the ten-step approach as a road map to recovery.

Only a very lucky few have the opportunity to attend in-patient centres where this whole process can be accelerated. This is mainly due to the high cost of such centres. It has been proven that community-level treatment can, and does, work, however. Everything depends on the level of insight of the addict, and how serious they are about fighting their addiction. Drug addiction takes a longer course of counselling and treatment in comparison to other addictions: withdrawing from a drug like heroin may involve many years of help, for example.

It is also important to recognise the danger of cross-addiction. I have seen cases where one addiction is admitted to and treated, only to find a second, hidden one emerging later. Addicts are very good at fooling not only the doctor but also themselves.

Addiction: Weakness or Illness?

The very word 'addiction' tends to evoke a strong reaction from the general public. Most feel that those who are addicted to alcohol, gambling or drugs have a weak personality. Many people think that addicts are entirely responsible for their own addiction. So is addiction merely a weakness which can be overcome?

A great deal of research has been carried out on the biological and genetic factors that underpin addiction. We now know that it is too facile to simply label addiction as a weakness. Addiction is an illness, caused by the exposure of a person with addictive traits to either substances or behaviour that can irrevocably alter that person's pleasure box in the brain. Such people are genetically or environmentally susceptible to the development of addictive behaviour.

We cannot choose our genes or upbringing; either of these can accelerate the addictive process. We *can* change our current environment, however. In diabetes, the predisposition is inherited genetically, but eating the wrong kinds of food and becoming obese will increase the likelihood of this illness appearing. On receiving the diagnosis, a diabetic could choose to ignore all medical advice, continue to eat the wrong foods, refrain from exercise, and refuse medications which would be of benefit, putting their health at risk in the process. This would of course be very foolish.

So, although the predisposition to develop an illness is usually genetically driven (in association with environmental factors), the person always plays an important role in how the illness is managed – to the benefit or the detriment of their health. Addiction is quite similar. A person does not directly cause their illness; they have inherited a strong predisposition (through genes or the environment, or both) towards it. By heavily misusing alcohol and drugs from an early age, however, the person increases the risk of this illness appearing.

There are also clear choices as to how they manage their own illness once they have been diagnosed. They can choose, as many do, to ignore all advice and help – to the detriment of their health, relationships and work prospects. Alternatively, they can choose to get help, and involve themselves in programmes which teach them how to deal with the cravings that this illness produces. This is the ground on which the battle against the illness must be fought.

Addiction is an illness, not a weakness. It is the way in which the sufferer deals with this illness that makes all the difference. If the addict chooses to hide in the addiction castle, they will spend most of their lives lonely and in poor health. Just as with diabetes and other illnesses, the addict also has the choice to get help from experts and fellow sufferers alike.

2: INDIVIDUAL ADDICTIONS

In this chapter, I will take a more detailed look at some individual addictions, such as alcohol, drugs, cigarettes and gambling.

Alcohol

This is the most prevalent cause of the Purple Flag. No other substance is so interwoven into the fabric of our society. In Ireland, we like to feel that we are world experts in this field. It is also a major problem in Britain and most of the northern European countries. Alcohol is a safe and enjoyable substance when used in moderation. But no other substance, with the exception of cigarettes, causes so much havoc when it is abused.

Why is alcohol enjoyable? Alcohol stimulates the serotonin and dopamine mood cables, and the pleasure box, so that the person feels quite euphoric. It also stimulates the GABA receptors; this has a relaxing effect. When used in moderation, alcohol helps us to relax and enjoy each other's company. If the 'mood machinery' is working normally, the effects are positive ones. Drinking does, however, affect our concentration and makes us more likely to become impulsive, so driving for example becomes hazardous with even small amounts of alcohol having been taken.

Excessive consumption of alcohol leads to loss of coordination, concentration and memory, and in some cases to complete memory blackouts. It releases self control, and can lead to violent, impulsive behaviour. This is particularly dangerous for those who are already suffering from undiagnosed mood problems, and can facilitate self-harm and suicide.

The negative effects of alcohol can be seen on our streets, leading to an increase in assaults, rape, road-traffic accidents and suicide. On an average weekend night, A&E departments all over Ireland witness the fallout. Teenagers arrive to get their stomachs pumped. People are brought in bleeding and reeling from vicious assaults. Others, less fortunate, are dead on arrival from road-traffic accidents caused by people drinking and driving. A final group are admitted after overdosing on a deadly mixture of drink and drugs. Some of these may suffer from the Red Flag of depression.

Alcohol is attractive because of the feelings of well-being and relaxation it induces, making the person think that the more that they consume, the better they will feel. This is not the case, especially when the person is already suffering from the Red Flag of depression.

Alcohol Misuse

Alcohol, when taken in moderate amounts, relaxes us by stimulating our GABA receptors, and makes us feel positive by stimulating our serotonin and dopamine cables and pleasure box. Once the amount of alcohol consumed becomes excessive, however, glutamate receptors in the brain are interfered with. As glutamate is important in almost every function of the brain, this results in chaos. We start to develop slurred speech and memory loss. We become completely uncoordinated in our movement and balance, our vision becomes blurred, and in some cases we become depressed and withdrawn.

A more serious side effect of alcohol is the removal of normal inhibitions. If we have a predisposition towards violent behaviour, alcohol reveals it. If we are depressed, alcohol may release suicidal thoughts and behaviour. Gross excess of alcohol can eventually lead to coma and death.

The results of alcohol misuse on a normal Irish weekend can be observed in almost every town and city in the country. Many people simply live and work to reach the weekend, so that they can meet up with their friends, go out on the town, and drink so much that they can forget about their problems for a couple of hours.

The side effects of alcohol inevitably emerge as the night goes on. A queue for a taxi or a takeaway becomes a flashpoint for a fight. Someone who was a normal young man at six in the evening has become an animal by 3 AM, kicking someone's head as they lie on the ground. This combination of alcohol and aggression has led to an alarming increase in serious assaults, rape and traffic accidents.

It is not only the younger generation who have an abusive relationship with alcohol; as a nation, we drink too much. Every Irish celebration ends up in the pub, from weddings to funerals, sports matches to birthdays. We have created and celebrated a culture which revolves around alcohol consumption. We turn a blind eye to the fallout. One of the difficulties in confronting people of all ages about alcohol misuse is that those involved will quickly say: 'It's not a problem for me', 'I'm not addicted to alcohol; I can happily do without it if necessary', 'I don't crave it; I just go out with my friends at the weekend to enjoy myself.'

In the majority of cases, these statements are probably correct. Many can misuse alcohol but do not become dependant or addicted. If I injure or kill someone in a violent incident as a result of alcohol misuse, however, the damage to my life, and to the life of the victim and his family, may be just as great as the damage wreaked by addiction itself. If I spend my Monday mornings feeling down and hung over, alcohol misuse is intruding on my life.

Alcohol misuse has become one of the greatest problems facing medical personnel and police in the country. It is a factor in up to 40 percent of fatal road-traffic accidents, and around a quarter of male and a tenth of female admissions to psychiatric hospitals are due to alcohol-related problems. In our A&Es, drink-related admissions cause a huge increase in workload for the already harassed and overworked medical and nursing staff who have to man these 'war zones'. It breeds violence, mayhem and unhappiness, and is one intimate relationship that we could do without.

Alcohol Abuse

This condition can be called by different names: alcoholism – an old term that is rapidly going out of use – alcohol abuse, or alcohol dependency syndrome, which is the most common definition. All of these terms refer to the same illness: the sufferer is addicted to alcohol. Alcohol abuse differs from alcohol misuse in that the person, through a combination of genetic predisposition and environmental factors, has become completely dependent on alcohol. This means that withdrawal of this substance will produce physical (sweating, shaking, nausea, headaches, sleep difficulties) and psychological (craving, anxiety, panic attacks, depression) symptoms.

Most people who are at risk will move from simple misuse, to extensive misuse, to finally becoming completely addicted to the substance. Tolerance, craving and dependency or withdrawal symptoms are the main indications of alcohol abuse. The changes seen in the pleasure box after extended use of the substance are the notable biological feature of this condition.

Excellent research in Sweden in the 1980s and 1990s has shown that there are two different groups of people who abuse alcohol. Each group has a different genetic basis, presentation and behaviour pattern.

The Type 1 Alcoholic

This relates to a group of people who do not need to drink constantly in order to feed their addiction. They are often described as binge drinkers or, more accurately, as binge alcoholics. They are able to stay clear of alcohol for weeks, or even months. But eventually, they feel the craving building up, and they start with their first drink. Once the drinking begins, it may go on for days and nights, until sickness, or more commonly lack of money, brings the binge to an end. Such binges are often triggered by celebratory occasions such as weddings, holidays and birthdays. Funerals in Ireland are also high-risk events. The partners and families of addicts learn to dread these periods.

The genetic basis for this illness, although clearly of relevance, is much weaker than for Type 2 alcoholics. It is almost certainly polygenetic in nature (i.e. varying numbers of malfunctioning genes in the chromosomes are involved from person to person). It affects both men and women in equal amounts, and often starts over the age of twenty-five.

Family upbringing, particularly if alcohol addiction is present, has a much stronger influence in this group. If alcohol abuse is present in both parents, or if poverty is present, the risk of severe illness increases. Parents of Type 1 alcoholics are much more likely to produce offspring suffering from

Type 1 rather than Type 2 alcoholism. The reasons for this seems to be a mixture of the genetic and environmental factors involved in the person's upbringing.

The Type 1 personality is generally passive, introverted and perfectionist. They may express guilt about their binges when they are sober. Such concerns rapidly disappear during binges. They frequently suffer from symptoms of anxiety. In many cases, they may start to misuse alcohol in order to deal with feelings of being inadequate, or if they are having difficulties with coping. They develop craving and tolerance quickly. They are more likely to worry about their image; this is part of the reason why they try to hide their addiction. They are also less likely to get into trouble with authority figures. A favourite statement from this group is: 'I don't have a drink problem because I don't drink every day', which is clearly a form of denial. They spend their lives in an endless cycle of anxiety, craving and binges, followed by guilt. Stress is often a trigger for a binge.

This group will show dopamine cable hyper-stimulation (which occurs during these binges), combined with the classical chemical changes in the pleasure box. It is these changes, both short- and long-term, which explain the craving, tolerance and lifelong nature of this illness.

The illness has a very damaging effect on the health, work and family life of the person. This group will have the usual 'addiction castle' symptoms of lying, stealing, cheating, and so on. But they are more likely to be secretive about their actions. This group are, however, more amenable to treatment and help than the Type 2 group. The addiction castle can be more easily breached by fear of losing family, housing, work, health or loved ones. AA is a particularly useful tool for this group if they eventually look for help and try to come to terms with their binges. One should not underestimate the power of their cravings, however, and many will struggle with this compulsion throughout their life.

These binges cause a great deal of damage to the person's health, in particular to the liver, pancreas and heart. Many will also suffer from the Red Flag of depression as a result of long periods of trying to cope with their illness. Sometimes, the Red Flag may follow the loss of family or work, as a result of their drinking. Suicide can eventually be the way out for many, especially if the Red Flag is already present.

This group contains a number of people who have been broken by life through abuse, loss or some other life problem. They may start to misuse alcohol as a way to cope, before moving on to binge drinking. Eventually, if they are susceptible (particularly if they come from a Type 1 abuse background), this turns into a full addiction.

Some similarly vulnerable people, initially suffering from depression, may also fall into this trap. In such cases, biological mechanisms take over, and a vicious circle of low mood, craving, binges and guilt take over. Many will become trapped in this cycle, eventually losing everything.

The female alcoholic in this group (many of whom may have a mother with the same illness) is particularly difficult to identify, and to treat. They are usually adept at hiding their problems and covering their tracks. Elderly females are exceptionally difficult, if not impossible, to help.

When people start using alcohol as a crutch, there is always a risk of developing this kind of addiction. If people are already susceptible, the crutch can become the main trigger. This is why the large number of people who misuse alcohol in Ireland is an extremely worrying phenomenon. As the numbers of people drinking heavily increases, so too does the risk of addiction. Misuse morphs into abuse.

The Type 2 Alcoholic

This alcoholic is driven to drink all the time. Symptoms of addiction can usually be seen before the age of twenty-five. This illness is strongly genetically inherited (up to 90 percent), and mostly involves males. It seems to be inherited as part of an overall personality disorder.

This group shows strong anti-social tendencies, often expressed in the form of violence, and has little remorse about the destruction that their behaviour causes in the lives of others. The combination of heavy alcohol use and violence often leads them into conflict with authority and the law. Some of the violence currently seen on our streets can be attributed to this group. Like all addicts, Type 2 alcoholics can be adept at minimising their own role in such situations, pushing the blame (and consequences) on to someone else. Sometimes, these violent impulses are self-directed, and suicide can be the final outcome. Drink-driving convictions are also common in this group.

In relationships, this group can cause major emotional and physical damage to their partners and children. The male children of this group run a greater genetic risk of developing the same violent destructive personality traits as the male parent, and of becoming young addicts themselves. The daughters of this group seem to inherit other personality characteristics, but not generally alcohol addiction.

It also seems as though environmental influences are far less important in this group than in Type 1 alcoholics. The fathers of this group will quite often have had similar personalities, and will often have a history of violence or conflict with the law.

This particular group of alcoholics can be classified as people who suffer from a strongly genetically inherited personality disorder, and who also happen to abuse alcohol (or any other substance they can get their hands on) because they find it pleasurable. They display the classical 'addiction castle', and this, together with their violent anti-social personality, causes untold misery in the lives of those who are close to them.

The primary difference between this group, and those who misuse alcohol and the Type 1 alcoholic, is their anti-social personality and continuous craving for alcohol. Lack of money is the only obstacle. They may lie, steal, cheat or use violence to get the money to feed their addiction. They will often also be abusing other drugs, like sleeping tablets, tranquillizers and street drugs.

Biologically speaking, the same addictive pathways involved in Type 1 alcoholism (with almost constant hyper-stimulation of the dopamine system and the pleasure box) are involved, but it is likely that the broader personality problems may have their origins in the serotonin cable (which may be under-active in some cases), and possibly in the early development of the brain.

Often, this group end up homeless or in prison (often for violent assault). Many reject any help or treatment. Their addiction castle wall is almost impenetrable, and often remains so for life. A substantial number suffer from serious health problems. Many continue drinking even as they are dying from their condition. They remain impervious to the loss of everything, including their own lives.

The prognosis for this group is, at present, quite poor. This is because they suffer from both addiction and personality problems. Many will develop serious medical problems, with damage to the liver, heart and other organs, which may lead to their death. Others may commit suicide, usually in a particularly violent manner. Only a very few manage to break their addiction castle walls, get treatment and end up living normal lives.

Not every alcoholic will fit neatly into either of the two groups above, but this general categorisation has proved to be of great help in improving our understanding of this illness.

It usually takes years for the full-blown emergence of alcohol addiction. Many are starting to look at this addiction as being part of a large spectrum of drinking problems, in all age groups. This starts with initial misuse, followed by increasingly hazardous, and then harmful, drinking, and finishes with eventual dependence or addiction. If one follows this approach, the major concern is the misuse of alcohol at younger and younger ages. Public discussion on the potentially harmful effects of alcohol on the developing brain and mood system must take place before the situation gets out of hand and a generation of alcoholics is forged. There is also increasing concern about the harmful effects of heavy drinking and addiction in the elderly, where the problem often remains hidden.

Some experts are uncomfortable with even describing alcohol dependency as an illness, and would prefer to call it a trait of particular personality types. Others feel that, if we could intervene at a much earlier stage in the cycle of development of this condition, many people would not reach a stage of full-blown dependency.

The example of being on a coach which stops regularly along its route across Ireland to allow passengers to disembark is often used by modern therapists. The coach is filled with heavy drinkers or alcoholics. It begins its journey in Galway and ends in Dublin outside the homeless shelter or the cemetery! The alcohol abuser, however, does not have to stay on the coach that is heading to ruin: they have the option of getting off anywhere along the way, and the earlier they do so, the less damage will be caused to themselves and their families. On the other hand, the closer they come to their final destination, the closer they are to ruin!

Encouraging as many heavy drinkers or alcoholics as possible to disembark early is now very much the target of many of those who work in this field. In my personal dealings with alcoholics and their families, I find that the 'coach' model seems to 'penetrate' the former, and the 'addict castle' the latter!

There is also a body of opinion that feels that early intervention might allow some heavy drinkers or alcoholics to continue to take alcohol in small amounts rather than having to face the prospect of abstinence for life. When alcohol dependency arrives, however (especially if serious physical or family difficulties are present), lifelong abstinence is usually the only solution.

Before leaving this discussion, let's examine what is happening in Ireland at present, bearing in mind everything we have learnt to date.

Firstly, we have to accept that a huge cultural change has occurred in the past decade in relation to how we view and use alcohol.

Ireland has always had an alcohol problem, with its fair share of alcoholics of both types, but in the past, young people in particular had neither the money nor the possibility of drinking heavily before the age of twenty-one. Now, increasing prosperity, plus greater freedom of movement in the twelve-to-eighteen age group has exposed a much larger population of young people in this country to the perils of alcohol misuse and abuse than hitherto. Many Irish teenagers are holding down part-time jobs when they are still studying to help feed their weekend drinking – something which is evident on a Monday morning, as many teachers will testify to!

The official position that alcohol is only available to those who are over eighteen belies the truth of what is happening in practice. Underage drinking increases the potential risk of alcohol dependency. Common sense would dictate that the greater the number of people who are exposed to alcohol at an early age, the greater the number of people who become alcoholics at an early age – and this is what is happening. From a biological point of view, this is inevitable. If the dopamine cable/pleasure box is hyper-stimulated from an early age, the chances of dependency emerging increase. If, as we are seeing, regular binge drinking becomes the norm at an early age, we are much more likely to see type 1 binge alcoholism appearing at earlier and earlier ages (sometimes before the age of twenty); once again, this is what is happening. There is also the potential for alcohol to alter the sensitive neurochemistry and neurobiology of the vulnerable developing brain in this age group.

This has many implications for us as a society. I often feel that the young person's peer group has taken control almost completely away from parents in this area. It now seems to be completely acceptable that GCSE and A Level students be allowed to binge-drink as they see fit! Graduation celebrations have become orgies of alcohol.

What we are all forgetting is that the young people involved have immature brains and mood systems. The controlling influence of the mature prefrontal cortex is not yet present, and pleasure rules. The risks outweigh the rewards. Because of these developments, the risk of future addiction, violence, accidents, depression and, most seriously, suicide dramatically increases. If we ignore the biology of the developing brain in this group, we will continue to pay a high price.

In older age groups, the combination of prosperity, high stress, an increasing acceptance of binge drinking, particularly among females, plus the easy availability of alcohol in off licences, pubs and nightclubs has led to an increasing risk of alcohol abuse (particularly of Type 1 binge alcoholism) in the adult population. Some experts think that we are at the start of an epidemic that will end up destroying many lives.

I am especially worried for the many young women who are drinking at levels they are neither physically (as women cannot process the same levels of alcohol as men) nor psychologically able to cope with. As this pattern often starts well before the age of eighteen, it is crucial that we try to reduce binge drinking at this stage. If we allow the dopamine system to develop a taste for alcohol at an early age, it is inevitable that the twenty-to-forty age groups will continue on the pattern. All of us have a responsibility in this area.

Common Questions Relating to Alcohol Abuse

How Big a Problem Is It?

At least 10 percent of our adult male drinking population, and 3 to 4 percent of the female drinking population, are dependent on alcohol – although even this may be a conservative estimate. At least another 10 to 20 percent is seriously misusing alcohol. There has been a gradual increase in the numbers of women developing serious drink problems in recent years.

It is estimated that around 25 percent of Irish adults drink above the recommended safe amounts of alcohol, and alcohol misuse is a factor in 25 percent of hospital admissions. Thirteen percent of patients attending A&E departments are intoxicated.

How Is Alcohol Abuse Treated?

Successful treatment for alcohol abuse depends on the level of insight that the person has into their own illness. Only those at Stages Three and Four are accepting of help and can really be reached by loved ones or professionals. The addiction castle wall of the alcoholic is very resilient, and many will lose everything rather than open up the addiction gate and look for help.

The current community approach to this problem is firstly to detoxify the person. This means helping them to stop drinking by using a combination of tranquillizers and vitamins to help them survive the withdrawal effects. Usually, this is done by the family doctor, but occasionally, for safety reasons, it will have to be done in a hospital.

Following this, the person is encouraged to attend an alcohol counsellor, and to start involving themselves with a group like Alcoholics Anonymous. Most are apprehensive about the thought of opening up to such a group. Those who genuinely try to follow the twelve steps of AA will often do extremely well. Many will also need relationship counselling if there are relationship difficulties as a result of their addiction. Those with an underlying depression in particular will need further help.

In a small number of cases, inpatient care is greatly beneficial. This is costly, however, and is only available to a small number of people. Increasingly, however, employers are becoming involved in encouraging workers to get such help. A company may pay for such a course of treatment and allow the person to repay the cost to them over a period of time. In reality, very few alcoholics can afford such treatments themselves. Another problem is that many end up being admitted to treatment units when they are still not at a stage where they genuinely want help.

If drugs could be designed to reverse completely the pleasure box changes, eliminating the craving and long-term dependence (while still allowing the person to enjoy normal pleasurable activities), the treatment of alcohol addiction could be revolutionised. There are some drugs which are available at the moment (see below), but none of them have yet achieved the goal of eliminating the cravings. Counselling and self-help groups remain the cornerstones of treatment.

At present, the best strategy for dealing with alcoholism is early detection of potential alcoholics, and efforts to alter their habits in order to limit the risk of addiction. As the brain is only fully mature by twenty-five years of age, however, it is difficult to reach anyone under this age (particularly those under eighteen) with a logical argument. Rather, one must appeal to their emotions, as this is the domain in which they are living. The drinks industry, for instance, is very aware of this vulnerability and is adept at using this strategy in their marketing. In the past, young people lacked the money, time and opportunity to drink at the level that we are now seeing. Now, by contrast, they are quickly developing a taste for alcohol at increasingly young ages. In the mid- to late teens, pleasure and experimentation are synonymous, especially if the money and opportunity to experience these things are readily available. This is worrying, as the developing mood system is more vulnerable to the effects of alcohol and other substances than the mature mood system.

What, If Any, Drug Treatments Are Available At Present For Alcohol Addiction?

Although we are still some distance from a 'wonder drug' which would banish all addictive cravings completely, a number of options are available. A drug called Campral (acamprosate) which acts on the GABA receptors, is sometimes prescribed for one year, in conjunction with counselling. It blocks some receptors in the pleasure box so the drinker will not experience a 'buzz' out of taking the substance, reducing the drive to binge drink.

An older drug called Antabuse is also occasionally still used. It is taken daily and works by causing severe vomiting if the person consumes alcohol within three days of taking the tablet. Although it is useful and of psychological help to spouses, who may supervise its consumption, there are many drawbacks to its use. Firstly, many alcoholics fake taking it, or 'forget' to take it; secondly, others will try and 'chance' drinking after taking it, with some becoming violently ill and requiring hospitalisation; thirdly, it does not deal with the cravings or the addiction castle symptoms. If used sensibly in conjunction with counselling and AA, it has a role in some cases.

Finally, if the Red Flag of depression is also present (as is often the case), the use of the SSRIs in particular has been shown both to treat the underlying depression and, by stimulating the serotonin cable, to reduce impulsive cravings for alcohol. Patients will often report a lessening of interest in the substance. Some will, however, keep drinking even when on antidepressants. This of course makes the antidepressants less effective, so the vicious circle of low mood, craving and drinking, followed by further withdrawal anxiety and drops in mood, continues. Although the SSRIs are helpful, their use is usually linked to the concomitant treatment of depression, with the side effects of reducing craving as a bonus.

What About The Addiction Castle Victims?

People close to the alcoholic often require more help than the alcoholic themselves. The constant collision with the addiction wall leaves them bruised and battered, both emotionally and physically. They often present as tense, anxious and depressed, and despairing as to what to do. They feel responsible for the alcoholic's condition, and admit to feeling guilt about their role, as they see it, in causing such problems. Many are ashamed about admitting the problem to family members or friends.

In many cases, where the alcoholic himself is not prepared to listen, explaining the stages of insight to those close to him can be a great help. They then understand the situation. If the alcoholic is at Stage One or Two, it is best for families and friends to detach emotionally, physically and financially. This saves them from future emotional hurt and pain. It may also force the alcoholic out into the open, as life is no longer so easy for them. Talking to an alcohol counsellor and attending AA support groups such as Alanon or Alateen is also recommended. Such groups provide great support and strength from others who have experienced similar problems.

If the addict is at Stage Three or Four, they are ready to look for help. At this stage, the alcoholic counselling may be a vital link. It is also important to rule out or treat any associated depression.

In some cases, where the addict is clearly lost and unlikely ever to look for help, their relationships may irrevocably break down, leading to separation between them and their loved ones. Sometimes, this is the only possible solution for the partner of the addict, in order that they can rebuild and continue with their own lives.

How Many Alcoholics Recover From Their Addiction?

'Recovering' here refers to stopping taking alcohol completely and making the changes necessary to live a fulfilled and happy life. The figures are not encouraging. Only about 25 percent of those with alcohol abuse will succeed in giving up alcohol for life. The rest will either never face their addiction or will spend their lives engaged in a tug-of-war between remaining sober and drinking heavily. In most of these cases, the drinking wins out in the end, and they lose their family and friends along the way. Some will die from complications due to their drinking. Others will end up homeless. Some will wave the White Flag and take their own lives. Many finish their lives lonely, embittered and stripped of all that they once held dear. The Purple Flag of alcohol addiction is a formidable one.

Is There A Cost To The Community?

The community pays a huge cost for this addiction. If one accepts that every alcoholic affects around five to seven people indirectly (i.e. family members, workmates, employers, friends, and so on), the ripple effect is enormous.

Family breakdown, violence and road-traffic accidents and illness resulting from alcohol abuse take a huge toll on our social and health-care systems. When one adds in alcohol misuse, the financial cost of the use and misuse of this substance is enormous.

Gambling

This addiction, also known as 'gambling-dependency syndrome' or pathological gambling, is a concealed addiction that causes major loss and hardship to the families of the person involved. While alcohol and drugs grab all the news headlines, gambling-dependency syndrome is secretly destroying lives in our community.

Many people are surprised to hear the word 'addiction' associated with gambling because it is an activity rather than a substance. Gambling, like alcohol, may start as a form of misuse, but in vulnerable people the craving sets in and the gambler starts to behave like the alcoholic. Once the gambler starts, they are unable to stop until all their funds run out. Interestingly, a substantial number of gamblers will cross-addict with alcohol.

This illness follows the same neurological pathways that other addictions do, i.e. stimulating the dopamine cable and the pleasure box, with chemical alterations resulting in the pleasure box. It is the latter that produces the craving, which is only relieved when the person starts gambling again. The gambler gets a euphoric feeling from this activity and ignores all other parts of his or her life, to focus purely on their addiction. They also live in the addiction castle. There may again be a genetic predisposition for this illness, as some come from an addictive background. Once again, environment may play a role in such cases.

The main methods of gambling in Ireland have traditionally been slot machines, horse racing and card games. In general, the addict will gamble on anything that is available. Young men, particularly those under twenty-five, seem to prefer slot machines, poker in particular. Members of this group are usually quite intelligent, and are convinced they can 'outsmart' the machine. Even if they win a substantial amount of money, they will usually keep playing until this money is gone. This is often followed by feeling down, and at this stage they often use alcohol to help them feel better.

A recent emerging problem is the arrival of internet gambling, where vast sums of money can be lost extremely quickly. This is believed to be a cause of increasing marital breakdown. The real risk here is the ability to run up huge credit-card debts.

As a group, gamblers are often tense, are superb liars, and are very good at stealing and cheating to feed their addiction. They will continue to conceal their illness until debt finally gives them away.

In the USA, it is estimated that between 1 and 2 percent of the population suffer from pathological gambling. Gambling is also a substantial problem in Ireland. Concrete figures are extremely difficult to obtain. Only figures from groups like Gamblers Anonymous on how many attend on a regular basis provide some clue as to the extent of this illness. A national figure of 20,000 was given to me on one occasion. For every one addict who is receiving help like this, there are almost certainly at least two or three who are not.

Gambling is particularly destructive to families and relationships. All finances are quickly (and often covertly) drained, leaving families in serious debt. This, combined with the constant denial of the gambler, living in his addiction castle, can lead to the breakdown of relationships. The gambler will risk losing everything – family, house and friends – to protect their addiction. They are usually good at holding on to their jobs, however: without this, they would have no money for gambling. In terms of stages of insight, gambling is similar to alcohol. Those who reach Stage Four and are genuinely looking for help have a much higher success rate than alcoholics, however. This may be explained by the fact that, unlike alcohol and drugs, there is no direct chemical effect on the neurons of the pleasure box. The problem is that very few gamblers reach this stage. The treatment for the condition is similar to that for alcohol. If people can afford it, inpatient care in treatment centres such as the Rutland Clinic can be very successful.

Very few reach a stage where they look for this help – or indeed can afford it – however. For the rest, the main treatment will be attending Gamblers Anonymous. Many will do well by attending addiction counsellors as well. All addiction counsellors are now trained to help in the area of gambling as well as substance addictions.

One possible treatment option in the not-too-distant future is the arrival of a sister drug to the one mentioned in the section on alcohol (Campral). This will probably work in a similar biological manner, to reduce the cravings associated with gambling. Once again, it will be combined with counselling. Although this approach looks promising, it remains to be seen how effective it will be in practice.

One further complication associated with gambling is cross-addiction with alcohol. Often the alcoholism is kept hidden, while the gambling is treated successfully.

Many young men fall into the trap of gambling abuse in the form of slot machines very early, in their mid-teens. Parents should always be vigilant for warning signs, such as behaviour changes, stealing, lying and denial. If large amounts of money are disappearing and the person does not appear to be using drugs or alcohol, it is possible that the person has a secret gambling addiction.

Those close to a gambler should study the addiction castle model before they also become seriously hurt by the behaviour of those they love. The addiction castle is just as powerful with this addiction as with alcohol. The families of gamblers can also get help from addict groups and gambling counsellors.

Nicotine Addiction

This is the most harmful and destructive drug ever sold to the public. It is responsible for more illnesses and misery than all the other substances combined.

Nicotine affects the same dopamine cable and pleasure box as all the other addictions. The chemical changes in the pleasure box produce the smoker's intense cravings. The fact that a third of the population smoke, knowing full well what it is doing to them, is testament to the power of this addiction.

Young people, girls in particular, think that smoking is attractive, and they like the fact that it helps control weight through metabolic enhancement and appetite suppression. In worldwide studies, this group seems to be impervious to all efforts to encourage them to quit.

This is due to the stage of brain development which they are at. They are quickly addicted, often at a very young age, and the changes in their brain may become permanent. A gene has been identified which predisposes some people to become addicted to cigarettes quickly. Thus, some will simply use nicotine and give it up after a while. Others will never break free from the 'death row' that is smoking.

To discuss the medical effects of nicotine addiction would require an entire book. A few key pieces of information, however, are useful to recognise. Firstly, nicotine increases blood clotting in the heart, brain and limbs. In those suffering from narrowing of the arteries due to plaque, particularly in the coronary arteries, nicotine causes clotting or thrombosis, which can block such arteries and eventually lead to a heart attack. The graveyards are full of men and women of all ages who only smoked ten to twenty cigarettes a day. Secondly, it destroys the bronchial tube linings of the lungs, filling them with thick, tarry material, and causing bronchitis, asthma and emphysema. Thirdly, it attacks the lung-cell genes, increasing the chances of lung cancer. Lastly, it destroys the blood vessels to the legs, increasing the chances of such long-term illnesses such as peripheral vascular disease, which causes pain and discomfort on walking, and gangrene.

Smokers destroy their bodies, and pay huge multinationals and their own governments large amounts of money for the privilege of doing so. All the other illegal drugs fade into insignificance in comparison with the number of people whose lives are destroyed by this substance.

The smoker also lives in their addiction castle and can only get help when they want to open the door. Like all addicts, many will lose their lives before giving up their pleasure and craving. 'I might as well be dead', is what the family doctor often hears from someone when they are told that they have to give up smoking. Unfortunately, many get their wish.

Nicotine addiction is also a powerful indicator in young people of other possible cross-addictions, such as alcohol and marijuana. If young people do not smoke before the age of twenty-one, they have a lower risk of being hooked on nicotine or other substances. Smoking therefore does not just destroy the health of the individual, it also takes up a huge amount of resources within the health system, resulting in other illnesses not getting the funding and attention they deserve.

What is tragic about the illnesses resulting from smoking is that it is self-inflicted and avoidable. Sadly, smokers generally only start to take responsibility for their actions when serious illness or the threat of death starts to blast holes in the addiction wall.

In terms of helping people to stop smoking, numerous techniques have been employed. The commonest method adopted by health professionals involves the withdrawal of cigarettes and their replacement with substitutes such as nicotine patches (my preference), chewing gum, inhalers and tablets. My own approach is to explain that these replacements are worthless unless a genuine decision to cease smoking has been made. The logical brain must be actively involved in this decision, or the attempt to give up is doomed to failure. Nicotine patches are normally used for a period of eight to twelve weeks, with a gradual reduction in the strength of nicotine over time.

Smoking clinics are now in place in most hospitals. Holding them in hospitals helps to consolidate the link between nicotine and illness. Many patients with cardiac or respiratory problems are directed towards these clinics. They can, along with smoking help lines, be a great help to many.

Some nicotine addicts have tried hypnosis, with varying success. Some people are immune to hypnosis, and others seem to get only temporary benefit from it. My own feeling is that, until the logical brain has truly decided to stop, even hypnosis may be ineffective. It is amazing how the most seasoned smoker who has tried (apparently unsuccessfully) to cease smoking may do so instantly (and often permanently) after a bout of angina!

There can be little doubt that the smoking ban in public and work areas, now being adopted in many other European countries, has been a great success. The ban has been reasonably well accepted and enforced. Once again, the 'stick' approach to this addiction has been much more effective in changing people's behaviour than decades of trying to persuade them of the health benefits of ceasing smoking.

Substance Abuse

This is an area which grabs all the headlines in the media when it comes to addiction. Experts in the field of addiction, however, know that alcohol and nicotine are the real problems. These two cause most of the carnage created by both misuse and addiction.

Many young people are being increasingly exposed to illegal substances, otherwise known as street drugs. Research has shown that, in Ireland, drug misuse is by far the most common problem among this group. In other words, many young people experiment with these drugs, but only a small number of them actually become addicted.

This distinction is vital, and is often not grasped by the public. Misuse of course carries its own risks, but compared to alcohol it is insignificant in terms of the damage done to the lives of young people. Parents worry about the dangers of drugs, but often ignore the more pressing and dangerous issue: alcohol. The real risk of drug misuse is that a small number of those who are predisposed, either genetically or through social circumstances, to it will move on into full addiction. In many cases, drug addiction is a downward spiral into illness and death. Although it is cumbersome to detail the contents and effects of all illegal and prescribed drugs, it is important to have a general understanding of the more common misused drugs.

Marijuana

Also known as hash or cannabis. This drug is the most commonly misused illegal substance in Ireland. Its use is often concomitant with nicotine, as they are usually smoked together. Users will feel relaxed and sluggish, with some impairment of concentration and short-term memory. It is quite dangerous to use marijuana if one is driving a car. Large amounts can produce hallucinations. It seems as though there is a definite subgroup in those using this drug who are particularly vulnerable to developing psychotic reactions (losing contact with reality). This almost certainly has a genetic basis. The difficulty is that such people find this out only when they start to use it. Many psychiatrists are also becoming concerned about the increasing appearance of schizophrenia in young teenagers following the use of marijuana. Suicide can unfortunately be another result in such cases, as can violence towards others. Most other people will simply misuse this drug, but those at risk of addiction may eventually become hooked on it. This group can, in my experience, be extremely difficult to treat.

The main fear is that misuse of this drug can lead to psychotic reactions in those who are genetically vulnerable, and can lead to the potential abuse of other, more serious drugs. For parents, a good way to spot whether a young person is misusing this drug is the presence of scorch-like burns on their clothes. Most parents assume these are due to smoking, but it is much more indicative of marijuana use. If this is accompanied by a change in behaviour or a disruption in school attendance or performance, one should start to ask questions. Often a timely chat can head off more serious problems.

A worrying longer term consequence is the appearance of the 'demotivational syndrome' in the mid-twenties onwards and most often seen in young males. They present with a mixture of mood and anxiety symptoms but also with a complete lack of either interest or pleasure in most of what life should have to offer them at this stage in their lives. They may have dropped out of college, can't hold down jobs, often live at home with parents at a loss as to what to do with them. The condition is caused by the dopamine receptors in the brain becoming reduced in number and harder to stimulate as they are flooded with this substance. So, it becomes more difficult for them to be either motivated or feel joy. It usually takes a year or two completely off the substance for the brain to recover.

Cocaine

There is increasing concern amongst medical personnel and the police that this drug is starting to become commonplace in Ireland. Cocaine can be extremely addictive from an early stage of use, particularly in those who are susceptible to addiction. This drug powerfully stimulates the dopamine cable and pleasure box, giving feelings of intense pleasure and confidence. It is usually sniffed up the nose (snorted) or smoked. A very addictive preparation smoked in poorer areas is called crack, and is almost instantly addictive.

Many young people and adults in the twenty-to-forty age group are experimenting with cocaine. Most will not become addicted, but unfortunately some susceptible people will. Chronic use of this drug will cause behaviour changes, impotence, paranoia and depression. Suicide is also a risk.

Those who misuse this drug will feel invincible, talkative and confident. They will also feel very sexually aroused. Overuse can lead to violent behaviour, paranoid thinking, and even schizophrenic-type symptoms. Withdrawal of the drug often results in depression and agitation.

There is great excitement among health professionals and others about the possibility of a new vaccination to help those who are addicted to cocaine. This will work by stimulating the body's immune system to attach a protein to the cocaine molecule, preventing the drug from being absorbed from the bloodstream into the brain itself. This of course prevents the drug from reaching the pleasure box, so the person gets no 'buzz' from using it. It is hoped that, in time, this may be used to help deal with other addictions, such as nicotine. Once again, understanding the biology of the mood system assists us in the treatment and prevention of this condition.

Amphetamines

These drugs, also known as uppers, are, like cocaine, stimulant in type. Those who use them feel hyper-alert, and full of energy and confidence. Large doses can lead to major paranoid delusions, which may translate into violence. Amphetamines work by activating the dopamine and pleasure box, and also strongly activate the noradrenalin cable. The latter explains why users become so 'high'.

Withdrawal from this drug often leads to exhaustion and depression. Chronic abusers, at a later stage in life, are also at risk of developing Parkinson's disease. Of note, if amphetamine users are driving cars, particularly at high speed, their driving may be aggressive and dangerous. Though there are no figures available, it would be interesting to know how many road-traffic accidents are caused by the use of these drugs.

Ecstasy

This drug, commonly used by young people in nightclubs, is a mixture of a stimulant and a hallucinogen. Ecstasy 'hypes up' its users, making them extremely emotional, increasing their energy reserves, and allowing them to dance the night away, before they collapse into exhaustion as the effects of the drug wear off. This drug affects all three mood cables, literally driving the user wild.

Ecstasy is primarily a drug of misuse in Ireland, although a small number may become addicted. The real risk is death through dehydration, as several tragic young deaths have shown. Some young people prefer this drug, as it is cheaper, and will last the duration of the night better, than alcohol. This drug may also release very violent behaviour in some of its users, and in other cases unmasks schizophrenia.

Heroin

This is the drug which lay people generally think of in relation to drug addiction. The classic picture of heroin addicts injecting themselves with dirty needles, prostituting themselves, stealing, being infected with HIV and hepatitis, and mugging others to get money to feed their habit is a strong stereotype. In practice, this picture is mainly confined to the bigger cities: there are an estimated 10,000 heroin addicts in Dublin today. The fallout from this addiction is all too clearly seen in the wasted bodies huddled on the city streets as night falls. A large percentage of these people are under twenty-five. This situation is the end result of a gradual progression from misuse to eventual abuse and addiction.

Not every person who uses heroin will become addicted, but misuse creates the potential in those who are susceptible to becoming dependent. Heroin addiction usually originates in areas where poverty, unemployment and lack of education are predominant: the drug is used to ease the pain and hopelessness of people's lives. Criminal gangs exploit this need, making massive profits from the misery of their victims. This group is in constant conflict with the law, are often homeless, and frequently end up in jail, where their habit is fed further.

Many end up suffering from malnutrition, hepatitis, needle abscesses and HIV, and are likely to die from illness or suicide.

Heroin mainly affects the dopamine cable and pleasure box, so when chemical changes become permanent, the craving becomes absolute. Any act, criminal or otherwise, is acceptable to feed the addiction. Our present response is to try to substitute heroin with oral methadone, a replacement opiate. This has met with only limited success, however, as those who walk the streets of Dublin at night can attest to. Long-term urban and rural treatment projects, with total detoxification for the individual, and a chance to spend a number of years learning new skills and doing manual work, might prove to be a more successful option.

Tranquillizers and Sleeping Tablets
Tranquillizer misuse and abuse is, after alcohol and nicotine, probably the most common drug problem in Ireland. It attracts little attention, because the drugs are not illegal.

As seen earlier in the Yellow Flag of anxiety, tranquillizers such as Valium, Xanax and Lexotane, which ideally are designed for the short-term treatment of episodes of acute anxiety, can end in lifelong addictions in susceptible people. This has been a particular risk in the past. Sleeping tablets such as Normison and Rohypnol (the so-called date-rape drug) have also joined the list. Efforts have been made to make these drugs more difficult to prescribe, because of the high risk of abuse of the drugs by addicts, and this has certainly helped to reduce the problem.

All addicts are at risk of cross-addiction with tranquillizers and sleeping tablets, particularly alcoholics and serious drug addicts. A major problem is where they have been prescribed by doctors for patients but have been diverted for sale on the streets. Addicts claim that they can get whatever they want on the streets; it's just a question of the price.

Apart from all the above traditional causes of substance abuse, newer ones have begun to appear in the last five to seven years. The streets have been flooded with synthetic new drugs which are often extremely powerful and with varying effects on the brain. There has been a battle with head shops supplying psychedelic substances 'legally' although new laws have tried to limit their input. There is also a thriving on line trade in all kinds of addictive substances.

Cross-addiction

All addictions have a common biological basis. This is of course a result of the chemical changes experienced in the pleasure box. It also explains the common scenario of cross-addiction seen by family doctors in their surgeries. Addicts are very comfortable slipping out of one mode of addiction and into another. Many will have two or three addictions: alcohol and gambling, alcohol and sleeping tablets, smoking and marijuana, cocaine and amphetamines, with tranquillizers to bring them down, and so on. I have even seen food addiction creeping in to take over from other addictions. This makes sense: the withdrawal effects of one can be eased by the administration of another, regardless of which addictive substance it is. Above all, this shows that the Purple Flag of addiction is truly an illness.

Summary

Many of us are affected, either directly or indirectly, by the Purple Flag of addiction. As a doctor, however, one can justifiably say that misuse of many of these substances can cause as many problems as addiction.

Of great interest is the capacity of the various flags to interact with the Purple Flag. For example, many people with the Red Flag of depression will use alcohol to numb their pain. Conversely, many people with the Purple Flag of addiction will suffer secondary problems with the Red Flag of depression.

Many people with the Purple Flag of addiction end up giving up the fight and succumbing to the White Flag of suicide. Misuse of alcohol can also play a contributory role in suicide among those who are already thinking about it.

Some people with the Yellow Flag of anxiety will try to mask their symptoms with either alcohol or prescribed drugs such as tranquillizers, and may become addicted as a result. Up to 50 percent of sufferers from the Grey Flag of schizophrenia (this mental illness, involving loss of grey matter in the prefrontal cortex, will be discussed later in the section on suicide) will become addicted to nicotine, alcohol, tranquillizers or other drugs. This, unfortunately, increases their chances of committing suicide. The Purple Flag of addiction is sadly often at half-mast, and rarely flies alone.

PART FIVE

The White Flag:
Suicide

1: NIALL'S STORY

Loss, disappointment and difficulty are all part of the journey of life. Sometimes, these things can be overwhelming, and we just want to give up. Despite this, we usually make it through such periods, with the help of those who are close to us.

A small minority of people will find life too distressing, and see suicide as the only way of escaping the situation. Many of these people succeed in taking their own lives every year. They often leave devastated and confused families behind them, along with many unanswered questions. The answers are multifaceted, and modern research is gradually uncovering the mystery of why a person consciously kills themselves.

Suicide attempts are often a mixture of a wish to annihilate oneself and a cry for help. This duality of wanting to be destroyed and wanting to be saved reflects the state of chaos and confusion that the mood system is in at the time of the suicide attempt. Sometimes, the cry for help is answered; at another time, the suicide attempt might be successful. The only positive legacy of suicide is the opportunity of intensive research into these tragic victims, to try to understand why it happened in order to prevent it happening again. Although this is of little consolation to those who have had their lives shattered by suicide, the hope is that such research can prevent another family from enduring the same hurt in the future.

I'm going to start our journey into the causes of suicide by telling the story of Niall. I am grateful to his parents, John and Ann, for allowing me the privilege of telling his story. I hope that their bravery will help others.

On 15 November 2002, Niall left his home for a night out. There was little that was different about him that day, other than that he had had a bad cold, and his mother, as all caring mothers do, had tried to persuade him to stay at home for the night. Niall was anxious to go out, however, so his dad, John, gave him a lift into the town centre at around 9.30. Little did John, or indeed the rest of his family, know that they would never see Niall alive again. A terrible tragedy was about to unfold. It is useful at this stage to describe Niall. He was a fine young man, nineteen years of age, with his life ahead of him. He was the second-youngest of a family of five children, a warm, loving and caring family unit where everyone looked out for each other. Niall was a good sportsman and was well liked and respected by his peers and friends alike. He was a quiet lad unless he was out socialising, when he was known for his sense of humour.

He had finished his Leaving Certificate a year before and had been very disappointed about not getting an apprenticeship to be an electrician, something he passionately wanted to do. He was advised to do an electronics course in the regional college to improve his knowledge, with a view to getting an apprenticeship later.

He was a normal young man in all other aspects. He had one close friend who had moved out of the area the previous year, but had plenty of acquaintances. Like all lads of his age, he dated girls, but apart from a previous relationship a year before, had no major relationship going on at the time. He worked part-time, like most students, in the pub at the weekend, but did not take alcohol the nights he was working.

Niall had only started taking alcohol at the age of eighteen and was not a very heavy drinker – unlike many of his peers. He did go out, however, usually once a week for a night out, when he was not working. This usually involved meeting friends in the pub and then sometimes moving on to a late-night disco. But Niall never arrived home drunk and was never in any difficulties in relation to misusing alcohol. He was a typical modern young lad, behaving in what would be seen by his peers to be a completely normal manner. In the days and months before his death, there was nothing to suggest that Niall was unwell or was unhappy in any way.

The first warning of problems appeared in the early hours of 16 November. Niall had a good friend who worked with him. They regularly shared a taxi to work, or on a night out. His friend rang Niall on his mobile to arrange to meet to catch a taxi home. Niall answered, telling his friend that he was down by the river. His friend immediately sensed that Niall was in trouble, and rushed down to find him. On arriving at the river, his friend found Niall in a very distressed state, wanting to throw himself in. His friend managed to calm him down, and tried to find out what was wrong. When he was asked about several possible areas of difficulties or stress, Niall replied that none of these were the problem. His next words revealed everything: 'It's just me.'

Thinking that things were now more settled, and that Niall was calm, they began to walk back along the river in order to get a taxi home. Suddenly, Niall left his friend's side and jumped into the cold, dark waters.

The next six weeks were a living nightmare for Niall's mother and father, together with all his family, close friends and peer group, for the river refused to hand up its dead. Days and weeks passed, and no body came to the surface, despite heroic efforts by the local search and rescue team, aqua divers, local people, fishermen and others.

His family waited in great sorrow, and with wonderful dignity, for Niall's remains to be discovered. A family of deep faith, they trusted in the power of prayer and the goodness of all those who helped them in any way. They also struggled desperately to come to terms with why Niall had taken his own life. How did this lovely, quiet young lad, so loved by them all, find himself late at night by cold, unforgiving waters wanting to end it all?

Finally, in answer to their prayers and all the hard work of all the rescue teams, Niall's body was discovered, tangled in moorings not far from where he had jumped in. The grieving family was able to lay their son's body to rest at last.

Niall's death had a huge impact on many in his town, and has acted as a catalyst for many new initiatives to try to ensure that his death would not be in vain. His father John, a wonderful and inspiring man, does not want other families to experience similar pain and loss, and also tries to help others who are attempting to come to terms with similar loss.

If Niall's death is to have real meaning, why it happened has to be examined. The following chapter is a search for the answer to this question.

2: THE BIOLOGY, CAUSES AND PREVENTION OF SUICIDE

Suicide Versus Self-Harm

The basic difference between suicide and self-harm is that suicide is a wholehearted attempt to kill oneself, and self-harm is not. 'Para' means 'faulty', indicating that the act was not intended to kill but to mimic suicide, either to get attention or partially to satisfy the suicidal urge which plagues the person. When one is addressing the issue of suicide in Ireland, these two distinct groups need to be examined.

Each year in Ireland, a large number of people will engage in self-harm. It is very difficult to put accurate figures on this phenomenon (as many cases go unreported), but some estimates put levels in the tens of thousands (probably between 50,000 and 60,000). From a medical perspective, this constitutes an epidemic.

Around 11,000 of these cases of deliberate self-harm (usually the most serious) will reach the casualty department. Forty percent of these individuals are between the ages of fifteen and twenty-four. Although worldwide figures indicate a higher number of females committing self-harm, there is a roughly equal number of men and women in this group in Ireland. Around two-thirds of cases will be from city areas.

Self-harm often involves an overdose of medication such as Paracetamol or tranquillizers. Alcohol is usually also found in the person's bloodstream. Another really popular, method of self-harm is self-mutilation, and this is done primarily by females.

Self-harm has traditionally been viewed as a cry for help – an indication that one is feeling suicidal, but not an attempt actually to kill oneself. Common events such as relationship breakdowns can combine with alcohol and lead to self-harm.

Some experts see self-harm and completed suicide in many cases as being part of a spectrum of deliberate self-harm.

Twenty-five percent of suicides are preceded by an act of self-harm the previous year. The fact that the other 75 percent showed no previous warning signs is worrying, and makes the task of preventing suicide extremely difficult. (This statistic must be read with caution, however, as an act of preceding self-harm among the latter group may have simply gone undetected.) In either case, this highlights the importance of screening for suicidal tendencies. Three-quarters of the time, these tendencies will be practically invisible.

Self-harm is also starting to emerge in younger and younger individuals. Children, particularly in the ten-to-twenty age group, are self-harming more frequently, which is a worrying trend.

A percentage of those who attend A&E departments following significant self-harm will be either assessed by a suicide liaison nurse or on occasions admitted for careful monitoring of their psychiatric state. Their assessment, and investigation into what makes them unique, is crucial in preventing further acts of suicide and self-harm.

Suicide

Those who are successful in ending their own lives represent a major challenge for researchers. In most cases, it is difficult to know with any certainty why they did it, and how they came to find themselves in a situation where that was the only choice that was available to them.

Every year in Ireland, around 450-500 people will die by suicide. In 2013 the figure was 475. This may be a conservative estimate, yet it is still greater than the number of people who die in road-traffic accidents every year. Despite the fact that, worldwide, more women than men commit self-harm, men are five times more likely than women to complete the act successfully.

Ireland lies fifth in the expanded EU for suicide among males in the fifteen-to-twenty-five age group. In 2011 145 died between the ages of 15 and 30 in Ireland from suicide. The fact that these victims are so young makes their suicide even more harrowing. It is an important statistic to report: if a form of cancer was specifically targeting this many young people between the ages of fifteen and thirty-five every year, there would be widespread concern.

I often wonder whether these statistics are an accurate estimation of the scale of the problem. How can one tell whether the many fatal road-traffic accidents involving young males late at night are deliberate? Some experts suggest a figure of 6 percent. Others may choose to drown themselves, and as suicide is often so unexpected, it may be considered an accident, rather than a conscious decision on the part of the victim. Every one of these hundreds of suicides destroys a family.

Methods of suicide will range from hanging (around 50 percent of cases) to drowning (20 percent), to massive overdoses. Unlike self harm, these are serious attempts to end the pain for good. In many cases, there is no warning of the impending suicide attempt. Although the attempt may look like an impulsive decision, the person will probably have had a definite method in mind for some time. These impulsive yet thorough acts of violence towards the self are the subject of this chapter. We cannot defeat suicide if we do not understand it.

Professor Patrick McKeown, medical director and founder member of Aware, estimates (along with many world experts) that there is a prevalence of mental illness in up to 90 percent of suicides. In other words, suicide is rarely the act of a healthy mind. The majority (between 60 percent and 70 percent) of cases are due to depression. The remainder are a mixture of addiction (10 percent to 15 percent) and schizophrenia (approximately 10 percent). Sometimes there is a personality disorder involved. Professor McKeown also believes that suicides are often triggered by loss and fuelled by alcohol. This is a valuable breakdown of the statistics, which helps us to understand the causes of suicide better.

The Biology of Suicide

Suicide is the end product of an illness in which the mood system is, biologically, in serious trouble, with a resultant loss of the normal control mechanisms which are so important to our survival. The rational, controlling part of the brain is swept away in a torrent of impulsive, self-destructive behaviour, which occurs as a direct result of illness (usually interacting with environmental influences) attacking the mood system. This process is usually preceded and triggered by a massive surge in the activity of the individual's stress system. The final act is often aided and abetted by alcohol. This may be a revolutionary interpretation for some readers of this book, and I hope that it will bring a great deal of comfort and relief to families who have lost loved ones to suicide.

Post-mortem neurological research into victims of suicide has revealed some interesting results. Our understanding of this area has also been advanced by neuro-imaging research on those who have survived suicide attempts. Genetic research into families with a history of suicide has also been of help. This research is beginning to reveal what is happening in the mood system before suicide. What follows are the results of this research, and an attempt to explain the possible relevance of such research. Once again, the flag system is beneficial in understanding this process. In suicide victims, the Green Flag of normal mood is definitely not flying.

The neurological basis of suicide lies in the prefrontal cortex in the frontal mood department, and in particular one key section, which for the purpose of this discussion we will call the 'impulse control centre', or ICC. (The technical name of this area is the ventral prefrontal cortex.) The ICC controls our tendencies towards impulsive thoughts and actions. The normal functioning of this box and this control centre depends in part on information supplied by parts of the serotonin mood cable .

Suicide victims, following post-mortem studies, revealed evidence of severe depletion of serotonin in the part of the cable supplying the ICC. This in turn leads to a reduction in the activity of this structure – a key finding.

This depletion of serotonin, together with under-activity in the ICC, leads to impulsive thoughts of self-harm that may make the urge to kill oneself overwhelming. This phenomenon seems to be common to all cases of suicide, whether the victim is suffering from depression, addiction or schizophrenia.

The prefrontal cortex has three very important functions that are relevant to our discussion:

1. It produces positive/logical thinking, and is the rational, controlling 'boss' of the mood system
2. It prevents violent behaviour towards the self or others; this is the function of the impulse box
3. It overrules negative thoughts emanating from the stress box

In suicide, due to the reduction of serotonin in the cable which supplies the prefrontal cortex, these three functions are impaired. This leads to negative thinking, so prevalent in this illness, and the inability to problem-solve or see a way forward, and also explains the increased likelihood of self-harm and suicide.

The stress box produces the negative emotional thinking, but the old saying that 'trouble happens when responsible people stand back and do nothing' is quite applicable here. The prefrontal cortex normally prevents trouble from happening by overruling these negative thoughts, and controlling impulsive thoughts and actions. Without an adequate supply of serotonin, however, the effectiveness of this box is greatly reduced.

The entire stress system is also dysfunctional in suicide. Stress peptides are elevated, and the adrenal glands are over-active, producing too much gluco-cortisol. This stress barrage causes chaos throughout the whole mood system and seems, in many cases, to have been present for some time before the person died. The noradrenalin mood cable has been found to be depleted, and this is felt to be further proof of a period of severe stress prior to the event.

These facts help explain why suicide occurs. The severe attack on the stress system, combined with a malfunctioning serotonin cable to the ICC section of the prefrontal cortex, go a long way towards explaining why some people suffering from depression, schizophrenia and addiction are more at risk of impulsive self-harm than others.

The mood department areas that are disrupted are as follows:

The Frontal Mood Department
A starvation of information due to a depleted serotonin cable renders key portions of the prefrontal cortex, in particular the ICC, ineffective and lets

impulsive thoughts of self-harm run rampant. This situation is worsened by a stress barrage attacking the prefrontal cortex – a barrage which is initiated by the peptide system. Of note, the frontal mood department prefrontal cortex is still developing up to the early to mid-twenties, which may put those in the fifteen-to-twenty-five age group at a greater risk of suicide. It is also a major player in both depression and schizophrenia. This fact is reflected in the statistics.

The Limbic Mood Department

The limbic system is also very much involved in the neurobiology of suicide. This is inevitable, since depression is so often present. This system also plays an important role in schizophrenia and addiction.

The stress box is over-active in suicide; this has been borne out in both post-mortem and neuro-imaging of high-risk groups. This box is normally restrained and regulated by the prefrontal cortex. When this control by the prefrontal cortex is undermined by illness (in the Red Flag, for example, we noted that Area 25, the 'gateway' between the mood departments, was over-active or 'open', allowing just such a negative flow of thoughts to run riot), feelings of helplessness and hopelessness dominate, and suicide becomes more likely.

This box is also commander-in-chief of the stress system, and as a result is the architect of the stress response which seems to predate the suicide attempt. It is the source of the flood of stress peptides and, through its links to the adrenal gland, the glucocortisol barrage, which in turn attacks the prefrontal cortex and further depletes the serotonin cable which supplies it.

The Adrenal Gland

Studies have shown that these glands are often enlarged in suicide. Adrenal glands increase when the demand for the stress hormone glucocortisol is increased at the command of the stress system. For this gland to increase in size, it would have to come under pressure for some time. This suggests that the body was under constant attack from stress for a period of time preceding the person's decision to take his or her own life.

Glucocortisol

This stress hormone is present in higher quantities in the bodies of those who have committed suicide. This excess level of glucocortisol damages the two mood departments and mood cables.

When they are combined, these findings show the common biological predecessors of the White Flag of suicide. They also suggest that mood-system difficulties are present in the victims of suicide for a period of time before their death. Due to the severity of the underlying illnesses of depression, addiction and schizophrenia, it can be very difficult for the person to explain how they are feeling.

The link, for example, between the Red Flag of depression and the White Flag of suicide is obvious. Both display a reduction in serotonin cable activity (due to serotonin depletion) and a constant stress response. In suicide, the depletion and stress barrage are particularly extreme. This suggests that in many cases suicide is simply the consequence of more severe (often hidden) forms of depression. This fact is borne out by clinical research.

But why is it that a greater number of people with depression do not experience severe suicidal thoughts, or that many more people who are experiencing depression, schizophrenia or alcohol or substance abuse do not take their own lives? The answer seems to lie in the ICC section of the prefrontal cortex. Marked under-activity of this centre, and the serotonin cable supplying it, seems to be a special risk factor.

This seems to be confined to a particular group who are at greater risk. So some people with this illness will not experience the same level of suicidal thoughts or behaviour. It may be that this impulsive self-harm trait lurks in the background and then, when depression arrives, with an accompanying general drop in both serotonin cable activity and behaviour box activity, it is unmasked. This trait also seems to be present in suicide involving the other illnesses mentioned above.

Research is already under way, particularly in the neuro-imaging area, into the behaviour box changes which distinguish between the high-risk and low-risk groups, in the hope that we can pick out those who are at particular risk of suicide.

So there does seem to be a definite at-risk group in the community displaying a greater predisposition towards the above biological changes and corresponding symptoms. This group is probably created by a mixture of genes and environment, with the former probably being of greater importance.

There is some evidence, for example, that genetic deficiencies in a particular enzyme which helps to produce serotonin may exist in some families and individuals who are more likely to develop suicidal difficulties. Much more research needs to be done to pin down the genes that are responsible. It is important to note, however, that this underlying genetic potential is actualised by illness and major stress triggers in the person's life.

Whatever the underlying illness, these major biological disturbances help explain the stress, anxiety, severe emotional pain, and helplessness which precede suicide. Although suicide can seem sudden, impulsive, irrational and perplexing to an outsider, it is more likely to be the end result of a long period of severe emotional pain, low mood and stress.

In many cases, the final link in the biological chain of suicide is alcohol: the Great Pretender. For those who are battling low mood and suicidal thoughts, alcohol becomes a potent poison. Its short-term effects make it attractive to a person with depression: it reduces anxiety and lifts their spirits, but in the long term is equivalent to extinguishing a fire by throwing petrol on it.

Alcohol targets the section of the brain which prevents suicidal actions. It impairs the ability to make rational decisions, and to consider the true consequences of an action. By doing this, it removes the brain's last line of defence against suicide. Furthermore, as it is a depressant, it exaggerates the emotional pain the person is in. Thus it gives the depressive a greater motivation to attempt suicide, while removing any inhibitions they may have about completing the act. Under the influence of alcohol, the links binding those at risk to loved ones and the beauty of life are discarded, with the full impulsive suicidal drive from a failing mood system arriving – with deadly consequences.

Many who have survived major suicide attempts try to describe the pain and hopelessness they were feeling at the time. I have often been asked what biological changes bring these feelings about. I reply as follows: a constant stress barrage, excessive negative thoughts from an over-active stress box, a particular lack of activity in the ICC section of the prefrontal cortex, and serotonin mood cable malfunctions. These cause low mood, anxiety, feelings of helplessness and hopelessness, impaired decision-making, and low self-esteem.

Summary

Research into suicide has revealed the following:

1. The prefrontal cortex, in particular one key section called the 'impulse control centre', in the frontal mood department is malfunctioning. This results in a lack of control by this part of the brain, which normally prevents suicidal thoughts and consequent impulsive actions.
2. The serotonin mood cable, which supplies this box is severely impaired. Many see this as the most important biological finding. This impairment contributes greatly to the breakdown of the prefrontal cortex in suicide.
3. The limbic mood system, particularly the stress box, is over-active, giving rise to a huge surge through the stress system. The latter is also the source of many of the negative emotional thoughts of despair, hopelessness and helplessness that are so prevalent in those at risk of suicide.
4. The adrenal stress gland is often enlarged or over-active, releasing large amounts of the stress hormone glucocortisol and other stress peptides. This may be the case for some time before the person's death. The stress box is the most likely culprit in initiating such anomalies.

The Causes of the White Flag

To help understand the nature of the cause of the White Flag, it is useful to imagine a seed fed by fertilizers, sown in suitable soil, and germinated by the heat of the sun. The seed represents genes, and the fertilizer represents the stress triggers, which can be summed up in one word: loss. The fertile soil is the environment, and the sun represents alcohol.

The Seed (Genetic Causes)

Genes control all aspects of the mood system. In depression, addiction and schizophrenia, there are clear genetic predispositions. Genes are also important in the development of certain at-risk personality disorders.

In many cases of the White Flag (irrespective of any underlying illness), there may be a particular genetic predisposition for the serotonin cable to malfunction severely. Serotonin in the rest of the body (blood platelets) is at a very low level in suicide victims. Suicide tends to 'run in the family', and some interesting work has been done in such groups. We discussed earlier how one gene site involved in producing an enzyme crucial for the manufacture of serotonin has been examined to see if it could be the problem. This research revealed clear genetic differences between members of such families and those without such a history.

It is likely, however, that many more genes will be shown to play a part in the potential of an individual, irrespective of underlying illness, to self-harm. A full decoding of the body's genes will be necessary to reveal the full story.

The Fertilizer (Loss)
The stress trigger activating many suicides is loss, of various types.

Loss of a Relationship
There is an increasing trend towards marriage and relationship breakdown at all levels and ages in Ireland. Such separations are often associated with a great deal of bitterness and recrimination. Children are often used as pawns, forced to take sides between two people both of whom they love. This conflict and confusion may lead susceptible people to self-harm. Where there are children and young teenagers involved in the relationship, they too must struggle with the stress and loss of family security, and can be at risk.

For young men in particular (and young women to a lesser extent), the breakdown of a relationship is a serious stress trigger. In many cases, the response to the loss of a major relationship is to drink excessively. Alcohol will only worsen the situation, however, and make it more likely that the person, particularly if they are already vulnerable, will attempt some form of self-harm.

Although the break-up of the relationship will act as a trigger, the person may already have been suffering from poor self-esteem, low mood and an underlying genetic vulnerability for some time. The relationship may have been the only thing keeping depression and suicidal thoughts at bay, because it was a source of love and support. Therefore, once it ends, there is nothing to stop these depressive symptoms from taking over. Loneliness too is a common but often unwanted friend to those who suffer from depression, and it often plays a role in the appearance of the White Flag.

Loss of Loved Ones

Bereavement is a potent stress trigger which may lead at-risk people to suicide. The death of a partner, child, sibling or close friend leaves a vacuum which is often filled only with pain and confusion.

Grief is a natural process that most people survive; this process usually consists of denial, realisation and, finally, acceptance. Sometimes, the grief is so profound that the body simply cannot cope with this process, and the person descends into depression. The loss and depression combine to increase the risk of the White Flag of suicide. The pain of bereavement can be so intense that death is seen as the only way to stop it. Naturally, if the person is drinking, the coping threshold is greatly reduced. Where brothers or sisters have committed suicide, or where a mother has lost her child, there is an increased risk of suicide.

Loss of Self-esteem

Self-esteem relates to how we perceive and value ourselves. Losing one's sense of self-worth removes another barrier towards suicide. It is a common result of bullying. This can occur anywhere where someone decides to assert their authority and make life a misery for the person concerned, at home, in school or at work.

Children are very sensitive to bullying, and the trigger here must therefore be neutralised as quickly as possible. If it is not, the annihilation of their self-esteem will lead to depression and possibly suicide, as a way of escaping the psychological torture they endure every day. It is important to ask young people about bullying, as they may be ashamed to talk about it. Bullying feeds on a feeling of helplessness. If children seem quiet, anxious or upset, the possibility of bullying must be addressed.

Flagging the Problem

Bullying can occur in the schoolyard, on the way home from school, or in places where children play together. Children are often bullied by older siblings who are jealous of the younger child's popularity within the home. The bullying can be well hidden by those involved.

Bullying can also occur in the workplace, causing crippling stress and anxiety in the victim. This bullying can take the form of sexual harassment, or bullying by superiors or work colleagues. In all of these cases, it can be difficult to know who to turn to for help in dealing with the problem. The bullying may be too subtle to attempt legal action over, but will nonetheless be extremely hurtful for the person involved. In this group also, suicide is in some cases seen as the only way out.

We mentioned in the Red Flag the particular problems experienced by young people in Northern Ireland who have been intimidated and bullied by paramilitary gangs. The profound effects of such thuggery have led many to take their own lives. This may be exacerbated by poverty and unemployment in some areas; all of these things reduce self-esteem.

Those incarcerated in prisons (particularly young men and women), those who live with addicts, and those who are victims of domestic abuse can also suffer a drop in self-esteem. The victims may feel that they are the problem and that the only way to fix the situation is to remove the problem through suicide.

Illiteracy is a little-noticed yet powerful cause of low self-esteem. People often leave school early for a variety of reasons, and as a result cannot read or write. I have counselled patients who have attempted suicide, only to find them deeply ashamed that they are illiterate. As this reduces their chances of gaining employment, they become frustrated and angry at themselves, and attempt self-harm. This issue must be brought into the open and addressed on a national level.

Low self-esteem is also a basic symptom of depression. Those with the Red Flag feel useless, worthless and deserving of their illness. They have no confidence in themselves. This may never be revealed to their family, and their inner world of self-hatred and low self-esteem ferments over time. As they feel that they are of no value, suicide does not seem like a big deal to them. Alcohol will help exacerbate their feelings of self-hate, and may remove any reservations they might have about completing the act.

Loss of Identity

The role of men in society is not as clear-cut as it used to be. Women are enjoying new-found independence, financially and emotionally, as their roles in society have become more diverse. Men often feel that their role as provider and protector has been made redundant and are left wondering where they fit in.

Girls have always been more expressive emotionally, and more able to support each other when there is a problem, than boys. For men, to talk about one's emotions is seen not only as unbecoming of a man because it is somehow weak or effeminate but also as conveying a sense of incompetence when it comes to dealing with one's own problems.

This results in a feeling of dislocation from others, and a sense on the part of the man that he cannot cope with his problems. This reduces self-esteem substantially. Some men try to escape this dilemma by drinking excessively, but this often leads them to release their frustration in violent acts against themselves and others.

Females with depression are more likely to talk about their feelings and look for help. Men are more likely to try to deal with it themselves, increasing the risk of suicide as their mood system is gradually destroyed. Is this loss of identity, combined with a fear of talking about the problem, a major factor in the large number of suicides among young males?

Loss of Employment

For many people, their job is their identity, and the place from which they derive their sense of worth and satisfaction in life. To these people, the loss of their job delivers a devastating blow to their self-esteem. This can combine with the loss of financial security to make them depressed. This is particularly difficult for a person who is lacking in other skills, or who is of an age where they will find it hard to get work. The longer the period of unemployment lasts, the more under pressure the person feels. The body's stress system comes under attack as a result of constant anxiety about what the future holds, especially if there is a fear of having one's house repossessed.

Apart from these obvious financial concerns, the person begins to feel useless. The combination of financial insecurity, loss of self-esteem and loss of a defined role in life can lead the person to believe that they have failed their families and are of no use to anyone.

In some countries, such as Japan, this is exacerbated by an obsession with duty to family and a long tradition of seeing suicide as an honourable option. Although in Ireland the latter is not the case, there are still increased risks of depression and suicide in such cases.

Loss of Freedom

Prison is often the final stop on a difficult journey for many young men and women. A difficult upbringing and drug and alcohol addiction will clearly not help the self-esteem of these people either. Many feel they were born into a life devoid of hope or opportunity. The removal of their freedom through incarceration will only confirm this feeling of predestined suffering. Many will not be properly educated and may not be able to read or write. Some will already be suffering from the Red Flag of depression due to a combination of the above factors. Prison delivers the final blow to their self-esteem, and suicide becomes an attractive solution. Our jails are also in many cases old and overcrowded. These young people need professional help with their addictions, education deficits and mood problems – not a life behind bars. Prison does not solve any of their problems; it merely hides them and increases the risk of the White Flag.

Another group who are at high-risk of depression are the homeless, who have lost everything: their homes, loved ones, self-esteem and dignity. Many are dealing with chronic alcohol or drug problems and are suffering from the Red Flag of depression as a result. Others are suffering from the Grey Flag of schizophrenia, casualties of a poorly funded mental-health system.

Of the five thousand homeless people in Ireland today, 40 percent are thought to be suffering from mental illness. These people feel that no one will miss them, and that they are only a burden on society. They often take their own lives as a result.

Loss of Health

Many people with debilitating or chronic illnesses feel hopeless. Their sense of joy in life can be impaired, and they may feel that it is useless for them to go on living the way they do. Suicide may seem to be the only way out in some cases. Those who care for people with long-term illness are not immune from the stress of this situation either. They have sometimes made huge financial and personal sacrifices to care for loved ones. Loss of financial security, loss of freedom, and loss of self-esteem can also create a fertile environment for depression and suicidal thoughts to develop in the carer.

Loss of Innocence

Those whose innocence in childhood is ravaged by sexual, physical or emotional abuse are at a lifelong risk of suicide. From an early stage of development in their mood system, this abuse creates a tendency towards living a life of anxiety, mixed with periods of low mood. This may facilitate suicide attempts later in life. The memory box in the limbic mood system has been shown in some cases to be reduced in size as a result of child abuse. Our past is indeed a part of our present.

The Soil (Environmental Influences)

Just as a seed needs not only fertiliser but also suitable soil to flourish, so does suicide. A stress-free and supportive environment reduces the pressure on a person and their mood system. The opposite is also true.

Materialism and Consumerism

The economy has undergone massive growth over the last ten years. This has been achieved at a high cost, however. Families and couples find themselves under increasing pressure to succeed financially in order to keep up with high mortgage payments and the rising cost of living. People are commuting longer distances and working longer hours. They find themselves under pressure to be financially successful, and often run into credit cards and other debt because they are living a life they cannot afford. This is another stress trigger.

Failure to reach these lofty financial goals makes young people feel like failures, unable to keep up with their peers. Sometimes, alcohol is used to blank out this feeling of worthlessness, leading in turn to a greater risk of self-harm. As long as self-worth is determined by the position you hold, the car you drive, or the house you live in, depression and suicide will be waiting for those at risk who don't make the cut.

Social Isolation

The French sociologist Emile Durkheim (1858–1917), renowned for his study and writings on suicide and religion, believed that the greatest deterrent to suicide in times of personal stress is a sense of identity and involvement with other people. Social isolation is a powerful environmental trigger in suicide. In many remote parts of the country, people are driven to the White Flag through a combination of loneliness, despair and depression.

Isolation need not only be physical. As technology advances, there is less and less need to communicate with other people, at least on a face-to-face level. This provides a dangerous breeding ground for depression and suicide. At home, televisions, DVDs and computer games have largely replaced conversation.

Technology eradicates the need for normal emotional expression, and can become a shield for many people with depression to hide behind. Watching television or playing computer games allows the person to avoid social contact and their problems, and e-mail and texting reduce the need to talk in person.

For those who are feeling low enough to be considering suicide, it is vital that they can talk to someone about how they are feeling. They already feel lonely and isolated because of their illness. The silence that is promoted by technology ensures that no one will notice or understand the pain they are in. Without interpersonal communication, there is no outlet for the person's emotions, and the White Flag can be seen as the only way out.

There are also worrying trends about overuse of the internet as a means of communication amongst our teenagers in particular. While the internet can be a positive development if it is used appropriately, many people worry about its potential for encouraging self-harm. One also must be concerned about the 'copycat' risks when suicide is glorified in communications between vulnerable twelve-to-twenty-year-olds. In general, there is concern that adolescents in particular are very vulnerable to the emotional 'hyping' or sensational reporting of suicide.

Loss of Spirituality

Ireland has gone from being a country that is heavily influenced and governed by the church to a more secular and affluent state. The church has been heavily hit by scandals of abuse and corruption. Religion has come to play a much smaller role than it did in the past. Are these changes, and the recent growth in suicide rates, just coincidence?

These changes in power and structure have had a number of important consequences. Firstly, the religious taboo which used to surround suicide has been broken. In the past, suicide was sometimes not mentioned by the family, due to the refusal of the church to bury the bodies of suicide victims in consecrated ground. As religion has come to play a smaller role (or no role at all) in people's lives, the concept of suicide as a mortal sin is no longer a deterrent to those who want to end the awful pain they are suffering. The documentation of suicide in the media has also contributed to the lifting of this taboo, with both positive and negative effects.

The second effect of this religious vacuum is more subtle, and difficult to quantify. An older generation still attempts to hold on to the value systems which they grew up with, but find it increasingly difficult to match these values with the world they are living in. The younger generation must devise their own value system, as they are not having one imposed on them. Materialism, money and hedonism, frowned upon by the old establishment, seem to many people to be the cornerstone of today's society.

Are they suitable and healthy replacements? Many experts agree that the dissipation of religious beliefs is removing a major inhibition towards suicide. If a person has no belief system, and consequently feels that life has no meaning, it is much easier for them to end their own lives in order to stop the pain.

The Sun (Alcohol)

If the above ingredients are present in adequate amounts, all that is needed for the seed of suicide to germinate is the warmth of the sun. Alcohol is effective in helping people to forget life's problems and the pain one is feeling. As a result, it is a drug that is easily abused, especially in depressives. Alcohol frequently offers the final motivation needed to drive a person to suicide. It is a factor in more than 75 percent of young male suicides between the ages of fifteen and twenty-five. In one study carried out in my own North-East Region, alcohol was found to be present in more than 90 percent of male suicides in the under-thirty age group. It is particularly dangerous in the fifteen-to-twenty-five group, where its effects on the developing brain can be detrimental. It is perhaps little surprise that the more alcohol consumption per capita increases, the higher the suicide rate climbs, particularly in the younger age groups.

Is Suicide the Result of Illness, Impulse or Accident?

This is the question that is most often asked by grieving families and loved ones who have lost someone to the White Flag of suicide. Often, there are no obvious warnings that the person is in trouble; those left behind struggle to come to terms with the mystery of the death.

Illness and impulse are linked biologically. Imagine a lake, which on the surface appears calm and serene, masking treacherous currents underneath. Many who take their own lives may appear to be normal to those around them, but are in fact experiencing hidden currents of stress, low self-esteem, low mood and negative thoughts. Impulsive suicidal thoughts are not far away from breaking through to the surface.

Accident

In certain cases, suicide was probably not intended but became the outcome. Self harm can involve a mixture of alcohol and an overdose of prescribed medication. In this situation, it is inevitable that mistakes will happen: people who expect to survive are often not found in time, or miscalculate the amount of the substance they have taken. Ironically, if the cry for help is too loud, it may never be heard.

It is also possible that many fatal accidents that occur late at night and involve single vehicles are a result of impulsive, reckless behaviour (often alcohol- or drug-related), rather than being planned suicide attempts. Within this group, there may also be a number of young people who plan to take their lives (often fuelled by alcohol, relationship breakdowns and depression) in such a manner. Some experts feel that at least 6 percent of these cases may be genuine suicides. It is difficult to clarify these situations, as the person was alone, and there are rarely witnesses.

There are other situations where people throw themselves into rivers but immediately cry out for help. In these situations, it would appear that, where fatalities occur, they are more accidental than a suicide. Accidents are most likely to occur where large amounts of alcohol or drugs have been consumed. This may distort the person's normal, rational thinking, and affect their judgement.

Impulse

This is the most deceptive factor of all. At first glance, most suicides appear to be spur-of-the-moment events, where the person makes a sudden, unplanned decision to end the pain and take their own life. In other cases, there may be obvious evidence of pre-planning, often up to several days before the event, with written notes left behind.

To understand the role of impulse in suicide, one must understand the biology of suicide. In many suicide victims, a long period of stress, low mood and low self-esteem will have preceded the act. We have already explained how some people are more biologically at risk due to an under-active ICC. This group is already more likely to be more impulsive than other people. Eventually, in such cases, impulsive thoughts of self-harm may creep into the mind: these thoughts are initially rejected but finally embraced.

Impulsive behaviour, therefore, is often linked to fleeting, impulsive thoughts which may have been present in the person for a longer duration of time. These impulses merely need a catalyst – an emotional event such as the break-up of a relationship – for the irrational urge to become a reality.

Alcohol plays an important role in unlocking this impulsivity. Alcohol is very adept at turning off the prefrontal cortex and allowing negative thoughts and actions to overpower the person's mood system – with fatal consequences. Many assume that it is the alcohol itself that produces the impulsive thoughts. This is not fully accurate: alcohol releases suicidal thoughts that were already there, hidden beneath the surface.

It is important to remember also that the frontal cortex mood department and prefrontal cortex is not fully developed until the age of twenty-five. So, from fifteen to twenty-five, when the limbic mood department is raging with hormones, and feelings of low mood and self-esteem are common, the brain lacks the crucial set of 'brakes' to stop the person from inflicting impulsive behaviour on themselves or others. One important exception is the use of powerful mind-altering drugs such as cocaine, LSD and magic mushrooms, where a major shift in neurochemistry may produce impulsive self-harm! This might happen in particular if the person is using the substance for the first time, or in a young adolescent whose brain is still immature.

So, yes, impulse is a vital ingredient of suicide, but only when we consider the broader picture. Contrary to popular opinion, most deaths by suicide are not merely a whim or a spur-of-the-moment occurrence.

Illness

This is usually the largest contributor to suicide. In most cases, suicide is not so much an accident or an impulse, but rather the consequence of an underlying illness attacking the mood system.

Most of those who die from the White Flag of suicide have the devastating turmoil of mental illness wreaking havoc beneath the surface of their seemingly calm exteriors. Many have very low mood and low self-esteem, and are in real pain. Others are suffering from the Grey or Purple Flags. In some cases, chronic stress, unemployment, bullying, or the breakdown of a relationship may, over time, combine with these illnesses to create a potential risk of suicide.

In such cases, impulsive, self-destructive thoughts start to intrude. The person's stress system is often over-acting; negative thoughts of hopelessness and helplessness take over. Solving problems becomes insurmountable. If we factor in the at-risk biological group's impulsive self-harm traits, these thoughts create the potential for suicidal action. It may then take only some relatively small event to trigger the conversion of such thoughts into action. When alcohol is added to the equation, tragedy can quickly ensue. In general, suicide is an illness with impulsive traits at its heart; only on occasion can suicide be clearly recognised as being accidental. There is obviously ongoing research and debate into this subject.

In my own career as a GP, I have learned a great deal from listening to people who have survived very serious suicide attempts, where death was truly the final goal. What these people have articulated to me supports the above concepts. In many cases, impulsive thoughts were usually restrained, but alcohol acted as a lethal catalyst.

To those who say that suicide is a 'coward's way out', I say this: suicide is often the final result of an underlying illness, with numerous stress triggers involved. Those who take their own lives simply want to end their pain permanently and may, in their confused mental state, give little thought to the impact that their death may have on those who are close to them. Those who have never experienced this pain will struggle to understand its intensity and the lengths to which people will go to end their inner torment. This pain, along with the release of impulsive thoughts and behaviour, lies at the heart of the White Flag.

The Last Word

It is fitting that we leave this subject by once again recalling Niall's words shortly before his death: 'It's just me.' These words carry profound meaning for us all. They challenge us and point us towards the fact that we all have a responsibility to unlock the mystery of the White Flag.

We need to reach out with love and compassion to all those who feel down – particularly young men and women under thirty-five – and encourage them to come forward for help. We must talk about the symptoms of depression, its causes, and how it can be tackled. We also need to challenge the role of alcohol in our society. The task is huge, but the prize is beyond value: the lives of many of our finest people, both young and old. If all of us do our part, Niall's words may become a beacon of hope for many others in the future.

BIBLIOGRAPHY

Altman, J. (1996). A biological view of drug abuse. Molecular Medicine Today, 2 (6). 237-241.

Anderson, R. (2003). Alcohol Abuse. Forum. Dublin: Newmedia.

Arango, V., Underwood, M. D. & Mann, J. J. (2002). Serotonin brain circuits in major depression. Progress in Brain Research, 136. 443-453.

Ballamier, M., Toga A.W., Blanton R.E., Sowell E.R., et al. (2004). Anterior cingulate , gyrus rectus, and orbito frontal abnormalities in elderly depressed patients: an MRI based parcellation of the pre frontal cortex. Am. Journal Psychiatic Assoc. 161: 99- 108.

Bates, T. (1999). Depression: the commonsense approach. Dublin: Newleaf.

Bates, T. (2004). Conversations that keep us alive. 3TS Conference, Dublin.

Benedetti, F., Mayberg, H. S., Wager, T. D., Stohler, C. S. & Zubieta, J. (2005). Neurobiological mechanisms of the placebo effect. The Journal of Neuroscience, 25 (45). 10390-10402.

Brendel, G. R., Stern, E. & Silbersweig, D. A. (2005). Defining the neurocircuitry of borderline personality disorder: functional neuroimaging approaches. Development and Psychopathology, 17. 1197-2206.

Brody,A.L., Saxena S., Matthew L. et al. (2001). Neuroimaging profiles and the differential therapies of depression. Arch. General Psychiatry, 58: 651-653.

Brophy, J. (2006). Bipolar Disorder. Forum. Dublin:Medmedia.

Butcher, J. N., Mineka, S., Hooley, J. M., Carson, R. C. (2004). Abnormal psychology.

Boston: Pearson Education.

Cahill, L. (2005). His brain, her brain. Scientific American.

Carlson, N. R. (2004). Physiology of behaviour. Boston: Pearson Education.

Chao, J. & Nestler, E. (2004). Molecular neurobiology of addiction. Annual Review of Medicine, 55. 113-132.

Cloningerm C. R., Sigvardsson, S., Gilligan, S. B., Von Knorring, A. L., Reich, T. & Bohman, M. Genetic heterogeneity and the classification of alcoholism. Advances in Alcohol and Substance Abuse, 7. (34). 3-16.

Coyle J.T., Schwarcz R., (2000). Mind glue – Implications of glial cell biology for psychiatry. Arch. General Psychiatry, 59: 90-93.

Cotter, D., Mc Kay, D. Landau S., Kerwin R., Everall I. (2001). Reduced glial cell density and neuronal size in the anterior cingulate cortex in major depressive disorder. Arch. General Psychiatry, 58: 545- 553.

Davison, G. C., Neale, J. M., Kring, A. M. (2004). Abnormal psychology. New Jersey: John Wiley & Sons.

De Paulo, J. R., & Horvitz, L. A. (2002). Understanding depression.New Jersey: John Wiley & Sons.

Dinan, T. G. (1994). Glucocorticoids and the genesis of depressive illness. A psychobiological model. The British Journal of Psychiatry, 164. 365-371.

Dinan, T. G. (1999). Psychiatry-physical consequences of depressive illness. Irish Medical Times.

Dineen, S. (1999). The genetics of alcoholism. Advances in psychiatry- Irish Medical Times.

Dobbs, D. (2006). Mastery of emotions. Scientific American.

Dobbs, D. (2006). Turning off depression. Scientific American Mind.

Drevets, W. C. (1999). Prefrontal cortical-amygdalar metabolism in major depression. Annals of Academy of Sciences, 877. 614-637.

Drevets, W. C. (2000). Neuroimaging of mood disorders. Biological Psychiatry, 48: 813–829.

Drevets, W. C. (2001). Neuroimaging and neuropathological studies of depression: implications for the cognitive-emotional features of mood disorders. Current Opinion in Neurobiology, 11. 240-249.

Dryden, W. (2003). Handbook of individual therapy. London: Sage.

Duman, R. S., Heniger, G. R., Nestler, E. J. (1997). A molecular and cellular theory of depression. Archives of General Psychiatry, 54 (7). 607-608.

Dumser, T., Barocka, A. & Schubert, E. (1998). Weight of adrenal glands may be increased in persons who commit suicide. American Journal of Forensic Medicine and Pathology, 19 (1).72-76.

Etkin, A., Pittenger C., Polan J., Kandal R. (2005). Towards a neurobiology of psychotherapy: Basic science and clinical applications. Journal of Neuropsychiatry- Clinical neuroscience, 17: 145- 158.

Ezzell, C. (2003). Why? The neuroscience of suicide. Scientific American.

Fitzpatrick, C. (2001). Suicide and mental health-whats new in childhood and adolescence? Irish Medical Times.

Gage, F. H. (2003). Brain repair yourself. Scientific American.

Geaney, C. (2003). The true picture of parasuicide in Ireland. Forum. Dublin: Medmedia.

George, M. S. (2003). Stimulating the brain. Scientific American.

Goldapple, K. (2004). Modulation of cortical-limbic pathways in major depression: treatment specific effects of cognitive behaviour therapy. Archives of General Psychiatry, 61. 34-41.

Goldberg, E. (2001). The executive brain. New York: Oxford University Press.

Greenwald, B. S., Ginsberg, E. K., Krishnan, K. R. R., Ashtari, M., Auerbacch, C., Patel, M. (1998). Neuroanatomic localization of MRI signal hyperintensities in geriatric depression. Stroke, 29. 613-612.

Gross, R. (2001). Psychology. The science behind mind and behaviour. London: Hodder and Staughton.

Harrison, P. J. (2002). The neuropathology of primary mood disorder. Brain, 125 (7). 1428-1449

Hemby, S. E. (1999). Recent advances in the biology of addiction. Current Psychiatry Reports, 1 (2). 159-165.

Hilty, D. M., Brady, K. T., Hales, R. E. (1999). A review of bipolar disorder among adults. Psychiatric Services. 50: 201-203.

Holford, P. (2003). Optimum Nutrition for the mind. London: Judy Piaktus ltd.

Hollaway, M. (2003). The mutable brain. Scientific American.

Hawton, K & VanHeeringen, K. (2002). The international handbook of suicide and attempted suicide. West Sussex: John Wiley and Sons.

Hyman, S. E. (2003) Diagnosing disorders. Scientific American.

Jameison, K., Dinan, T. G. (2001). Glucocorticoids and cognitive function: from physiology to pathophysiology. Human Psychopharmacology: Clinical and Experimental, 16 (4). 293-302.

Julian, R. M. (2001). A primer of drug action. New York: Henry Holt and Company, LLC.

Kamali, M., Oquendo, M. A. & Mann, J. J. (2001). Understanding the neurobiology of suicidal behaviour. Depression and Anxiety, 14. 164-176.

Kennedy, S. H., Javanmard, M., Vaccarino, F. J. (1997). A review of functional neuroimaging in mood disorders: positron emission tomography and depression. Canadian Journal of Psychiatry, 42. 467-475.

Khan, A., Warner H.A., Browne W.A., (2000). Symptom reduction and suicide risk in patients treated with placebo in antidepressant clinical trials – an analysis of the FDA database. Arch. Gen. Psychiatry, 57:311-317.

Kolb, B & Whishaw, I. Q (2002). An introduction to brain and behaviour. New York: Worth.

Koob, G. F. (2006). The neurobiology of addiction- a neuroadaptive view relevant for diagnosis. Addiction, 101. 23-30.

Kramer, P. D. (1994). Listening to prozac. London: Fourth Estate.

Lam, R. W., Levitan R. D. (2002). Pathophysiology of seasonal affective disorder : a review. Journal psychiatry neuroscience 25(5): 469 – 80.

LeDoux, J. E. (2002). Emotion, memory and the brain. Scientific American.

Lingford-Hughes, A. & Nutt, D. (2003). Neurobiology of addiction and implications for treatment. The British Journal of Psychiatry 182, (97-100).

Logan, A. C. (2004). Omega-3 fatty acids and major depression: a primer for the mental health professional. Lipids in Health and Disease, 3 (25).

Logan, A. C. (2003). Neurobehavioral aspects of Omega-3 fatty acids: possible mechanisms and therapeutic value in major depression. Alternative medical review; 8 (4): 410-425.

Lucey, J. V. (1999). Obsessive compulsive disorder. Irish Medical Times.

Lucey, J. V., (2004). Generalised Anxiety Disorder. Forum. Dublin: Medmedia

Lynch, T. (2001). Beyond prozac. Dublin: Marino Books.

Manji, H. K., Drevets, W. C. & Charney, D. S. (2001) The cellular neurobiology of depression. Nature Medicine, 7 (5).

Manji, H. K., Quiroz J.A., Payne J.L., Singh J., Lopes B.P., Viegas J. L., and Zarate C. A. (2003): The underlying neurobiology of bipolar disorder. World Psychiatry, October , 2(3): 136-146.

Mann, J. J. (2003). Neurobiology of suicidal behaviour. Nature Review/Neuroscience, 4.

Mann, J. J. (2004). National strategies for suicide prevention. 3TS Conference, Dublin.

Marano, H. E. (1999). Depression beyond serotonin. Psychology Today.

Marano, H. E. (2002). The many faces of depression. Psychology Today.

Marchand, W. R., Dilda D. V., Jensen C. R. (2005). Neurobiology of mood disorders. Hospital Physician. September, 17-26, 43.

Mayberg, H. S., Silva, J. A., Brannan, S. K., Tekell, J. L., Malhurin, R. K., McGinnis, S., Jerabek, P. A. (2002). The functional neuroanatomy of the placebo effect.

Mayberg, H. S. (2003). Modulating dysfunctional limbic-cortical circuits in depression: towards development of brain-based algorithms for diagnosis and optimised treatment. British Medical Bulletin, 65. 193-207.

Mayberg, H. S. (2005). Deep brain stimulation for treatment resistant depression. Neuron, 45 (5). 651-660.

McGaugh, J. L. (2002). Memory consolidation and the amygdala: a systems perspective. Trends in neurosciences, 25 (9). 456-480.

McGauran, A. T., Barry, D & Commins, S. (2006). Disruption of consolidation of long term spatial memories: a role for protein synthesis and glutaminergic (NMDA/AMPA) receptors. FENS Abstracts, 3. 68.

McKeown, P. (1995). Coping with depression and elation. London: Sheldon Press.1996

McKeown, P. (1999). Depression and suicide. Forum. Dublin: Medmedia

Mc Keown P., Healy J., Bailey G., Ward G. (2000). Depression – Keeping hope alive. Aware.

Mirza, K. A. H., Michael, A., Dinan, T. G. Recent advances in paediatric psychopharmacology: a brief overview. Human Psychopharmacology: Clinical and Experimental, 9 (1). 13-24.

Murck, H., (2003). Atypical depression spectrum disorder – neurobiology and treatment. Acta Neuropsychiatrica, 15 (4). 227 – 241.

Nestler, E. (2001). Molecular neurobiology of addiction. American Journal of Addiction, 10. (3). 201-217.

Nestler, E. J. & Malenka, R. C. (2004). The addicted brain. Scientific American.

Obrien, S. M., Scott, L. V., Dinan, T. G. (2004). Cytokines: abnormalities in major depression and implications for pharmacological treatment. Human Psychopharmacology: clinical and experimental, 19 (6). 397-403.

Ochsner, K. N., Bunge, S. A., Gross J. J Gabrieli J. D. (2002). Rethinking feelings: an fMRI study of the cognitive regulation of emotion. Journal of Cognitive Neuroscience,14:1215-1229.

Öngür, D., Drevets, W. C. & Price, J. L. (1998). Glial reduction in the subgenual prefrontal cortex in mood disorders. Proclamation of the National Academy of Sciences, 95 (22). 13290-13295.

Oquendo, M. A., Placidi, G. P., Malone, K. M., Campbell, C., Keilp, J., Brodsky, B., Kegeles, L. S., Cooper, T. B., Parsey, R. V. & VanHeertuum, (2003). Positron emission tomography of regional brain metabolic responses to a serotonergic challenge and lethality of suicides attempts in major depression. Archives of General Psychiatry, 60 (1). 144-22.

Oquendo, M. A. (2003). Identifying neurobiological correlates of suicide risk in depression. Psychiatric Times (3).

Park, A. (2004). What makes teens tick. Time (June ed).

Philips, M. C., Drevets W.C., Rauch S. L., Lane R. (2003). Neurobiology of emotion in psychiatric disorders. Biological Psychiatry, 54: 515-528.

Pinel, J. P. J. (2003). Biopsychology. Boston: Pearson Education.

Plomin, R., DeFries, J. C., MacClearn, G. E., McGuffin, P. (2001). Behavioural genetics. New York: Worth Publishers.

Plotsky, P. M., Owens, M. J. & Nemeroff, C. B. (2000). Neuropeptide alterations in mood disorders.

Puri, B. K. & Boyd, H. (2005). The natural way to beat depression. London: Hodder and Stoughton.

Quitkin, F. M., Rabkin, J. G., Gerald, J., Davis, J. M. & Klein, D. F. (2000). Validity of clinical trials of antidepressants. American Journal of Psychiatry, 157. 327-337.

Quitkin, F. M., Klein, D. F. (2000). What conditions are necessary to assess antidepressant efficacy? Archives of General Psychiatry, 57. 323-324.

Raine, A., Lenz, T., Bihrle, S., LaCasses, L. & Colletti, P. (2000). Reduced Prefrontal grey matter volume and reduced autonomic activity in antisocial personality disorder. Archives of General Psychiatry, 54 (7). 607-608.

Ressler, K. J. & Nemeroff, C. B. (2003) Depression. In Rosenberg, R. N., Prusiner, S. B., DiMauro, D. S., Barchi, R. L. & Nestler, E. J. (2003) The Molecular and Genetic Basis of Neurologic and Psychiatric Disease, 3rd Ed. Woburn, MA: Butterworth Heinemann.

Reyna V.F., Farley F. (2006). Is the teen brain too rational? Scientific American Mind.

Sabbagh, L. (2006). The teen brain. Scientific American Mind.

Sapolsky, R. (2003). Taming stress. Scientific American.

Servan-Screiber, D. (2004). Healing without Freud or prozac. London: Rodale.

Sheline Y.I., Wang P. W., Gado M.H.,Csernansky J.,G.Vannier M.W. (!996). Hippocampal atrophy in recurrent major depression. Proc. Nat. Academic Science USA Vol. 93: 3908-3913.

Szigethy, E., Cornwell, Y., Forbes, N. T., Cox, C. & Caine, E. D. Adrenal weight and morphology in victims of completed suicide. Biological Psychiatry, 36 (6). 374-380.

Thomas, A.J., O' Brien J.T., Davis S., Ballard C., Barber R., Kalaria R., Perry R.H. (2002). Ischemic basis for deep white matter hyperintensities in major depression – a neuropathological study. Arch. Gen. Psychiatry 59: 785-792.

Ulian,E.M., Sapperstein S.K., Christopherson K. S., Barres B. A. (2001). Control of synapse number by glia. Science, 5504: 657- 661.

Vythilingam, M., Heim C., Newport J., Miller A., et al. (2002). Childhood trauma associated with smaller hippocampal volume in women with major depression. (2002). Am. Journal Psychiatry,159: 2072- 2080.

Walsh, M. T., Dinan, T. G., Condron, R. M., Ryan, M. & Kenny, D. Depression is associated with an increase in the expression of the platelet adhesion receptor glycoprotein Ib. Life sciences, 70 (26). 31555-3165.

White, F. J. (2002). A behavioural/systems approach to the neuroscience of drug addiction. The Journal of Neuroscience, 22 (9). 3303-3305.

Wickens, A. (2005). Foundations of biopsychology. Essex: Pearson Education.

Willenberg, H. S., Bornstein, S. R., Dumser, T., Ehrhart-Bornstein, M., Barocka, A., Chrousos, G. P. & Scherbaum, W. A. (1998). Morphological changes in adrenals from victims of suicide in relation to altered apoptosis. Endocrine Research, 24 (3-4). 963-967.

Zubenko, G.S., Hughes H.B, Maher, D.S., Stiffler J.S., Zubenko, W.N., Marazita, M.L. (2002). Genetic linkage of region containing the Creb1 gene to depressive disorders in women from families with recurrent early onset major depression. Am. Journal Medical Genetics. 114(8): 980-87.

SELF-HELP GROUPS

Alcoholics Anonymous

Alcoholics Anonymous 'AA' is an international organisation with over 2,000,000 members who have recovered or are suffering from alcohol abuse or addiction. AA is concerned solely with the personal recovery and continued sobriety of individual alcoholics; it does not engage in the fields of alcoholism research, medical or psychiatric treatment, education, or advocacy in any form but provides peer-to-peer support within a Fellowship structure. There are approximately 4,400 group meetings each week throughout Great Britain. The AA is fully self-supporting and does not accept donations from non-members: all contributions are voluntary.

Helpline: 0800 917 7650
help@aamail.org | www.alcoholics-anonymous.org.uk

Anxiety UK

Anxiety UK is a national registered charity formed in 1970 to provide help for anyone affected by anxiety, stress and anxiety-based depression. The website maintains an up-to-date list of independent, verified self help groups located across the UK and provides a wealth of self help resources online.

Helpline: 08444 755 744
support@anxietyuk.org.uk | www.anxietyuk.org.uk

Aware

Aware is a voluntary organisation established in 1985 to support those experiencing depression and their families. Aware endeavours to create a society where people with mood disorders and their families are understood and supported, and to obtain the resources to enable them to defeat depression. Weekly support group meetings at approximately fifty locations nationwide, including Northern Ireland, offer peer support and provide factual information, and enable people to gain the skills they need to help them cope with depression. Aware's 'Beat the Blues' educational programme is run in secondary schools.

Helpline: 1890 303 302 (Ireland only)
support@aware.ie | www.aware.ie | 01 661 7211

ChildLine

ChildLine, a service run by the ISPCC, seeks to empower and support children using the medium of telecommunications and information technology. The service is designed for all children and young people up to the age of eighteen.

Helpline: 0800 1111

Grow

Established in Ireland in 1969, GROW is Ireland's largest mutual-help organisation in the area of mental health. It is anonymous, nondenominational, confidential and free. No referrals are necessary. GROW aims to achieve self-activation through mutual help. Its members are enabled, over time, to craft a step-by-step recovery or personal-growth plan, and to develop leadership skills that will help others.

Helpline: 1 890 474 474 (Ireland only)
info@grow.ie | www.grow.ie

Mind

Mind is one of the UK's leading mental health charities. The organisation has been committed to making sure that mental health advice and support is accessible for anyone who needs it. In 2013 the charity successfully campaigned against the Mental Health (Discrimination) Act, removing the last significant forms of discrimination that prevented people with mental health problems from serving on a jury, being a director of a company or serving as an MP. With over 375,000 local Minds across England and Wales, the charity provides millions with services that include supported housing, crisis helplines, drop-in centres, employment and training schemes, counselling, peer support, information and befriending.

Helpline: 0300 123 3393
info@mind.org.uk | www.mind.org.uk

No Panic

No Panic is a charity which aims to facilitate the relief and rehabilitation of people suffering from panic attacks, phobias, obsessive compulsive disorders and other related anxiety disorders, including tranquilliser withdrawal, and to provide support to sufferers and their families and carers. Founded by Colin M. Hammond in the UK, this group has extended its activities to Ireland, where it is organised by therapist Caroline McGuigan.

Helpline: 0844 967 4848
Youth Helpline: 0175 384 0393
admin@nopanic.org.uk | nopanic.org.uk | 0195 268 0460

Samaritans

Samaritans was started in 1953 in London by a young vicar called Chad Varah; the first branch in the Republic of Ireland opened in Dublin in 1970. Samaritans provides a twenty-four-hour-a-day confidential service offering emotional support for people who are experiencing feelings of distress or despair, including those which may lead to suicide.

Helpline: 116 123
jo@samaritans.org | www.samaritans.org

Sane

Established in 1986 to improve the quality of life for all those affected by mental health problems, SANE is a UK-wide charity with three main objectives: to raise awareness and combat stigma about mental illness; to provide emotional support and care; to aid research into the causes and treatments of serious mental health conditions such as schizophrenia and depression. SANE provides confidential emotional support, information and access to self-management strategies.

Helpline: 0300 304 7000
info@sane.org.uk | www.sane.org.uk

ACKNOWLEDGEMENTS

I would like to start by thanking my editorial team at Orion for all their wonderful assistance in republishing this book. In particular, I want to thank Olivia Morris who has believed in the Flag series from the beginning and who has been so supportive. I also owe a huge debt of gratitude to Vanessa Fox O'Loughlin and Dominic Perrim my two agents who have made all of this possible.

There are so many others who have played a part in this project. To John and Anne, who allowed me to share Niall's story, and to businessman Dr Michael Smurfit for his support and encouragement, and for writing the foreword, I can only say 'thank you'. I know the death of his nephew Jason affected him deeply. A special thanks to his personal secretary Kate Kelly for all her help.

I would also like to thank my dear friend and colleague Dr Muiris Houston for taking the time to review the text, and for his friendship and support. His reports in the excellent *Irish Times* Health Plus supplement are respected by us all. And I include a special word of thanks to Carol Hunt of the *Sunday Independent* for her kind review and constant support. We are lucky to have journalists of this quality in Ireland. I would also like to say 'thank you' to Maria Carmody for taking time out of her busy schedule to review the text.

I send the warmest thanks to Cathy Kelly (best-selling author and UNICEF ambassador) for her constant kindness and support throughout the years. I am, as always, indebted to my friend and colleague Enda Murphy former Irish College of General Practice CBT Project Director, (and his wife Mei) for his invaluable assistance. He was of great assistance in introducing myself and many GPs around Ireland into the world of CBT. I hope I have been faithful to his teachings! We both value our national radio slot with the Sean O' Rourke show very highly and I would like to take this opportunity to thank Sean and his wonderful team for allowing us to highlight key areas of mental health.

I would also like to thank Breda O'Brien for her kind comments and my special thanks as always to Professor Patricia Casey, Professor of Psychiatry, University College Dublin, for all her support over the years. I would also like to thank Professor Ted Dinan of University College Cork, renowned for his work on the consequences of stress in our lives. I would also like to thank psychologist Marie Murray who has also been so supportive.

There are a number of people who sadly will not be here to see this published. The first is my brother David (who died shortly before this book was published, following a short illness), and I dedicate this book to him and his family (as well as to Niall and the other people mentioned in the dedication). We will miss you. The second is our great family friend Sister Kieran Saunders MMM. She was by my side during many difficult times in the Developing World and remained close to our little unit over many years till her death. It was she who persuaded me to stay in Ireland rather than return to the Developing World, explaining that there was poverty of a different kind at home. How right she was, for despite our affluence, there are many problems (some of which are dealt with in this book) in modern Ireland. We miss you so much, Kieran, and pray that you will remain our 'spiritual guide' throughout this mysterious journey through life and beyond.

I say a special thanks to my sons Daniel and Joseph (and his wife Sue and beautiful granddaughter Saoirse) and to my daughter Lara, her husband Hans (and my two grandsons Ciaran and Sean) for all their love and support and for keeping me well grounded!

As always, I reserve my biggest 'thank you' to my wife Brenda, whose love, friendship, support, encouragement, and particularly patience has made this book and indeed the whole series possible. You are my light in the darkness, and truly my soulmate. '*Mo ghra, mo chroi.*' (My love, my heart).

Also by

DR HARRY BARRY

TOXIC STRESS

A step-by-step guide to managing stress

DR HARRY BARRY

ANXIETY AND PANIC

How to reshape your anxious mind and brain

DR HARRY BARRY

DEPRESSION

A practical guide

DR HARRY BARRY

FLAGGING THE THERAPY

Pathways out of depression and anxiety

DR HARRY BARRY

FLAGGING THE PROBLEM

A new approach to mental health

DR HARRY BARRY